iPhone 14
7th Edition

by Guy Hart-Davis

Visual
A Wiley Brand

Teach Yourself VISUALLY™ iPhone 14, 7th Edition

Copyright © 2023 by John Wiley & Sons, Inc. All rights reserved.

Published by John Wiley & Sons, Inc., Hoboken, New Jersey.

Published simultaneously in Canada and the United Kingdom.

ISBN: 978-1-394-15604-7

ISBN: 978-1-394-15621-4 (ebk.)

ISBN: 978-1-394-15605-4 (ebk.)

For general information on our other products and services or for technical support, please contact our Customer Care Department within the United States at (800) 762-2974, outside the United States at (317) 572-3993 or fax (317) 572-4002.

For technical support please visit https://hub.wiley.com/community/support.

If you believe you've found a mistake in this book, please bring it to our attention by emailing our Reader Support team at wileysupport@wiley.com with the subject line "Possible Book Errata Submission."

Wiley also publishes its books in a variety of electronic formats. Some content that appears in print may not be available in electronic formats. For more information about Wiley products, visit our web site at www.wiley.com.

Library of Congress Control Number: 2022947347

Cover images: Phone courtesy of Devon Cajas; Screenshot courtesy of Guy-Hart Davis

Cover design: Wiley

Contact Wiley at (877) 762-2974 or fax (317) 572-4002.

SKY10055344_091523

About the Author

Guy Hart-Davis is the author of more than 175 computer books, including *Teach Yourself VISUALLY MacBook Pro and MacBook Air*, *Teach Yourself VISUALLY Google Workspace*, *Teach Yourself VISUALLY Chromebook*, *Teach Yourself VISUALLY Word 2019*, *Teach Yourself VISUALLY iPad*, and *Teach Yourself VISUALLY Android Phones and Tablets*, 2nd Edition.

Author's Acknowledgments

My thanks go to the many people who turned my manuscript into the highly graphical book you are holding. In particular, I thank Jim Minatel for asking me to write the book; Lynn Northrup for keeping me on track; Kim Wimpsett for skillfully editing the text; Ryan Williams for reviewing the book for technical accuracy and contributing helpful suggestions; Susan Hobbs for proofreading the book minutely; and Straive for laying out the book.

How to Use This Book

Who This Book Is For

This book is for the reader who has never used this particular technology or software application. It is also for readers who want to expand their knowledge.

The Conventions in This Book

1 Steps

This book uses a step-by-step format to guide you easily through each task. **Numbered steps** are actions you must do; **bulleted steps** clarify a point, step, or optional feature; and **indented steps** give you the result.

2 Notes

Notes give additional information — special conditions that may occur during an operation, a situation that you want to avoid, or a cross-reference to a related area of the book.

3 Icons and Buttons

Icons and buttons show you exactly what you need to click to perform a step.

4 Tips

Tips offer additional information, including warnings and shortcuts.

5 Bold

Bold type shows command names, options, and text or numbers you must type.

6 Italics

Italic type introduces and defines a new term.

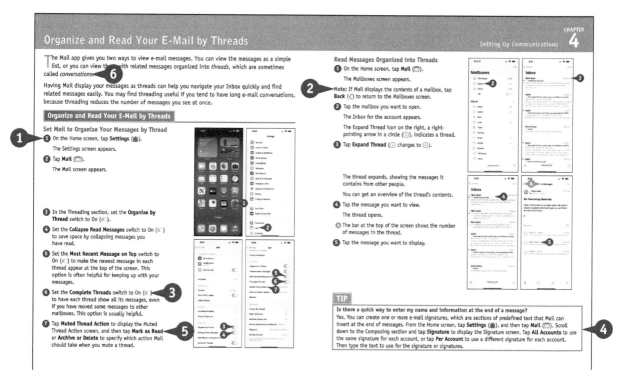

Table of Contents

Chapter 3   Using Voice, Accessibility, and Continuity

Chapter 4   Setting Up Communications

Table of Contents

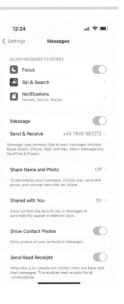

Chapter 7   Working with Apps

Chapter 8   Browsing the Web and E-Mailing

Table of Contents

Chapter 9   Keeping Your Life Organized

Chapter 10   Enjoying Music, Videos, and Books

Chapter 11   Working with Photos and Video

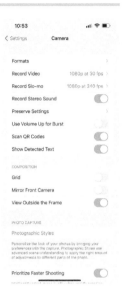

Chapter 12   Advanced Features and Troubleshooting

CHAPTER 1

Getting Started with Your iPhone

In this chapter, you set up your iPhone to work with your computer or iCloud. You choose items to sync and learn to use the iPhone's interface.

Identify and Compare the iPhone Models

The iPhone is a series of hugely popular smartphones designed by Apple. As of this writing, Apple sells seven iPhone models that differ in size, power, features, and price. This section explains the seven models, their common features, and their differences to enable you to distinguish them and choose among them.

Understanding the Seven iPhone Models

As of this writing, Apple sells seven iPhone models. Four models are in the iPhone 14 family, which Apple introduced in September 2022. The base model in this family is called simply iPhone 14; it has a sibling called iPhone 14 Plus that has a larger screen but is otherwise almost identical. The other two models are in the Pro line and have different sizes. The iPhone 14 Pro is the smaller of the two, and the iPhone 14 Pro Max is the larger.

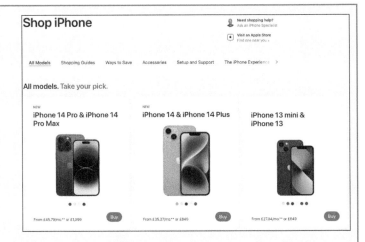

- **iPhone 14.** The iPhone 14 has a 6.1-inch OLED screen with 2532×1170-pixel resolution. OLED is the acronym for organic light-emitting diode; these screens are considered top of the range and have a wide viewing angle.

- **iPhone 14 Plus.** The iPhone 14 Plus has a 6.7-inch OLED screen with 2778×1284-pixel resolution.

- **iPhone 14 Pro.** The Pro has a 6.1-inch OLED screen with 2556×1179-pixel resolution.

- **iPhone 14 Pro Max.** The Pro Max has a 6.7-inch OLED screen with 2796×1290-pixel resolution.

As well as the four iPhone 14 models, Apple sells three older models: the iPhone 13, the iPhone 12, and the iPhone SE third generation.

- **iPhone 13.** Introduced in 2021, the iPhone 13 has a 6.1-inch screen with 1792×828-pixel resolution.

- **iPhone 12.** Introduced in 2020, the iPhone 12 has a 6.1-inch screen with 1792×828-pixel resolution. The iPhone 12 is similar in size and design to the iPhone 13 but contains slightly less powerful hardware and less memory.

Each of these six models has a design featuring thin bezels, rounded screen corners, and a "notch" cutout at the middle of the top edge of the screen. The notch contains the front camera and various sensors for features such as Face ID face recognition. The notch on the iPhone 14 Pro models changes shape to display various types of information and controls in a feature called Dynamic Island.

The third of the older iPhone models, the iPhone SE third generation, has a 4.7-inch screen with 1334×750-pixel resolution and an older design with two main differences from the newer designs. First, this phone has thicker bezels and no notch at the top of the screen; the front camera and its sensors are in the top bezel. Second, in the lower bezel, below the screen, is the Home button, a round button used for navigation and for the Touch ID fingerprint-recognition authentication system. Touch ID is easy to use and can be preferable to Face ID if you are wearing a face mask or other personal protective equipment.

The iPhone SE has long been popular among those with smaller hands, smaller pockets, or less need for a huge screen. Since the introduction of its first generation in 2016, the iPhone SE has been considered the cutest iPhone.

Understanding What Is Included in the Box

As of this writing, each iPhone box contains only the iPhone itself and a USB-C to Lightning cable for charging the iPhone and connecting it to a PC or a Mac.

Understanding Charging and Connectivity

Each iPhone features wireless charging, which you may find easier and more convenient than using a cable. You will need to get a wireless charger separately.

iPhone 14 models sold in the United States use eSIMs, virtual SIM cards that you manage electronically, rather than physical SIM cards, to connect to cellular networks. iPhone 14 models sold in some other markets use physical SIM cards, as do all other current iPhone models, but can use one or more eSIMs as well.

All current iPhone models have 5G connectivity, enabling them to connect to fifth-generation cellular networks. 5G can be up to 100 times faster than 4G, but it is not yet widely available. Check the current and, if possible, future availability of 5G in the areas you will use your iPhone before using 5G as a deciding factor for buying an iPhone.

Understanding the Operating System

Each iPhone runs iOS 16, the latest operating system from Apple, which comes with a suite of built-in apps, such as the Safari web browser and the Mail e-mail app. If you buy an older iPhone model, you may need to upgrade it to iOS 16, but this is easy to do, and there is no charge for the update. The iPhone 8 and all later models — iPhone X, iPhone SE second generation and third generation, iPhone 11, iPhone 12, iPhone 13, and iPhone 14 — can run iOS 16.

Know Which Colors Are Available for Which iPhone Model

The iPhone 14 Pro models come in four colors: Space Black, Silver, Gold, and Deep Purple.

The iPhone 14 and iPhone 14 Plus come in five colors: Blue, Purple, Midnight, Starlight, and (PRODUCT)RED.

The iPhone 13 comes in six colors: Green, Pink, Blue, Midnight, Starlight, and (PRODUCT)RED.

The iPhone SE third generation comes in three colors: Starlight, Midnight, and (PRODUCT)RED.

In addition to physical size and key features, you should consider the storage capacity of the iPhone model you are thinking of buying. Having plenty of storage is especially important for shooting videos with your iPhone.

Having more storage enables you to install more apps and carry more music, movies, and other files with you; however, if you stream your music and movies, offload unused apps, and store your files online, you may not need a huge amount of storage.

Understanding the Cameras on iPhone Models

The iPhone 14 Pro models have a 48-megapixel main camera on the back, accompanied by a 12-megapixel Ultra Wide camera and a 12-megapixel Telephoto camera that switches between 2X and 3X magnification using the quad-pixel sensor. On the front is a 12-megapixel camera with depth-sensing features that enable the Face ID authentication and unlocking system.

The iPhone 14 and iPhone 14 Plus have dual 12-megapixel cameras on the back — Main and Ultra Wide. The iPhone 13 and iPhone 12 also have dual 12-megapixel rear cameras, but these are Ultra Wide and Wide. On the front, all these models have a 12-megapixel camera with depth-sensing features for Face ID.

The iPhone SE third generation has a single 12-megapixel camera on the back and a 7-megapixel camera on the front.

Compare the iPhone 14 Models with the Earlier iPhone Models

The iPhone 14 Pro models offer a substantial upgrade over the iPhone 13 Pro models, their direct predecessors, in three key ways.

First, the iPhone 14 Pro models have Apple's A16 Bionic chip, which is faster and more powerful than the A15 Bionic chip used in the iPhone 13 Pro and iPhone 13. The A15 Bionic chip also powers the iPhone 14 and iPhone 14 Plus and the iPhone SE third generation.

Second, the iPhone 14 Pro models have brighter screens and slightly higher resolution than the iPhone 13 Pro models. The iPhone 14 Pro models have an Always-On display feature that displays information on the lock screen, plus the Dynamic Island feature for displaying context-sensitive information and controls.

Third, the 48-megapixel camera on the iPhone 14 Pro models is a huge improvement over the 12-megapixel camera on the iPhone 13 Pro models. Other camera improvements, including a larger sensor and better optical image stabilization, make the iPhone 14 Pro models the best choice for taking serious photos and videos.

The iPhone 14 and iPhone 14 Plus use the same A15 Bionic chip as the iPhone 13 models and have the same screen type, Super Retina XDR. The iPhone 12 has the A14 Bionic chip and a Super Retina XDR screen. The iPhone SE third generation has the A15 Bionic chip and the less sophisticated Retina HD screen.

All currently available iPhone models except the iPhone SE third generation have an IP68 rating, which means water resistance for up to 30 minutes in up to 6 meters of water — almost 20 feet. The iPhone SE third generation has an IP67 rating — up to 30 minutes in 1 meter of water, or just over three feet.

Evaluate iPhone Storage Capacity

The iPhone models are available with different amounts of storage capacity. The following table shows the capacities with sample amounts of contents to give you some idea of what the amounts mean in real terms.

The iPhone 14 Pro models come in 128GB, 256GB, 512GB, and 1TB capacities. The iPhone 14, iPhone 14 Plus, and iPhone 13 come in 128GB, 256GB, and 512GB capacities. The iPhone 12 and iPhone SE third generation come in 64GB, 128GB, and 256GB capacities.

Higher capacities command substantially higher prices, so you must decide how much you are prepared to spend. Generally speaking, higher-capacity devices get more use in the long run and are worth the extra cost.

Capacity	Songs	Photos	Video
64GB	5,000	4,000	10 hours
128GB	10,000	8,000	20 hours
256GB	20,000	16,000	40 hours
512GB	40,000	32,000	80 hours
1TB	80,000	64,000	160 hours

Understanding the Reachability Feature

iOS includes a feature called Reachability to help you use your iPhone with one hand when necessary. With the Reachability feature enabled, swipe down on the bottom edge of the screen to slide the screen down so that you can easily reach the top of it. On the iPhone SE, you double-tap **Home** — double-tap rather than double-press — to slide the screen down. After you give a command, the screen slides back up again; if you decide not to give a command, tap **Restore** (B) (⬛) to slide the screen back up; on an iPhone SE, double-tap **Home** again. Alternatively, wait a few seconds, and the iPhone slides the screen back up automatically.

To enable Reachability, first tap **Settings** (⚙), tap **Accessibility** (⚙), and then tap **Touch** (⬛). Near the top of the Touch screen, set the **Reachability** switch (A) to On (⬤).

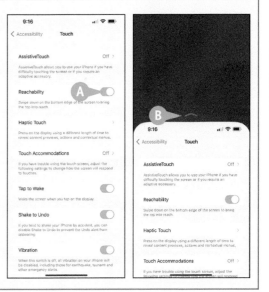

Understanding the Live Photos Feature

All of the current iPhone models include a feature called Live Photos that enables you to capture short sections of video before and after a still photo. After capturing the Live Photo, you can make the video segments play by tapping and holding the photo.

You can view your Live Photos on other Apple devices, such as your iPad or your Mac. You can also use a Live Photo as the wallpaper for your iPhone's lock screen.

Using Your iPhone's Controls

With the touchscreen used for most actions, the iPhone 14 models have only four other hardware controls: the Side button in the middle of the right side; the Ringer On/Off switch at the top of the left side; and the Volume Up button and Volume Down button below the Ringer On/Off switch. This section illustrates and explains these controls, plus the methods for unlocking the iPhone and locking it again.

Identify the Hardware Controls

The right side of the iPhone has only one control, a button called the Side button. The Side button has multiple functions on its own and in combination with the Volume Up button and the Volume Down button. The remainder of this section explains how to use the Side button.

Volume Down button
Volume Up button   Side button
Ringer On/Off switch

The left side of the iPhone has three controls:

- The Ringer On/Off switch turns the ringer on and off. Move the switch toward the rear of the iPhone, exposing an orange background, to turn the ringer off. Move the switch to the front again to turn the ringer back on.

- The Volume Up button and Volume Down button enable you to control the volume quickly without having to use the touchscreen. These buttons also work in combination with the Side button for other actions.

Turn Your iPhone On and Off

To turn on your iPhone when it is powered off, press and hold **Side** until the Apple logo (A) appears on-screen; then release the Side button. Your iPhone continues to start, and then the lock screen appears.

To turn off your iPhone, press **Volume Up** once, press **Volume Down** once, and then press and hold **Side** until the Power Off screen appears; then swipe **slide to power off** (B, ⏻) to the right.

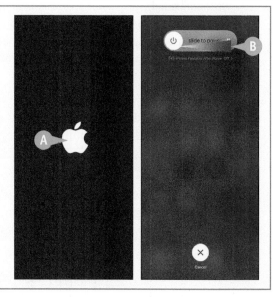

Unlock and Lock Your iPhone

Most iPhone models have Face ID, which enables you to unlock the iPhone by scanning your face. However, iPhone models that have the Home button, such as the iPhone SE third generation, instead use Touch ID, which scans your fingerprint.

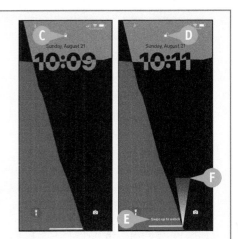

To unlock your iPhone via Face ID, hold the iPhone so the front cameras can scan your face. The iPhone unlocks (🔒, C, changes to 🔓, D), and the *Swipe up to unlock* prompt (E) appears at the bottom of the screen. Swipe up from the bottom of the screen (F). The iPhone unlocks, and you can start using it.

To unlock your iPhone via Touch ID, hold your registered finger against the Home button. When the *Press Home to open* prompt appears, press the Home button.

To lock your iPhone and put it to sleep, press **Side** once. Depending on how the iPhone is configured, the iPhone may also go to sleep automatically after a period of inactivity.

Using Sleep and Wake, Siri, App Store, and Apple Pay

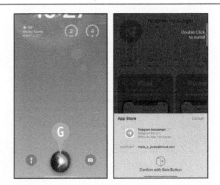

When the iPhone is awake, press **Side** once to put it to sleep. When the iPhone is asleep, press **Side** once to wake it.

On a Face ID iPhone, press and hold **Side** at any time to activate Siri, which plays a tone and displays its icon (G) near the bottom of the screen.

On a Touch ID iPhone, press and hold **Home** at any time to activate Siri.

When installing an app from the App Store on a Face ID iPhone, double-click **Side** to authenticate yourself via Face ID and continue installing the app. On a Touch ID iPhone, hold your registered finger against the Home button to scan your fingerprint.

When making a purchase via Apple Pay on a Face ID iPhone, double-click **Side** to authenticate yourself via Face ID and confirm the purchase. On a Touch ID iPhone, hold your registered finger against the Home button to scan your fingerprint.

Force the iPhone to Restart

If the iPhone becomes unresponsive, a software problem may have occurred. Wait for a minute or two to see if iOS can resolve the problem.

If the iPhone remains unresponsive, you will need to restart it. Press **Volume Down** once, press **Volume Up** once, and then press and hold **Side** for 10–15 seconds. When the screen turns off, release **Side**. The iPhone then restarts, and the Apple logo appears on-screen.

Set Up and Activate Your iPhone

Before you can use your iPhone, you must set it up and activate it. First, you choose your language and specify your country or region. You can then either use the Quick Start feature, if you have an iPhone running iOS 11 or an iPad running iPadOS 13 or a later version, or continue setup manually. Assuming you continue manually, you connect the iPhone to the Internet through either a Wi-Fi network or the cellular network, choose whether to use Face ID unlocking or Touch ID fingerprint unlocking, and choose a passcode.

Power On Your iPhone

First, power on your iPhone by pressing and holding **Side** — the button on the right side of the iPhone — until the Apple logo appears on-screen. The Hello screen then appears.

Swipe up from the bottom of the screen (A) to start setup. The Language screen appears. Tap the language you want to use, such as **English**.

On the Select Your Country or Region screen that appears, tap your country or region (B).

Choose Quick Start or Manual Setup, and Connect to Wi-Fi

The Quick Start feature lets you set up your iPhone more quickly by sharing settings from an existing iPhone running iOS 11 or a later version or an existing iPad running iPadOS 13 or a later version. If you have such a device, bring it close to the new iPhone and follow the prompts. If not, tap **Set Up Manually** (C).

On the Choose a Wi-Fi Network screen, tap the wireless network (D) you want to use; if the Wi-Fi network's name does not appear because the network does not broadcast its name, tap **Choose Another Network** (E), and then type the network's details. Enter the network password when prompted, and then tap **Join**. To set up your iPhone via the cellular network rather than via Wi-Fi, tap **Continue Without Wi-Fi** (F).

Set Up Face ID

On the Face ID screen, tap **Continue** (G) if you want to set up Face ID now, which is usually the most convenient unlock method; if not, tap **Set Up Later** (H). Assuming you proceed, Face ID then walks you through the process of scanning your face twice, either by rotating your head (I) or by moving the iPhone around. If you have difficulty completing Face ID, you can tap **Accessibility Options** (J) at the bottom of the screen and then tap **Use Partial Circle**.

When Face ID is set up, tap **Continue**.

Create a Passcode

After setting up Face ID, you create a passcode for unlocking your iPhone when Face ID does not work or when iOS requires extra security, such as when the iPhone has restarted. On the Create a Passcode screen, tap the keypad to enter a six-digit numeric passcode, and then reenter the same passcode when prompted.

If you want to create a different type of passcode, tap **Passcode Options** (K). In the Passcode Options dialog, tap **Custom Alphanumeric Code** (L), **Custom Numeric Code** (M), or **4-Digit Numeric Code** (N), as needed. A long custom alphanumeric code is most secure, a long custom numeric code can be highly secure, and a four-digit numeric code is inadvisable.

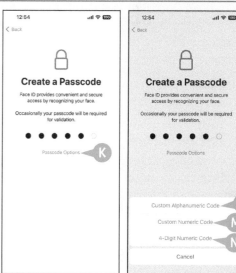

If you enter an easily guessed passcode, such as *111111* or *abcdef*, iOS warns you and suggests you enter a stronger passcode. Tap **Use Anyway** or **Change Passcode**, as needed.

continued ▶

Set Up and Activate Your iPhone (continued)

After setting up Face ID and choosing a passcode, you choose how to complete setting up the iPhone. If you have not used an iOS device before, you can set up the iPhone as a new iPhone. If you have used an iOS device, you can restore an iCloud backup or an iTunes backup of that device to the iPhone. If you have been using an Android device, you can use the Move to iOS app to move data to the iPhone.

Choose How to Set Up Your iPhone

On the Apps & Data screen, you choose between five ways of setting up your iPhone:

- Tap **Restore from iCloud Backup** (O) if you have a backup of your previous iPhone or an iPad stored in iCloud. Sign in (P) on the iCloud screen that appears, and then continue with the instructions in the next subsection on this page.

- Tap **Restore from Mac or PC** (Q) if you have a backup of your previous iPhone or other iOS device on your computer. See the next section, "Set Up Your iPhone Using Finder or iTunes," for further details.

- Tap **Transfer Directly from iPhone** (R) if you are upgrading iPhones and have your old iPhone at hand. The Quick Start screen appears, and you can connect the iPhones wirelessly by bringing them close together.

- Tap **Move Data from Android** (S) if you are switching from an Android phone or tablet to the iPhone and you want to transfer data from your old device. You will need to install the Move to iOS app on your Android device. You then run the app, connect the iPhone and Android device by using a pairing code, and choose which data to transfer.

- Tap **Don't Transfer Apps & Data** (T) if you want to set up your iPhone from scratch. Follow the prompts to set up the iPhone manually; see the later subsection, "Set Up Your iPhone Manually," for highlights.

Set Up Your iPhone from an iCloud Backup

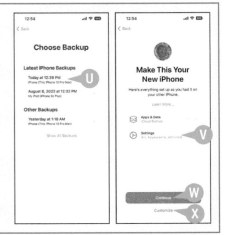

Follow the prompts to sign in to iCloud; if you have two-factor authentication enabled, iCloud sends a verification code to your registered device to enable you to authenticate yourself to your new iPhone. On the Terms and Conditions screen, tap **Agree** if you want to proceed.

On the Choose Backup screen, tap the backup (U) you want to use. Then, on the Make This Your New iPhone screen, tap **Settings** (V) and review the settings that you can restore or customize. Then tap **Continue** (W) or **Customize** (X), as appropriate.

Set Up Your iPhone Manually

When you choose to set up your iPhone manually, iOS walks you through a long sequence of configuration screens that enable you to customize how the operating system looks and behaves. The following list explains the key items you configure:

- **Apple Pay.** You can set up Apple's payment system on your iPhone, enabling you to make electronic transactions easily, including sending payments to your contacts via the Messages app. If you prefer to set up Apple Pay later, tap **Set Up Later in Wallet** (Y).

- **Siri.** You can set up Apple's voice-driven virtual assistant on your iPhone. Siri enables you to give various commands, such as sending an e-mail message or a text message and asking for a wide variety of information — for example, getting directions in the Maps app or looking up information on Wolfram|Alpha or on the web. If you prefer not to set up Siri now, tap **Set Up Later in Settings** (Z).

- **Appearance.** iOS gives you the choice between a Light appearance and a Dark appearance. During setup, you choose an appearance on the Appearance screen. The appearance you choose controls the way much of the iOS interface appears. Tap **Light** (AA, changes to ✓) or **Dark** (AB, changes to ✓) to see which you prefer, and then tap **Continue** (AC). You can subsequently change the appearance by tapping **Settings** (⚙) on the Home screen, tapping **Display & Brightness** (🔆), and then working on the Display & Brightness screen. Here, you can also set the **Automatic** switch to On (⬤) and specify the schedule — either **Sunset to Sunrise** or **Custom Schedule** — on which you want iOS to switch appearances automatically.

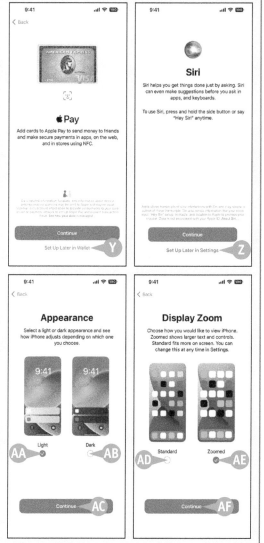

- **Display Zoom.** iOS offers two views, Standard View and Zoomed View. During setup, you choose a view on the Display Zoom screen. Tap **Standard** (AD, changes to ✓) or **Zoomed** (AE, changes to ✓) to compare the two views, and tap **Continue** (AF) once you have made your choice. You can subsequently change views by tapping **Settings** (⚙) on the Home screen, tapping **Display & Brightness** (🔆), tapping **View** on the Display & Brightness screen, and using the controls on the Display Zoom screen.

Set Up Your iPhone Using Finder or iTunes

You can manage your iPhone from your Mac using Finder on recent versions of macOS. For macOS Mojave and earlier versions, and for Windows PCs, you use iTunes. You can either restore a backup to the device or set up the iPhone from scratch using Finder or iTunes. This example shows macOS Ventura.

When setting up your iPhone for the first time, you can restore it from a backup of another iPhone — for example, your previous iPhone. If you have already set up this iPhone and have backed it up, you can restore it from its own backup.

Set Up Your iPhone Using Finder or iTunes

1 Begin setup as explained in the previous section, "Set Up and Activate Your iPhone."

2 On the Apps & Data screen, tap **Restore from Mac or PC**.

The Connect to Computer screen appears.

3 Connect your iPhone to your computer via the USB cable.

Ⓐ The Connected to Computer screen appears on your iPhone.

Ⓑ On macOS, click **Finder** (🙂) on the Dock to open a Finder window if one does not open automatically showing the iPhone's management screens, and then click the iPhone.

On your computer, a Finder window opens or iTunes opens or becomes active.

The Welcome to Your New iPhone screen appears.

4 Make sure the **Restore from this backup** radio button is selected (◉).

5 Click the pop-up menu button (🔼) and select the appropriate iPhone from the menu.

6 Click **Continue**.

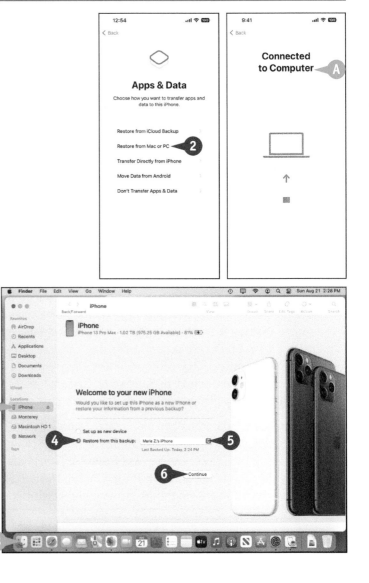

iTunes restores your iPhone from the backup.

When the restore is complete, your iPhone restarts.

The Restore Completed screen appears on the iPhone.

7 Tap **Continue**.

Your iPhone's control screens appear in the Finder window or iTunes window.

You can now choose sync settings for the iPhone as explained in the next section, "Choose Which Items to Sync from Your Computer."

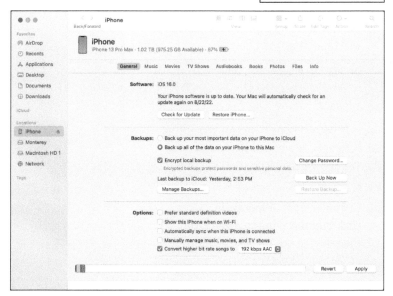

TIP

How do I set up my iPhone from scratch using Finder or iTunes?

On the Apps & Data screen, tap **Restore from Mac or PC**, and then connect your iPhone to your computer via the USB cable. When the Welcome to Your New iPhone screen appears in Finder or iTunes on your computer, click **Set up as new device** (⃝ changes to ◉). Click **Continue**. On the Sync screen that appears, click **Get Started**. The iPhone's management screens appear, and you can set up synchronization as described in the next section, "Choose Which Items to Sync from Your Computer."

Choose Which Items to Sync from Your Computer

After specifying that you will use Finder or iTunes to sync your iPhone, as explained in the previous section, "Set Up Your iPhone Using Finder or iTunes," you use the iPhone's control screens in Finder or iTunes to choose which items to sync. On the General tab in Finder or the Summary tab in iTunes, you can change your iPhone's name, specify the backup location, and set general options for controlling syncing.

Choose Which Items to Sync from Your Computer

Connect Your iPhone and Choose Options on the General Tab or Summary Tab

1. Connect your iPhone to your computer via the USB cable.

A. On macOS, click **Finder** (🙂) on the Dock to open a Finder window if one does not open automatically showing the iPhone's management screens, and then click the iPhone.

On macOS Mojave or older versions or on Windows, the iTunes window appears.

Note: If your iPhone's control screens do not automatically appear in iTunes, click **iPhone** (📱) on the navigation bar at the top of the screen.

2. In Finder, click **General**; in iTunes, click **Summary** in the sidebar on the left.

3. To change the iPhone's name, click the existing name, type the new name, and press Return or Enter.

4. Click a radio button (◯ changes to ⦿) to specify where to back up your iPhone.

5. If you choose to back up to this computer, click **Encrypt local backup** or **Encrypt iPhone backup** (☐ changes to ☑).

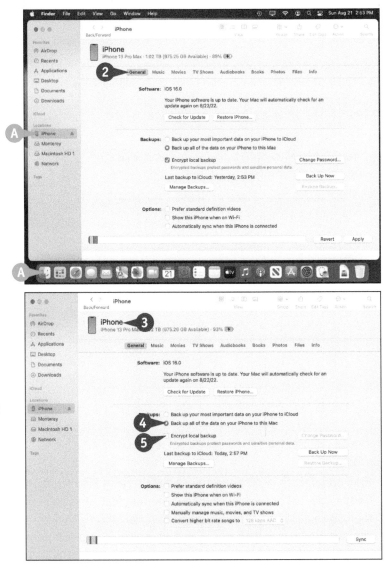

16

A dialog opens for setting a password.

6 Type a password in the Password box and again in the Verify Password box.

7 On a Mac, click **Remember this password in my keychain** (☐ changes to ☑) if you want to save the password in your keychain.

8 Click **Set Password** to close the dialog.

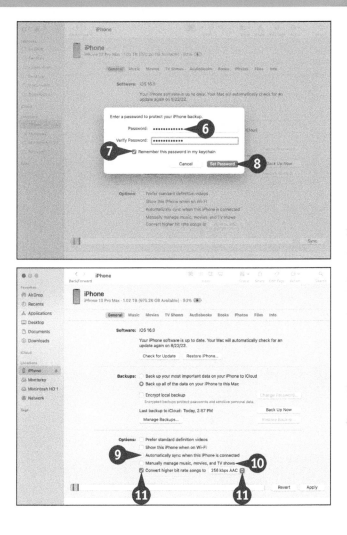

9 Click **Automatically sync when this iPhone is connected** (☐ changes to ☑) if you want to sync your iPhone automatically when you connect it.

10 Click **Manually manage music, movies, and TV shows** (☐ changes to ☑) if you want to load these items on your iPhone manually rather than using the automated features in Finder or iTunes.

11 Click **Convert higher bit rate songs to** (☐ changes to ☑) if you want to compress larger songs to fit more on your iPhone. Click the pop-up menu button (🔽) and select the bit rate and encoding type, such as **256 Kbps AAC**.

TIP

Should I back up my iPhone to my computer or to iCloud?

If you plan to use your iPhone mostly with your computer, back up the iPhone to the computer. Doing so makes iTunes store a full backup of the iPhone on the computer, so you can restore all the data to your iPhone or to a replacement iPhone, if necessary. You can also encrypt the backup; doing so enables you to store and restore your passwords. To keep your data safe, you must back up your computer as well. For example, you can use Time Machine to back up a Mac.

Backing up your iPhone to iCloud enables you to access the backups from anywhere via the Internet and to take advantage of Apple's reliable storage, but make sure your iCloud account has enough storage to contain the backups. An iCloud backup stores less information than a Finder or iTunes backup.

continued ▶

Backing up your iPhone to your computer is convenient but takes up space. You may want to delete old backups manually to reclaim space.

You can easily choose which items to sync to your iPhone. By selecting the iPhone in the sidebar in Finder on recent versions of macOS and clicking the appropriate tab or by selecting the iPhone on the navigation bar in iTunes and then clicking the appropriate item in the Settings area of the Source list, you can specify which music, movies, books, and other items to sync from your computer.

Choose Which Items to Sync from Your Computer (continued)

Manage Your iPhone Backups

1. In Finder, click **General**; in iTunes, click **Summary**.

2. Click **Manage Backups**.

   A dialog opens, showing a list of backups.

3. Click the backup you want to delete.

4. Click **Delete Backup**.

5. Click **OK**.

   The dialog closes.

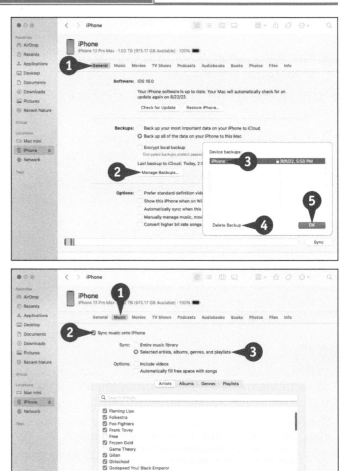

Choose Which Content to Sync

Note: This section uses the Music category to illustrate choosing content to sync. The controls in most of the other categories — such as Movies, TV Shows, and Podcasts — work in the same way, although the specific controls vary.

1. Click the category or tab, such as **Music**.

   The contents of the category or tab appear.

2. Click **Sync music onto iPhone** (☐ changes to ☑).

   The remaining controls become enabled.

3. To load a selection of music, click **Selected artists, albums, genres, and playlists** (○ changes to ◉) instead of **Entire music library**.

4 Click **Include videos** (☐ changes to ✓) if you want to include music videos.

5 Click **Automatically fill free space with songs** (☐ changes to ✓) only if you want to put as much music as possible on your iPhone.

Note: Filling free space with songs may limit your ability to shoot photos or videos.

6 Click **Artists**, **Albums**, **Genres**, or **Playlists**.

That type of content appears.

7 Click the check box (☐ changes to ✓) for each artist, album, genre, or playlist to include.

Apply Your Changes and Sync

B If a content category is being synced via iCloud, you cannot sync it via Finder or iTunes. To turn off iCloud sync, tap **Settings** (⚙) on the iPhone's Home screen; tap **Apple ID**, the button bearing your name; tap **iCloud** (☁); and then use the controls in the Apps Using iCloud list. You may need to tap **Show All** to display the Apps Using iCloud screen.

1 Click **Apply** or **Sync**, depending on which button appears.

iTunes syncs the items to your iPhone.

2 When the sync finishes, disconnect your iPhone.

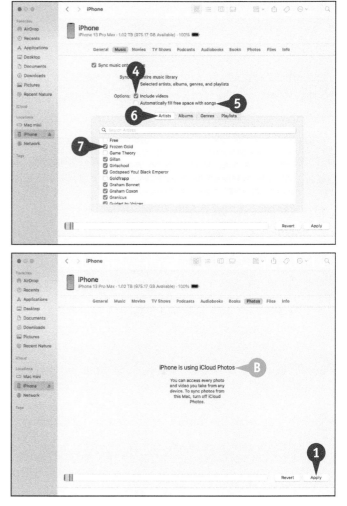

TIP

How can I fit more content on my iPhone?
You cannot install a memory card to increase your iPhone's storage capacity, but you can use the iPhone Storage feature to remove items you do not need.

Tap **Settings** (⚙) on the Home screen to display the Settings screen, and then tap **General** (⚙). On the General screen, tap **iPhone Storage** to display the iPhone Storage screen. You can then follow suggestions in the Recommendations box, such as tapping **Enable** for Optimize Photos or for Offload Unused Apps; or you can tap buttons in the lower section to see which apps and files are consuming the most space.

Explore the Interface and Launch Apps

After you set up your iPhone with iCloud or iTunes, you are ready to start using the device. When you wake the iPhone from sleep, it displays the lock screen. You then unlock the iPhone to reach the Home screen, which contains icons for running the apps installed on the iPhone.

You can quickly launch an app by tapping its icon on the Home screen. From the app, you can return to the Home screen by swiping up from the bottom of the screen. You can then launch another app as needed.

Explore the Interface and Launch Apps

1 Tap the screen.

Note: You can also press **Side** to wake the iPhone.

The iPhone's screen lights up.

The lock screen appears.

2 Raise the iPhone, pointing the screen at your face.

Face ID scans your face and attempts to match it to the stored data. If it succeeds, the iPhone unlocks; if it fails, the iPhone prompts you to enter your passcode.

Note: If the iPhone prompts you to enter your passcode, do so.

The iPhone unlocks.

3 Swipe up from the bottom of the screen with one finger.

The Home screen appears.

The iPhone has two or more Home screen pages. When you swipe between Home screen pages, the Search field changes to an indicator (•••) showing how many Home screen pages there are. The white dot indicates the current Home screen page.

4 Tap **Notes** ( ).

The Notes app opens.

Note: If you chose to sync notes with your iPhone, the synced notes appear in the Notes app. Otherwise, the list is empty until you create a note.

5 Tap **New** ( ).

A new note opens, and the on-screen keyboard appears.

6 Type a short note by tapping the keys.

A If the middle button in the suggestion bar shows the word you want, tap `Spacebar` to accept it. If one of the other buttons shows the right word, tap that button.

7 Tap **Done**.

The on-screen keyboard closes.

8 Tap ‹. This button shows the name of the folder, such as All iCloud.

B The Notes list appears, with your note in it.

9 Swipe up from the bottom of the screen.

The Home screen appears again.

10 Swipe left.

C When you start swiping, the Home screen pages indicator (● ● ●) appears, showing you which Home screen page is currently displayed.

The second Home screen page appears.

You can now launch another app by tapping its icon.

11 Press **Side**.

Your iPhone goes to sleep.

Where do I get more apps to perform other tasks?

You can find an amazingly wide selection of apps on Apple's App Store. Some apps are completely free, whereas other free-to-download apps have "in-app purchases" that make you pay for premium features. Other apps are ones you must pay for, either as a single payment or as a subscription payment. See Chapter 7 for instructions on finding and downloading the apps you need.

Using Cover Sheet and Today View

Your iPhone handles many different types of alerts, such as missed phone calls, text messages, and invitations to events such as meetings. Your iPhone integrates these alerts into Cover Sheet so that you can review them easily.

The iPhone's Today View enables you to view snippets of important and helpful information, such as weather, calendar appointments, and stock updates. You can access Today View either via Cover Sheet or directly from the Home screen.

Using Cover Sheet and Today View

Open Cover Sheet and Deal with Notifications

1 Swipe down on the left side of the screen from the top.

Cover Sheet appears.

Note: See the section "Choose Which Apps Can Give Notifications" in Chapter 2 for instructions on customizing the notifications that appear on Cover Sheet.

A You can tap **Clear** (⊗) to clear all notifications in a category such as Notification Center.

2 To remove a single notification, swipe it left.

Action buttons for the notification appear.

B You can tap **Options** to view other actions available for the notification.

3 Tap **Clear**.

The notification disappears from Cover Sheet.

4 Tap and hold a notification.

The pop-up panel opens, together with action buttons.

5 Tap the action you want to take. For example, for an e-mail message, tap **Mark as Read** to mark the message as read.

Note: To go to the app that raised a notification, tap the notification.

6 When you finish working on Cover Sheet, swipe up from the bottom of the screen.

The Home screen appears.

Open Today View

1 On the first Home screen page, swipe right.

Note: If the Home screen page that appears is not the first page, swipe up to display the first page. You can also swipe right one or more times, as needed.

Today View appears.

Note: You can customize the selection of widgets in Today View. See the section "Customize Today View" in Chapter 2 for details.

2 Swipe up.

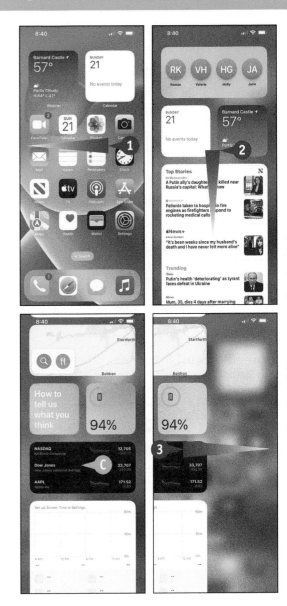

Other items appear.

C You can tap a widget to go straight to the related app.

3 Swipe left.

The Home screen appears.

TIP

What happens if I receive a notification when my iPhone is locked?
This depends on the type of notification. For most types of notifications, your iPhone displays an alert on the lock screen to alert you to the notification. Unlocking your iPhone while the alert is showing takes you directly to the notification in whatever app it belongs to — for example, to an instant message in the Messages app. You can configure your iPhone to put less important notifications in a scheduled summary; see the section "Choose Which Apps Can Give Notifications" in Chapter 2 for details.

Using Control Center

Control Center puts your iPhone's most essential controls at your fingertips. From Control Center, you can turn Airplane Mode, Wi-Fi, Bluetooth, Do Not Disturb Mode, and Orientation Lock on or off; control music playback and volume and direct your iPhone's audio and video output to AirPlay devices; change the setting for the AirDrop sharing feature; and quickly access the Flashlight, Clock, Calculator, and Camera apps.

Using Control Center

Open Control Center

1. Swipe down from the upper-right corner of the screen.

   Control Center opens.

A. You can drag the **Brightness** slider to control screen brightness. Tap and hold the **Brightness** slider to display a larger slider and the icons for toggling Night Shift (●), Dark Mode (●), and True Tone (●).

B. You can drag the **Volume** slider to control audio volume.

Control Essential Settings

1. Tap **Airplane Mode** (● or ●) to turn Airplane Mode on (●) or off (●).

2. Tap **Wi-Fi** (● or ●) to turn Wi-Fi on (●) or off (●).

3. Tap **Cellular Data** (● or ●) to turn Cellular Data on (●) or off (●).

4. Tap **Bluetooth** (● or ●) to turn Bluetooth on (●) or off (●).

5. Tap **Orientation Lock** (● or ●) to turn Orientation Lock on (●) or off (●).

6. Tap **Focus** (● or ●) to display the Focus screen in Control Center.

7. Tap and hold the **Communications** box.

   The Communications panel opens.

8. Tap **AirDrop** (●) to change the AirDrop setting.

9. Tap **Personal Hotspot** (● or ●) to turn Personal Hotspot on (●) or off (●).

10. Tap outside the Communications panel.

    The Communications panel closes.

Choose an AirPlay Device for Audio

C You can tap the song information to go to the song in the Music app.

D You can tap **Previous** (◄◄) to go back to the start of the song. Tap again to play the previous song.

E You can tap **Next** (►►) to play the next song.

F You can tap **Pause** (❙❙) to pause playback.

1 Tap and hold the Audio box.

The Audio panel opens.

G You can drag the playhead to move through the song.

2 Tap **AirPlay** (◉).

The list of AirPlay devices appears.

3 Tap the audio device to use for output.

The iPhone starts playing audio on that device.

4 Tap the song name.

The Now Playing On panel closes.

5 Tap the screen outside the Audio panel.

The Audio panel closes.

6 Tap at the bottom of the screen.

Control Center closes.

TIP

What are the buttons at the bottom of Control Center?

Tap **Flashlight** (🔦) to turn on the Flashlight. Tap and hold **Flashlight** (🔦) to display the Flashlight panel, which lets you choose among four levels of brightness. Tap **Timer** (⏱) to display the Timer screen in the Clock app. Tap and hold **Timer** (⏱) to display the Timer panel, which enables you to set timers for preset times from 1 minute up to 2 hours. Tap **Calculator** (🧮) to display the Calculator app; tap and hold **Calculator** (🧮) to get the result of the last calculation. Tap **Camera** (📷) to display the Camera app. Tap and hold **Camera** (📷) to display the Camera panel, which contains commands such as **Take Selfie** and **Record Video**.

CHAPTER 2

Personalizing Your iPhone

To make your iPhone work the way you prefer, you can configure its many settings. In this chapter, you learn how to control iCloud sync, notifications, audio preferences, screen brightness, and other key aspects of the iPhone's behavior.

Find the Settings You Need

The iOS operating system includes many settings that enable you to configure your iPhone to work the way you prefer. The central place for manipulating settings is the Settings app, which contains settings for the iPhone's system software, the apps the iPhone includes, and third-party apps you have added. To reach the settings, you first display the Settings screen and then the category of settings you want to configure.

Find the Settings You Need

Display the Settings Screen

1 On the Home screen, tap **Settings** (⚙).

The Settings screen appears.

A You can tap **Search** (🔍) and type a setting name or keyword to locate the setting. You may need to drag down the screen to reveal the Search bar.

B The Apple ID button, which shows your Apple ID name, gives access to settings for your Apple ID and your accounts for iCloud, iTunes, and the App Store.

C The top section of the Settings screen contains settings you are likely to use frequently, such as Airplane Mode, Wi-Fi, and Bluetooth.

2 Tap and drag up to scroll down the screen.

D This section contains settings for built-in apps and features developed by Apple.

3 Tap and drag up to scroll farther down the screen. You can also swipe up to move more quickly.

E This section contains settings for apps you install. These apps can be either from Apple or from third-party developers.

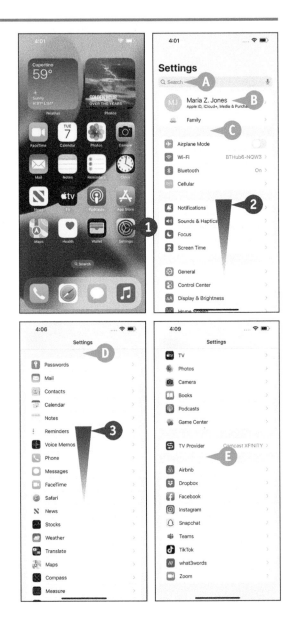

Display a Settings Screen

 On the Settings screen, tap the button for the settings category you want to display. For example, tap **Sounds & Haptics** (🔊) to display the Sounds & Haptics screen.

 Tap **Settings** (<) when you are ready to return to the Settings screen.

Note: Tap at the very top of the screen — for example, tap the clock readout or the battery icon — to scroll quickly to the top of the screen. This shortcut action works in most iOS apps.

Display the Settings for an App

1 On the Settings screen, tap the button for the app whose settings you want to display. For example, tap **Safari** (🧭) to display the Safari settings.

2 Tap **Settings** (<) when you are ready to return to the Settings screen.

3 Swipe up from the bottom of the screen.

The Home screen appears again.

Note: When you next open the Settings app, it displays the screen you were last using. For convenience, it is usually best to return to the main Settings screen when you finish choosing settings.

TIP

Where do I find other settings for an app?

As well as the settings that you access by tapping the button bearing the app's name on the Settings screen, some apps include settings that you configure directly within the app. For such apps, look for a Settings icon or menu item.

To configure notifications for an app, tap **Notifications** (🔔) on the Settings screen, and then tap the app's button. To configure Location Services settings for an app, tap **Privacy & Security** (✋) on the Settings screen, tap **Location Services** (➤), and then tap the app's button.

Apple's iCloud service enables you to sync many types of data — such as your e-mail account details, your contacts, and your calendars and reminders — online so you can access them from any of your devices. You can use the iCloud Backup feature to back up your iPhone's important data to iCloud to reduce the risk of losing data. To use iCloud, you set your iPhone to use your Apple ID and then choose which features to use.

Choose Which iCloud Items to Sync

1 On the Home screen, tap **Settings** (⚙).

The Settings screen appears.

2 Tap the Apple ID button. This button shows the name you have set for your Apple ID.

3 Tap **iCloud** (☁) to display the iCloud screen.

4 In the Sync with iCloud section, tap **Show All**.

The Sync with iCloud screen appears.

5 Set each app's switch to On (🔵) or Off (⚪), as needed.

6 Tap **Photos** (✿) to display the Photos screen.

7 Set the **Sync this iPhone** switch to On (🔵) to store all your photos and videos in iCloud.

8 Tap **Optimize iPhone Storage** (✓ appears) to store lower-resolution versions of photos on your iPhone to save space. Tap **Download and Keep Originals** (✓ appears) if you prefer to keep original, full-quality photos on your iPhone.

9 Set the **Shared Albums** switch to On (🔵) to use the Shared Albums feature.

10 Tap **Sync with iCloud** (〈).

The Sync with iCloud screen appears again.

11 Tap **iCloud** (〈).

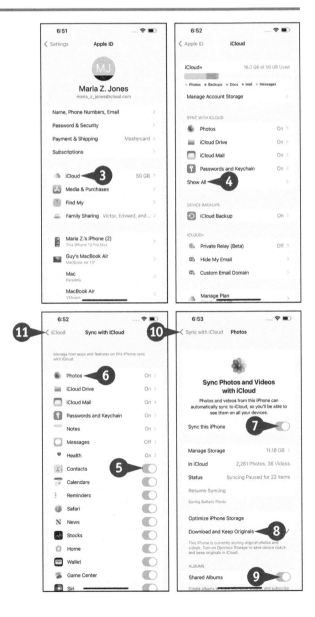

The iCloud screen appears again.

12 Tap **iCloud Drive**.

The iCloud Drive screen appears.

13 Set the **Sync this iPhone** switch to On (⬤) to enable iCloud Drive.

Ⓐ You can tap **Manage Storage** to manage your iCloud storage.

14 Tap **iCloud** (〈).

The iCloud screen appears again.

15 Tap **iCloud Mail**.

The iCloud Mail screen appears.

16 Set the **Sync this iPhone** switch to On (⬤) to enable iCloud Mail.

17 Tap **iCloud** (〈).

The iCloud screen appears again.

18 Tap **iCloud Backup** (🔄).

The Backup screen appears.

19 Set the **iCloud Backup** switch to On (⬤).

20 Set the **Back Up Over Cellular** switch to Off (⬤) unless you have an unlimited data plan.

Ⓑ You can tap **Back Up Now** to run a backup immediately.

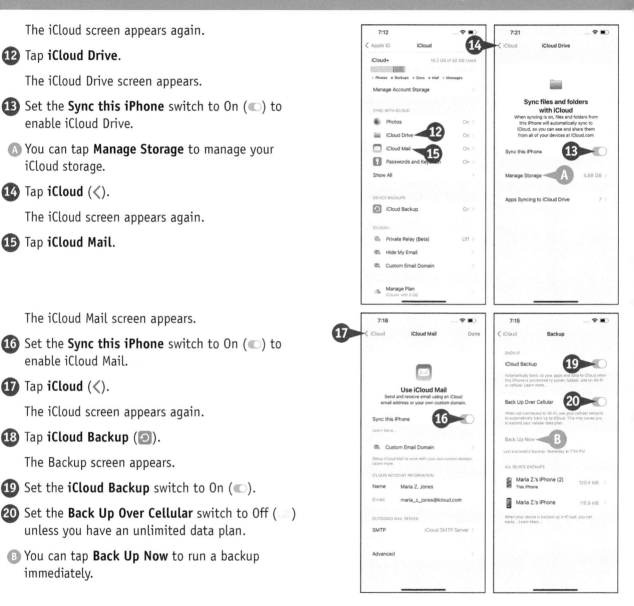

TIP

How much space does iCloud provide?

iCloud provides 5GB of space for a free account. Content and apps you acquire from Apple do not count against this space, nor do your Photo Stream photos or songs included in iTunes Match — but Shared Albums do count. You can buy more space by tapping **Manage Storage** and then tapping **Buy More Storage** on the iCloud Storage screen that appears.

Configure the Find My Feature

Apple's Find My feature enables you to locate your iPhones, iPads, Macs, and other supported devices, such as Apple Watch and Apple's AirTag location trackers. Find My also enables you to share your location with individual family members, allowing them to learn where you are at any time.

Normally, you will want to enable the Find My iPhone feature and the Find My network so that you can locate your iPhone if you misplace it. Enabling the Send Last Location feature, which makes the iPhone send its location to Apple when its battery is critically low, is usually helpful, too.

Configure the Find My Feature

1 On the Home screen, tap **Settings** (⚙️).

The Settings screen appears.

2 Tap the Apple ID button. This button shows the name you have set for your Apple ID.

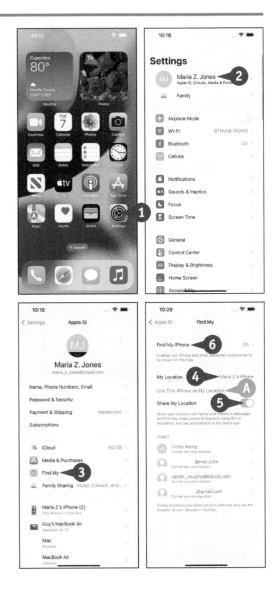

The Apple ID screen appears.

3 Tap **Find My** (📍).

The Find My screen appears.

4 Verify that the My Location button shows the appropriate device for determining your location.

Ⓐ You can tap **Use This iPhone as My Location** to set this iPhone to provide your location.

Note: The Use This iPhone as My Location button appears only when your iPhone is not providing the location.

5 Set the **Share My Location** switch to On (🔘) to share your location with family and friends.

6 Tap **Find My iPhone**.

The Find My iPhone screen appears.

7 Set the **Find My iPhone** switch to On (⬤).

8 Set the **Find My network** switch to On (⬤) if you want to use the Find My network.

9 Set the **Send Last Location** switch to On (⬤) if you want your iPhone to send Apple its location when the battery is critically low.

10 Tap **Find My** (‹).

The Find My screen appears again.

B In the Family section, the readout *Cannot see your location* appears on each family member who cannot see your location.

11 Tap the family member for whom you want to configure sharing your location.

The Information screen for that family member appears.

12 Tap **Share My Location** to share your location.

Note: If you are already sharing your location with the family member, tap **Stop Sharing My Location**.

The Find My screen appears again.

C The button for the family member no longer shows the *Cannot see your location* readout.

TIP

Should I be concerned that the government can track me via the Find My feature?
Such tracking is possible but is arguably not worth worrying about, as most known government agencies would need to get a warrant to access Find My data. They are more likely to track you via data from cell-phone towers or law-enforcement cell-site simulators; such data requires no warrant in most of the United States.

Cell-site simulators are commonly known by the proprietary term *Stingray* and the generic term *IMSI catcher*. IMSI stands for International Mobile Subscriber Identity, a unique identifier for a SIM card. If you are seriously concerned about tracking, see the section "Lock Down Your iPhone Against Serious Hackers" in Chapter 12.

Choose Which Apps Can Give Notifications

Some iPhone apps can notify you of events that occur, such as messages arriving or updates becoming available. You can choose which notifications an app gives or prevent an app from giving notifications. You can also have iOS summarize notifications for you at one or more scheduled times; choose between displaying notifications as a count, as a stack, or as a list; and choose which notifications appear on the lock screen and in Notification Center.

iPhone apps use three types of notifications: badges on app icons, temporary banners, and persistent banners. See the tip for details.

Choose Which Apps Can Give Notifications

1 On the Home screen, tap **Settings** (⚙).

The Settings screen appears.

2 Tap **Notifications** (🔲).

Note: The Count view displays a straightforward number showing how many notifications are waiting for you. The Stack view arranges the notification cards in a stack at the bottom of the screen, with the topmost card fully displayed and the lower edges of the other cards appearing below it. The List view shows each notification separately, taking up all the vertical space on the screen.

The Notifications screen appears.

3 Tap **Display As**.

The Display As screen appears.

4 Specify the notification view to use by tapping **Count** (✓ appears), **Stack** (✓ appears), or **List** (✓ appears).

5 Tap **Notifications** (‹).

The Notifications screen appears again.

6 Tap **Scheduled Summary**.

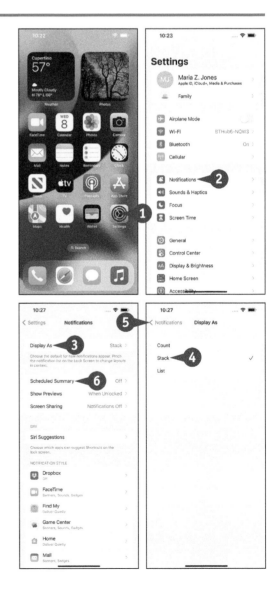

The Scheduled Summary screen appears.

7 Set the **Scheduled Summary** switch to On (⬤).

The Notification Summary screen appears.

8 Tap **Continue**.

The Choose Apps for Your Summary screen appears.

9 Tap each app you want to include in the summary (changes to ✓).

A You can tap **Show More** to display other apps.

10 Tap **Add Apps**.

The Set a Schedule screen appears, suggesting two default scheduled summaries.

11 To change a summary's time, tap the time readout, and then tap the new time on the pop-up menu.

B You can tap **Remove** (⊖) to remove a scheduled summary.

C You can tap **Add Summary** (⊕) to add another scheduled summary.

12 Click **Turn on Notification Summary**.

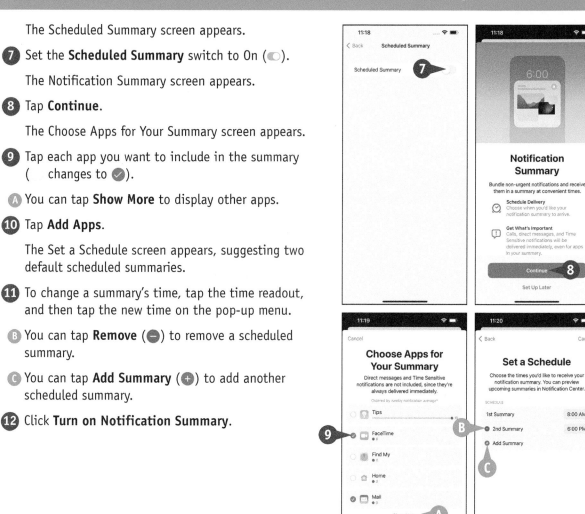

TIP

What are the three kinds of notifications?
A *badge* is a red circle or rounded rectangle that appears on the app's icon on the Home screen and shows a white number indicating how many notifications there are. A *temporary banner* is a pop-up notification that appears briefly at the top of the screen and then disappears automatically after a few seconds. A *persistent banner* is like a temporary banner, but you must dismiss it before you can take other actions on your iPhone. Whichever notification type you choose, you can set the **Sounds** switch to On (⬤) to have your iPhone play a sound to get your attention.

continued ▶

iOS gives you close control over when notification previews appear. First, you choose a default setting for notification previews: You can choose **Always** to always display previews, **When Unlocked** to display previews only when your iPhone is unlocked, or **Never** to always suppress previews. This default setting applies to all apps, but you can choose a different setting for each app, as needed. For example, you might choose **When Unlocked** as the default setting but then specify the **Always** setting for a high-priority app, such as Messages. You can also hide notifications while sharing your iPhone's screen.

Choose Which Apps Can Give Notifications (continued)

The Scheduled Summary screen appears again.

D The Schedule section shows the scheduled summaries you added.

13 Tap **Back** (<).

The Notifications screen appears again.

14 Tap **Show Previews** to display the Show Previews screen; specify the default setting by tapping **Always**, **When Unlocked**, or **Never**, as needed; and then tap **Notifications** (<).

15 Tap **Screen Sharing** to display the Screen Sharing screen; set the **Allow Notifications** switch to On (◉) or Off ( ), as needed; and then tap **Notifications** (<).

16 Tap **Siri Suggestions**.

The Siri Suggestions screen appears.

17 Set the **Allow Notifications** switch to On (◉) to enable notifications.

18 Set the switch for each app to On (◉) to allow Siri suggestions or to Off ( ) to not allow them.

19 Tap **Notifications** (<).

The Notifications screen appears again.

20 Tap the app for which you want to configure notifications. This example uses **Calendar** ( ).

The screen for configuring the app's notifications appears.

21 Set the **Allow Notifications** switch to On (⬤) to enable notifications.

22 In the Notification Delivery section, tap **Immediate Delivery** (🔔) or **Scheduled Summary** (▤), as needed.

23 Set the **Time Sensitive Notifications** switch to On (⬤) to always receive time-sensitive notifications immediately.

24 In the Alerts section, tap **Lock Screen**, **Notification Center**, and **Banners** to control where alerts appear (✅) or do not appear (   ).

25 Tap **Sounds**.

26 Tap the sound you want to use.

Ⓔ You can tap **None** for no sound.

Ⓕ You can tap **Vibration** and choose the vibration pattern for the notification type.

27 Tap the **Back** button (〈).

28 Tap **Banner Style**; tap **Persistent** or **Temporary**, as needed; and then tap the **Back** button (〈).

29 Set the **Badges** switch to On (⬤) to show badges.

30 To exempt this app from your default preview setting, tap **Show Previews**; tap **Always**, **When Unlocked**, or **Never**, as needed; and then tap the **Back** Button (〈).

31 Tap **Notification Grouping**; tap **Automatic**, **By App**, or **Off**, as needed; and then tap the **Back** button (〈).

32 If the Customize Notifications button appears, tap **Customize Notifications** and work on the Customize Notifications screen. See the tip for more information.

TIP

What settings does the Customize Notifications screen provide?
The Customize Notifications screen contains notification settings specific to the app whose notifications you are configuring; only some apps have the Customize Notifications screen. For example, on the Customize Notifications screen for the Calendar app, you can set the **Upcoming Events** switch, the **Invitations** switch, the **Invitee Responses** switch, and the **Shared Calendar Changes** switch to On (⬤) or Off ( ) to control which of those items can raise notifications.

Choose Sounds and Haptics Settings

The Sounds & Haptics screen in Settings enables you to control what audio feedback and vibration feedback your iPhone gives you. You can have the iPhone always vibrate to signal incoming calls or vibrate only when the ringer is silent. You can set the ringer and alerts volumes, choose your default ringtone and text tone, and choose which items can give you alerts. Your iPhone can play lock sounds to confirm you have locked or unlocked your iPhone. It can also play keyboard clicks to confirm each key press.

Choose Sounds and Haptics Settings

1 On the Home screen, tap **Settings** (⚙).

The Settings screen appears.

2 Tap **Sounds & Haptics** (🔊).

The Sounds & Haptics screen appears.

3 Drag the **Ringer and Alert Volume** slider to set the volume.

Ⓐ When the **Change with Buttons** switch is set to On (⬤), you can change the Ringer and Alert Volume setting by pressing **Volume Up** and **Volume Down** on the side of the iPhone.

4 Tap **Headphone Safety**.

The Headphone Safety screen appears.

Ⓑ The Headphone Notifications button shows the number of headphone notifications the iPhone has issued in the time period shown.

5 To reduce the volume of loud sounds while using headphones, set the **Reduce Loud Sounds** switch to On (⬤).

6 Drag the slider to set the sound pressure threshold level in decibels.

Ⓒ The readout shows the number of decibels and an everyday comparison, such as *As loud as a noisy restaurant* or *As loud as heavy city traffic*.

7 Tap **Back** (‹).

The Sounds & Haptics screen appears again.

8 Tap **Ringtone** to display the Ringtone screen.

9 Tap the ringtone you want to hear.

D You can tap **Tone Store** to browse and buy ringtones.

10 Tap **Vibration** to display the Vibration screen.

11 Tap the vibration pattern you want to feel.

E To create a custom vibration, tap **Create New Vibration** in the Custom area. On the New Vibration screen that appears, tap your rhythm, and then tap **Stop**. Tap **Play** to play back the vibration. Tap **Save** to open the New Vibration dialog, type a name, and then tap **Save**.

12 Tap **Ringtone** (‹) to display the Ringtone screen.

13 Tap **Sounds & Haptics** (‹).

The Sounds & Haptics screen appears again.

14 Repeat steps **8** to **13** to set other tones, such as text tones.

15 Set the **Lock Sound** switch to On (⬤) or Off (◯), as needed.

16 Set the **Play Haptics in Ring Mode** switch and the **Play Haptics in Silent Mode** switch to On (⬤) or Off (◯), as needed.

17 Set the **System Haptics** switch to On (⬤) or Off (◯) to control whether your iPhone plays haptics for system controls and touches.

18 Tap **Keyboard Feedback** to display the Keyboard Feedback screen.

19 Set the **Sound** switch and the **Haptic** switch to On (⬤) or Off (◯), as needed.

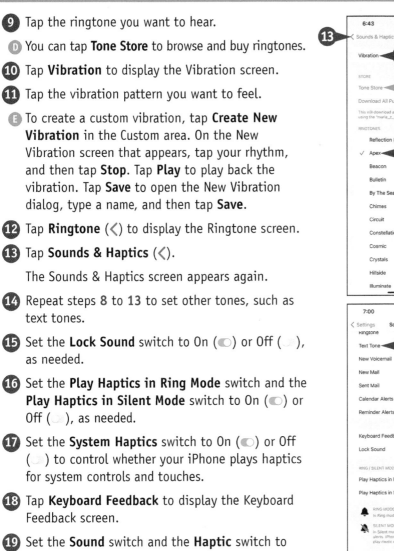

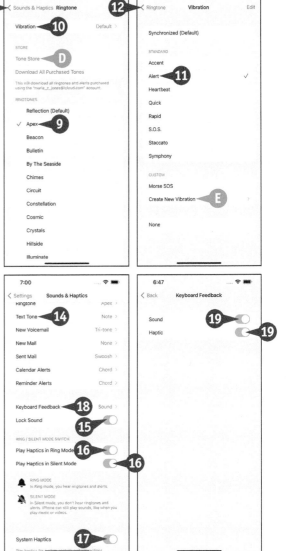

TIP

How do I use different ringtones for different callers?

The ringtone and text tone you set in the Ringtone area of the Sounds & Haptics screen are your standard tone for phone calls, FaceTime calls, and messaging calls. To set different tones for a contact, display the Home screen, tap **Phone** (📞), and then tap **Contacts**. In the Contacts list, tap the contact, tap **Edit**, and then tap **Ringtone**. On the Ringtone screen, tap the ringtone, and then tap **Done**. You can also change other settings, such as the Text Tone vibration for the contact. Tap **Done** when you are finished.

Set Appearance, Brightness, and Auto-Brightness

You can choose between a Light appearance and a Dark appearance for iOS, or you can set iOS to switch automatically between Light and Dark. You can adjust your iPhone's screen's brightness to improve visibility, and you can turn the True Tone feature on to make colors appear consistent.

As well as manual controls for screen brightness, iOS has an Auto-Brightness setting that adjusts the screen's brightness automatically to match the ambient light conditions. Auto-Brightness is enabled by default and helps save battery power, but you may prefer to turn it off so you have full control over screen brightness.

Set Appearance, Brightness, and Auto-Brightness

1 On the Home screen, tap **Settings** (⚙).

The Settings screen appears.

2 Tap **Display & Brightness** (🔆).

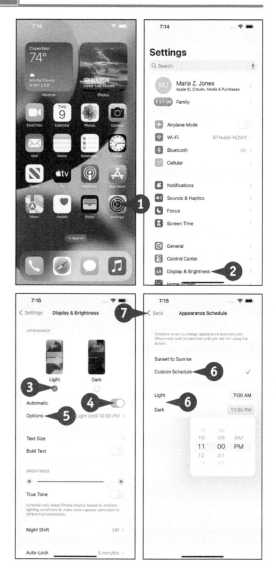

The Display & Brightness screen appears.

3 In the Appearance area, select **Light** ( ) or **Dark** ( ), as appropriate.

4 If you want iOS to switch between Light and Dark for you, set the **Automatic** switch to On (⬤).
If not, go to step **8**.

5 Tap **Options**.

The Appearance Schedule screen appears.

6 Either tap **Sunset to Sunrise** (✓) or tap **Custom Schedule** (✓) and then set custom times on the Light row and the Dark row.

7 Tap **Back** (‹).

The Display & Brightness screen appears again.

Ⓐ You can tap **Text Size** to set your preferred text size.

Ⓑ You can set the **Bold Text** switch to On (⬤) to make the system text bold.

⑧ Drag the **Brightness** slider to set the screen brightness.

⑨ Set the **True Tone** switch to On (⬤) if you want colors to appear consistent in different lighting conditions.

⑩ Set the **Raise to Wake** switch to On (⬤) to make the iPhone wake when you raise it.

⑪ Tap **Settings** (‹).

The Settings screen appears again.

⑫ Tap **Accessibility** (⊙).

The Accessibility screen appears.

⑬ Tap **Display & Text Size** (AA).

The Display & Text Size screen appears.

⑭ At the bottom of the screen, set the **Auto-Brightness** switch to On (⬤) or Off ( ), as needed.

TIP

How else can I make the screen more readable?

Try the Smart Invert Colors feature. From the Settings screen, tap **Accessibility** (⊙), tap **Display & Text Size** (AA), and then set the **Smart Invert** switch to On (⬤).

Change the Wallpaper

iOS enables you to choose what pictures to use as the wallpaper on each of your Home pages and your lock screens. iOS provides a wide variety of built-in wallpaper pictures but also lets you use your own photos as wallpaper.

iOS organizes the wallpapers into categories such as People, Photos, Emoji, Weather, Astronomy, and Color. Each category has a different design and different configurable options, enabling you to customize the wallpaper to your liking.

Change the Wallpaper

1 On the Home screen, tap **Settings** (⚙️).

The Settings screen appears.

2 Tap **Wallpaper** (⚙️).

The Wallpaper screen appears.

Ⓐ The left side of the preview shows the wallpaper applied to the current lock screen. Tap **Customize** to edit this wallpaper.

Ⓑ The right side of the preview shows the wallpaper applied to the current Home screen. Tap **Customize** to edit this wallpaper.

Ⓒ You can also change wallpaper from the lock screen. Tap and hold the lock screen to display the wallpaper controls.

3 Tap **Add New Wallpaper**.

The Add New Wallpaper screen appears.

Ⓓ You can tap **Photos** (🖼️), **People** (👤), **Photo Shuffle** (🔀), **Emoji** (☺️), **Weather** (🌧️), **Astronomy** (🌑), or **Color** (⬤) to display those categories.

Ⓔ The Featured, Suggested Photos, and Photo Shuffle categories show examples. Scroll down to see the Weather & Astronomy, Emoji, Collections, and Color categories.

4 Tap the wallpaper you want to view. To follow this example, tap **Astronomy**.

The wallpaper appears.

5 If a row of dots appears, swipe left or right to change the picture displayed. The white dot indicates the current picture.

The picture appears.

 If a widget box appears, tap **Add Widgets** (+).

The Add Widgets panel opens.

 Tap each widget you want to add.

The widgets appear in the widget box.

8 Tap **Close** (×).

The Add Widgets panel closes.

9 Tap **Add**.

The Set as Wallpaper dialog opens.

10 Tap **Set as Wallpaper Pair**.

Note: You can tap **Customize Home Screen** to customize the Home screen layout.

iOS applies the wallpaper.

11 Swipe up from the bottom of the screen.

The Home screen appears, showing the new wallpaper.

Note: To see the lock screen wallpaper, press **Side** to lock the iPhone, and then press **Side** again to wake it.

 TIP

How do I use only part of a picture as the wallpaper?
When you choose a photo as wallpaper, the iPhone displays the central part of the photo as the wallpaper. Pinch in or out to zoom the photo out or in, and drag with two fingers to move the picture around.

Configure Night Shift and Display Zoom

Blue light from the screens of devices can prevent or disrupt your body's sleep, so the iPhone includes a feature called Night Shift that reduces blue light from the screen. You can configure Night Shift to run automatically each night, manually enable it until the next day, and adjust the color temperature to look more warm or less warm.

On large-screen iPhones, you can choose whether to zoom the display in to a larger size or to keep it at the standard size.

Configure Night Shift and Display Zoom

1 On the Home screen, tap **Settings** (⚙).

The Settings screen appears.

2 Tap **Display & Brightness** (🔤).

The Display & Brightness screen appears.

3 Tap **Night Shift**.

The Night Shift screen appears.

4 Drag the **Color Temperature** slider along the Less Warm–More Warm axis to set the color temperature you want for Night Shift.

A You can set the **Manually Enable Until Tomorrow** switch to On (⬤) to enable Night Shift immediately.

5 Set the **Scheduled** switch to On (⬤) to run Night Shift each night.

6 Tap **From, To**.

The Schedule screen appears.

7 Tap **Sunset to Sunrise** if you want Night Shift to follow sunset and sunrise times for your location; go to step **10**. Otherwise, tap **Custom Schedule**.

8 Tap **Turn On** and set the time.

9 Tap **Turn Off** and set the time.

10 Tap **Night Shift** (ᐸ).

The Night Shift screen appears.

11 Tap **Back** (ᐸ).

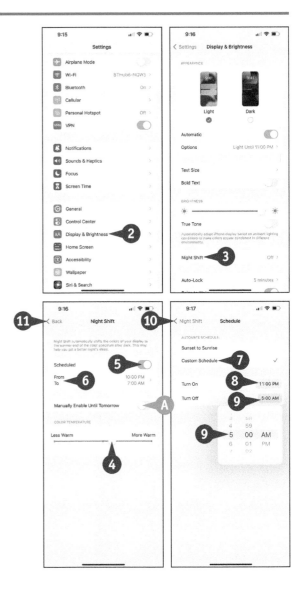

The Display & Brightness screen appears again.

12 Tap **Display Zoom** in the Display area at the bottom of the screen.

The Display Zoom screen appears.

13 Tap the unselected zoom type (✓ changes to).

The preview shows the zoom effect.

The preview cycles through several images to illustrate how the zoom types look.

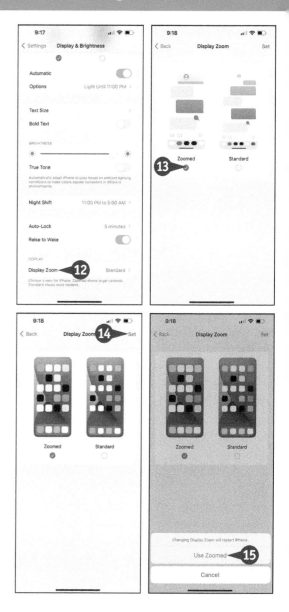

14 Tap **Set**.

The Changing Display Zoom Will Restart iPhone dialog opens.

15 Tap **Use Zoomed** or **Use Standard**, depending on which button appears.

Your iPhone restarts, but you do not need to unlock it again.

The display appears with the zoom effect you chose.

TIP

How does Night Shift know when sunset and sunrise are?
Your iPhone uses Location Services to determine your location and then looks up the sunset time and sunrise time online. If you disable Location Services, you will need to turn on Night Shift either on a custom schedule or manually.

Choose Privacy, Security, and Location Settings

Your iPhone contains a huge amount of information about you, the people you communicate with, what you do, and where you go. To keep this information secure, you need to choose suitable privacy, security, and location settings.

Privacy and security settings enable you to control which apps can access your contacts, calendars, reminders, and photos. You can also choose which apps can use your iPhone's Location Services, which apps can get your precise location and which can get only your approximate location, and which apps can track the iPhone's location via the Global Positioning System, or GPS.

Choose Privacy, Security, and Location Settings

1 On the Home screen, tap **Settings** (⚙).

The Settings screen appears.

2 Tap **Privacy & Security** (✋).

Note: To limit how ads can track your iPhone usage, tap **Apple Advertising** near the bottom of the Privacy & Security screen. On the Apple Advertising screen, set the **Personalized Ads** switch to Off ( ). On this screen, you can also tap **View Ad Targeting Information** to display the Ad Targeting Information screen, which shows information used to deliver ads targeting you on the App Store, Apple News, and Stocks.

The Privacy & Security screen appears.

3 Tap the app or service you want to configure. This example uses **Photos** (🌸).

The screen for the app or service appears, showing apps that have requested access to the app or service. In this example, the Dropbox app and the Facebook app have requested access to the Photos app.

4 Tap the app you want to configure.

The screen for the app appears.

5 Tap the appropriate permission level.

6 Tap ‹ to return to the previous screen.

7 Tap **Privacy & Security** (‹) to return to the Privacy & Security screen.

8 Configure other apps and services as needed.

9 Tap **Location Services** (➤).

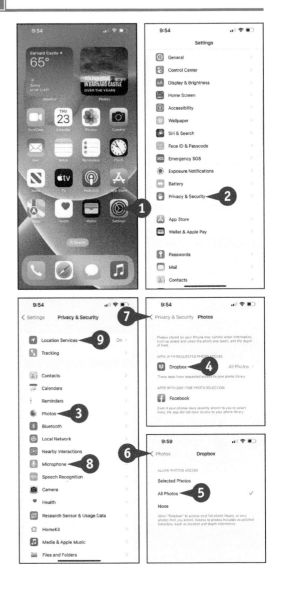

46

The Location Services screen appears.

10 If you need to turn Location Services off completely, set the **Location Services** switch to Off ( ). Usually, you would leave it set to On ( ).

11 Tap the app or feature you want to configure.

The screen for the app or feature appears.

12 In the Allow Location Access box, tap the appropriate button, such as **While Using the App**, **While Using the App or Widgets**, or **Never**.

Note: The buttons in the Allow Location Access box vary depending on the app or feature.

13 Set the **Precise Location** switch to On ( ) or Off ( ), as needed.

14 Tap **Location Services** (‹).

The Location Services screen appears again.

15 Set location access for other apps and features.

16 Tap **System Services** (⚙).

The System Services screen appears.

17 Set the switch for each system service to On ( ) or Off ( ), as needed. For example, set the **Location-Based Suggestions** switch to Off ( ) to turn off suggestions based on your location.

Note: The Exposure Notifications feature, which tracks COVID-19 and similar threats, requires the Location-Based Alerts feature to be enabled.

18 Set the **Status Bar Icon** switch to On ( ) to see the Location Services icon in the status bar when an app requests your location.

TIP

Why do some apps need to use Location Services?

Some apps and system services need to use Location Services to determine where you are. For example, the Maps app requires Location Services to display your location, and the Compass service needs your location to display accurate compass information.

If you allow the Camera app to use Location Services, it stores GPS data in your photos. You can then sort the photos by location in applications such as Photos on the Mac. Other apps use Location Services to provide context-specific information, such as information about nearby restaurants. For privacy, review the apps using Location Services and turn off any you prefer not to have this information.

Configure and Use Search

Your iPhone can put a huge amount of data in the palm of your hand, and you may often need to search to find what you need.

To make your search results more accurate and helpful, you can configure the Search feature. You can turn off searching for items you do not want to see in your search results.

Configure and Use Search

Configure Search

1 On the Home screen, tap **Settings** (⚙).

The Settings screen appears.

2 Tap **Siri & Search** (🔷) to display the Siri & Search screen.

3 Set the **Show in Look Up** switch to On (⬤) to see Siri content suggestions when you use Look Up.

4 Set the **Show in Spotlight** switch to On (⬤) to see Siri content suggestions when you use Spotlight.

5 Set the **Allow Notifications** switch to On (⬤) to see notifications for Siri suggestions.

6 Set the **Show in App Library & Spotlight** switch to On (⬤) to see Siri suggestions in the App Library and in Spotlight.

7 Set the **Show When Sharing** switch to On (⬤) to see Siri suggestions when you share items.

8 Set the **Show When Listening** switch to On (⬤) to see Siri suggestions when it is listening to you.

9 In the list of apps, tap the app you want to configure. This example uses **App Store** (🅰).

The screen for that app appears.

10 Set the **Learn from this App** switch to On (⬤) if you want Siri to learn from your use of this app.

11 Set the **Show App in Search** switch to On (⬤) if you want Search to include this app.

48

12 Set the **Show Content in Search** switch to On (◯) if you want Search to include this app's content.

13 Set the **Show on Home Screen** switch to On (◯) to make Siri suggestions for this app appear on the Home screen.

14 Set the **Suggest App** switch to On (◯) to let Siri suggest this app.

Note: Siri suggests apps you have used frequently.

15 Set the **Suggestion Notifications** switch to On (◯) to allow Siri to raise notifications when it suggests this app.

16 Tap **Siri & Search** (〈) to display the Siri & Search screen.

17 Tap the next app you want to configure.

Search for Items Using Search

1 Tap **Search** (🔍) on the Home screen.

A The Search panel appears.

Note: You can also start a search by swiping right from the Home screen, pulling down, and then tapping the search box that appears at the top of the screen.

The keyboard appears.

2 Start typing your search term.

A list of results appears.

3 Tap the result you want to view or open.

TIP

Which items should I search?

This depends on what you need to be able to search for. For example, if you do not need to search for music, videos, or podcasts, you can exclude the Music apps, the Videos app, and the Podcasts app from Siri & Search Suggestions.

Choose Locking and Control Center Settings

After a period of inactivity whose length you can configure, your iPhone automatically locks itself. It then turns off its screen and goes to sleep to save battery power. Setting your iPhone to lock itself quickly helps preserve battery power, but you may prefer to leave your iPhone on longer so that you can continue to work and then lock your iPhone manually. You can also choose which controls to display in Control Center and the order in which they appear.

Choose Locking and Control Center Settings

1 On the Home screen, tap **Settings** (⚙).

The Settings screen appears.

2 Tap **Display & Brightness** (🔠).

Note: If your iPhone is managed by an administrator, you may not be able to set all the options explained here. For example, an administrator may prevent you from disabling automatic locking for security reasons.

The Display & Brightness screen appears.

3 Tap **Auto-Lock**.

The Auto-Lock screen appears.

4 Tap the interval — for example, **30 Seconds**.

Note: Choose **Never** for Auto-Lock if you need to make sure your iPhone never goes to sleep. For example, if you are playing music with the lyrics displayed, turning off auto-locking may be helpful.

5 Tap **Back** (＜).

The Display & Brightness screen appears again.

6 Tap **Settings** (＜).

The Settings screen appears again.

7 Tap **Control Center** (■).

The Control Center screen appears.

8 Set the **Access Within Apps** switch to On (●)
if you want to be able to access Control Center from
apps rather than only from the Home screen.

A The Included Controls section shows the controls
currently in Control Center that you can remove.

B The More Controls section shows controls you
can add.

9 To remove a control from Control Center, tap
Remove (●), and then tap the textual **Remove**
button that appears.

Note: You can also remove a control by dragging it
from the Include list to the More Controls list.

10 To add a control to Control Center, tap **Add** (●).

C The control moves to the Included Controls list.

11 To change the order of controls in Control Center,
drag a control up or down by its handle (≡).

TIP

How do I put the iPhone to sleep manually?

You can put the iPhone to sleep at any point by pressing **Side**.

Putting the iPhone to sleep as soon as you stop using it helps to prolong battery runtime. If you apply
a passcode or other means of locking, as discussed in the section "Secure Your iPhone with Face ID and a
Passcode," later in this chapter, putting the iPhone to sleep also starts protecting your data sooner.

Create Custom Lock Screens

Whereas earlier versions of iOS provided a single lock screen and let you customize it only by changing the wallpaper, iOS enables you to create multiple lock screens and customize them extensively with your choice of wallpaper, your preferred fonts and colors, and a selection of widgets.

After creating a custom lock screen, you can link it with a particular Focus; see the next section, "Configure and Use Focus Mode," for details. For example, you might create a lock screen that provides the widgets and notifications you need when focusing on work. You could then link that lock screen with your Work Focus.

Create Custom Lock Screens

1 If your iPhone is not locked, press **Side** to put it to sleep, and then press **Side** again to wake it again.

Your iPhone displays the current lock screen.

2 Tap and hold the screen.

The lock screen switches to Customization Mode.

A You can customize this lock screen by tapping **Customize**.

3 Tap **Add** (⊕).

The Add New Wallpaper screen appears.

B You can tap **Photos** (▣), **People** (▣), **Photo Shuffle** (▨), **Emoji** (☺), **Weather** (☁), **Astronomy** (◉), or **Color** (◉) to display those categories.

C You can scroll through the categories: Featured, Suggested Photos, Photo Shuffle, Weather & Astronomy, Emoji, Collections, and Color.

4 Tap the wallpaper you want to use.

The wallpaper appears.

5 Tap the clock readout.

The Font & Color panel opens.

6 Tap the font you want.

7 Tap the color you want.

8 Tap **Close** (×).

The Font & Color panel closes.

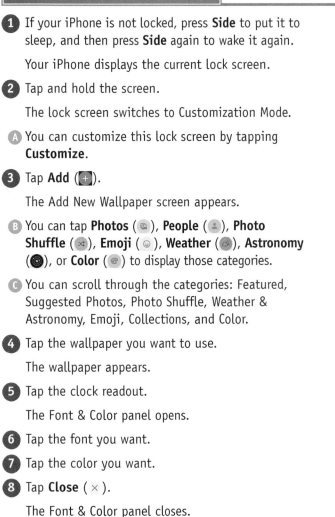

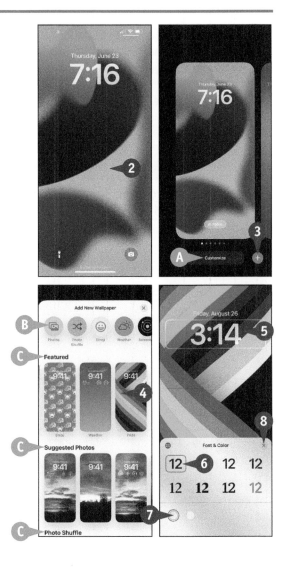

9 Tap the widgets box.

The Add Widgets panel opens.

10 Tap each widget you want to add.

Note: To control widget placement, tap and hold a widget in the Add Widgets panel or in the widgets box, and then drag it to where you want it.

The widgets you tap appear in the widgets box.

11 Tap **Close** (×).

The Add Widgets panel closes.

12 Tap **Done**.

The Set as Wallpaper dialog opens.

D You can tap **Customize Home Screen** if you want to customize the Home screen.

13 Tap **Set as Wallpaper Pair**.

The Wallpaper dialog closes.

The lock screen wallpaper appears.

E You can tap **Focus** (🔗) to assign a Focus Mode to this lock screen.

14 Tap the lock screen.

iOS applies the lock screen, and your iPhone starts using it.

TIPS

How do I switch among my custom lock screens?
Tap and hold the lock screen until it switches to Customization Mode. You can then swipe right or left to switch the lock screen. When you reach the lock screen you want, tap it.

How do I delete a custom lock screen?
Tap and hold the lock screen until it switches to Customization Mode. Swipe up on the lock screen you want to delete, moving it up and revealing the Delete (🗑) icon. Tap **Delete** (🗑).

Configure and Use Focus Mode

When you want to reduce distractions or perhaps eliminate them altogether, you can use Focus Mode on your iPhone and your other Apple devices. Focus Mode enables you to set up multiple Focuses designed to help you accomplish specific tasks. iOS includes various built-in Focuses — including Driving, Sleep, and Work — but you can also create custom Focuses as needed.

Your Apple Watch picks up Focus from your iPhone automatically, but you can also share Focus from your iPhone with your iPad and your Mac. You can share status from one or more Focuses so your contacts know you are focusing.

Display the Focus Screen and Configure Focus Status

On the Home screen, tap **Settings** (⚙️) to display the Settings screen, and then tap **Focus** (🌙). The Focus screen appears, showing a list (A) of existing Focuses. The prompt *Set Up* (B) appears on any built-in focus you have not yet set up.

Set the **Share Across Devices** switch (C) to On (⚪) to share Focus across all your Apple devices that support the feature. This functionality is usually helpful. For example, if you turn on Focus on your iPhone, Share Across Devices applies Focus to your iPad too.

Tap **Focus Status** (D) to display the Focus Status screen. Set the **Share Focus Status** switch (E) to On (⚪) to share your Focus status. Then, in the Share From list (F), set each Focus' switch to On (⚪) or Off (⚪), as needed.

Create a New Focus

On the Focus screen, tap **New** (+) to display the What Do You Want to Focus On? screen, which shows a list of available templates for Focus types — in the example, Custom (➕), Fitness (🏃), Gaming (🎮), Mindfulness (🌸), and Reading (📖). If one of the Focus types listed seems — either exactly or roughly — what you need, tap that Focus. Otherwise, tap **Custom** (G, ➕) to get generic Focus settings. Whichever Focus you choose, you can adjust its settings as needed.

If you tap **Custom** (➕), the Name Your Focus screen appears; if you tap a named Focus, you skip this step. Tap **Name** (H) and type a descriptive name for the Focus; tap the color (I) and glyph (J) you want to give the focus; and then tap **Next** (K).

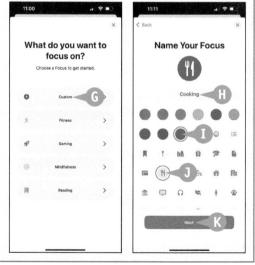

Create a New Focus (continued)

The summary screen for the Focus appears, showing its settings, such as "Silence notifications you don't want — across all your devices" and "Share with friends you have notifications silenced."

If the Focus has just the settings you want, you can tap **Close** (L, ×) to close the summary screen. The Focus appears on the Focus screen, and you can enable it from there.

Normally, however, you will want to tap **Customize Focus** (M) to display the customization screen for the Focus. At the top of this screen, you can tap **Edit** (N) to change the Focus' name, color, or glyph. Further down, you can make a wide range of changes, as discussed in the following sections.

Silence Notifications for a Focus

To reduce distractions, you can silence notifications entirely for a Focus. Alternatively, you can allow notifications only from selected people, selected apps, or both.

In the Silence Notifications area on the customization screen for the Focus, tap **Choose People** to display the Choose People screen. Tap either **Silence Notifications From** (O, 🔔) or **Allow Notifications From** (P, ✅), tap **Add People** (Q, ＋), tap each person (changes to ✅), and then tap **Done**. Tap **Next** (R) to display the Choose Calls To Allow screen.

Tap **Everybody** (S, 📇), **Allowed People Only** (T, ✅), **Favorites** (U, ⭐), or **Contacts Only** (V, 📇); or tap **Contact Group** (W, 😊) and then tap the group, such as **Friends** (X, 👥). After making your choice, tap **Done** (Y).

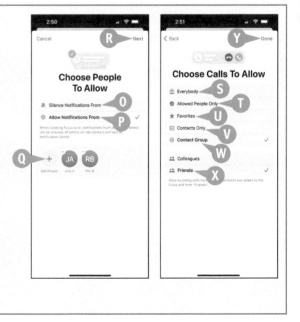

continued ▶

When you create a custom Focus, you base it on either the Custom template or another existing template, such as the Reading template. You give the Focus a name, icon, and color of your choosing, and you decide whether to accept the template's default settings or to customize them.

You can tie each Focus to a particular lock screen and Home screen page and apply Focus filters to limit the information a given app shows when the Focus is enabled. You can set any Focus to run automatically or turn them on and off manually from Control Center.

Specify the Lock Screen Face and Home Screen Page for a Focus

In the Customize Screens area of the customization screen, tap **Choose** under the lock screen thumbnail — the left thumbnail — to display the Choose a Lock Screen screen. In the Create a New Lock Screen area, you can tap **Gallery** (Z) to start creating a new lock screen. Alternatively, in the Choose from Your Lock Screens area, tap the existing lock screen (AA) you want to use (changes to ✓), and then tap **Done** (AB) to return to the customization screen.

To specify the Home screen page for the Focus, tap **Choose** under the Home screen thumbnail — the right thumbnail — to display the Choose a Home Page to Turn On screen. Tap the Home screen page (AC) you want to use (changes to ✓), and then tap **Done** (AD).

Set the Focus to Turn On Automatically

If you want iOS to turn on the Focus automatically via Automation based on how it observes you using the Focus, tap **Smart Activation** (AE, ☾) on the customization screen. On the Smart Activation screen, set the **Smart Activation** switch (AF) to On.

If you want to add an automation of your own, tap **Add Automation** (AG). On the New Automation screen, specify the type of automation by tapping **Time** (AH, 🕐), **Location** (AI, ➤), or **App** (AJ, 🔵), and then work on the subsequent screens to set up the automation.

Apply a Focus Filter

To control how your iPhone and its apps behave when this Focus is active, you can add one or more Focus filters to the Focus. For example, you can set the Mail app to get new messages for only a particular account while the Focus is active, sparing you the distraction that incoming messages on your other accounts might cause.

On the customization screen, tap **Add** (AO) in the Focus Filters box to display the Focus Filters screen, which contains the App Filters list and the System Filters list.

Tap the filter you want to apply. For example, tap **Safari** (AK,) to display the Safari screen, tap **Tab Group** (AL) to display the Tab Group screen, and then tap the tab group (AM) the filter should allow. Back on the Safari screen, set the **Allow opening external links in your Focus Tab Group** switch (AN) to On ( ) or Off ( ), as needed. Then tap **Add** (AO) to add the filter to the Focus.

Apply Your Focus Filters Manually

To apply a Focus filter manually, first open Control Center by swiping down from the upper-right corner of the screen. Tap the text part of the **Focus** button (AP) to display the Focus screen in Control Center. Do not tap the icon shown on the Focus button, because tapping the icon enables or disables the Focus that icon represents.

To simply enable or disable a Focus, tap its button. For more choices, tap **Options** (AQ,), and then tap the appropriate button, such as **For 1 hour** (AR).

Customize Today View

Today View, which you display by swiping right on the first Home screen page, shows a list of widgets to provide you with quick information about the weather, the news, and your time commitments. You can configure Today View by removing widgets you do not need, adding widgets you find useful, and arranging the widgets into the order you find most helpful.

Customize Today View

1 From the first Home screen page, swipe right.

Today View appears.

2 Swipe up to scroll down to the bottom of the screen.

More items in Today View appear.

3 Tap **Edit**.

Today View opens for customization and goes into Jiggle Mode, in which the icons jiggle to indicate they are movable.

4 Tap **Remove** (−) in the upper-left corner of a widget you want to remove.

The Remove Widget? dialog opens.

5 Tap **Remove**.

iOS removes the widget from Today View.

6 To add a widget, tap **Add** (+).

The Add Widgets panel appears.

Ⓐ You can find widgets by tapping **Search Widgets** (Q) and then typing your search term.

❼ Tap the widget you want to add.

The Information panel for the widget appears.

❽ Swipe left to browse through the available versions of the widget, as needed.

❾ Tap **Add Widget** (⊕).

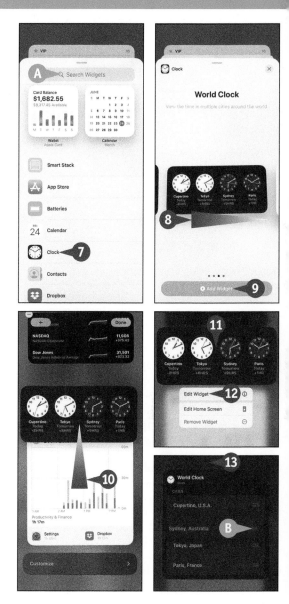

The widget appears on the Today View screen.

❿ Drag the widget to where you want it to appear.

⓫ To customize the widget, tap and hold it.

The pop-up menu opens.

⓬ Tap **Edit Widget** (ⓘ).

The widget displays customization options.

Ⓑ For example, for the World Clock, you can drag the cities into a different order.

⓭ Tap outside the widget.

The widget appears with the changes you made to it.

TIP

How do I get more widgets to add to Today View?

The widgets in Today View come built into apps, so the only way to get more widgets is to install more apps that have widgets.

When choosing an app to add to your iPhone, consider whether the app is one for which a widget in Today View would be useful. If so, look for an app that offers a widget.

Secure Your iPhone with Face ID and a Passcode

The primary method of unlocking your iPhone is Face ID, which uses depth cameras to scan your face in 3D and match it to stored data. During the initial setup of your iPhone, iOS walks you through setting up Face ID, together with a passcode as a backup method of unlocking your iPhone for when Face ID does not work. After setup, you can configure Face ID, reset Face ID, or add an alternate appearance. For added security, you can set your iPhone to automatically erase its data after ten failed attempts to enter the passcode.

Secure Your iPhone with Face ID and a Passcode

1 On the Home screen, tap **Settings** (⚙).

The Settings screen appears.

2 Tap **Face ID & Passcode** (😀).

Note: If the Enter Passcode screen appears, type your passcode.

The Face ID & Passcode screen appears.

3 Set the **iPhone Unlock** switch to On (⬤) to use Face ID to unlock your iPhone.

4 Set the **iTunes & App Store** switch to On (⬤) to use Face ID to authorize purchases on the iTunes Store and the App Store.

5 Set the **Wallet & Apple Pay** switch to On (⬤) to use Face ID to authorize payments in Wallet and via Apple Pay.

6 Set the **Password AutoFill** switch to On (⬤) to use Face ID to authorize filling in passwords automatically.

7 To add an alternate appearance, such as wearing glasses or makeup, tap **Set Up an Alternate Appearance** and follow the prompts.

8 Set the **Face ID with a Mask** switch to On (⬤) to allow Face ID when you are wearing a mask. This is convenient but may be less accurate and less secure.

9 Tap **Add Glasses** to start the process of adding glasses to Face ID.

A You can tap **Reset Face ID** if you want to redo Face ID, including any alternate appearance.

10 Set the **Require Attention for Face ID** switch to On (⬤) for added security.

11 Set the **Attention Aware Features** switch to On (⬤) to have Face ID detect whether you are using the phone before it dims the screen or turns down alerts.

B To change the passcode type, you can tap **Change Passcode**, tap **Passcode Options**, and then tap **Custom Alphanumeric Code**, **Custom Numeric Code**, or **4-Digit Numeric Code**.

C You can set the **Unlock with Apple Watch** switch to On (⬤) to use your Apple Watch as an unlocking device for your iPhone.

D iOS normally requires a passcode immediately after locking it. If your iPhone is configured via management policy, you may be able to tap **Require Passcode** and implement a delay, such as 30 Seconds.

12 Set the **Voice Dial** switch to On (⬤) or Off (◯), as needed.

13 In the **Allow Access When Locked** area, set the switches to On (⬤) or Off (◯), as needed.

Note: Allowing access to Wallet when your iPhone is locked enables you to make payments and reach boarding passes and similar documents more quickly when you need them.

14 If you want the iPhone to erase all its data after ten failed passcode attempts, set the **Erase Data** switch to On (⬤).

The iPhone displays a confirmation dialog.

15 Tap **Enable**.

TIP

Which type of passcode should I use?

The default, a six-digit numeric passcode, provides reasonably good security and is easy to enter. But if you need strong security, choose **Custom Numeric Code** and use 12 or more digits. For extra-strong security, choose **Custom Alphanumeric Code** and create a passcode of 12 or more characters, including upper- and lowercase letters, numbers, and symbols. Do not use a four-digit passcode, because it leaves your iPhone dangerously unsecure.

Configure Screen Time and Restrictions

Mobile phones can be not only extremely useful but great productivity tools as well — yet they can also be addictive time-sinks promoting disengagement and isolation. iOS provides the Screen Time feature to enable you to track and manage the time spent using an iPhone and other Apple devices, enforce downtime away from the screen, and set limits on apps, either on your own iPhone or on an iPhone you manage. You can also enforce restrictions on content and privacy — for example, preventing the iPhone's user from buying content in apps or watching adult-rated movies.

Access the Screen Time Features

To access the Screen Time features, tap **Settings** (⚙) on the Home screen to display the Settings screen, and then tap **Screen Time** (A, ⧗) to display the Screen Time screen.

The Daily Average histogram (B) shows your daily average usage for this week. You can tap **See All Activity** (C) to display the usage details broken down by the week (D).

Set Downtime Hours

To enforce downtime on the iPhone and other iPhones, iPads, or Macs using the same iCloud account, tap **Downtime** (⧗) on the Screen Time screen, and then work on the Downtime screen. Set the **Scheduled** switch (E) to On (⬤) to enable the controls; then either tap **Every Day** (F) to use the same hours each day or tap **Customize Days** (G) and tap a day (H) to customize its hours. On the screen for a day, such as the Sunday screen, you can disable downtime by setting the switch (I) to Off ( ), or you can simply specify custom hours.

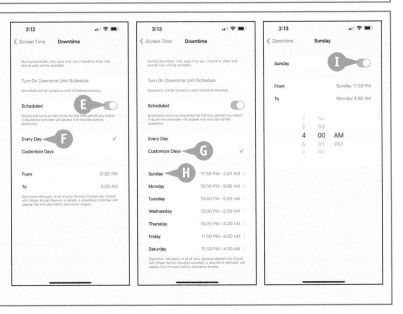

Set App Limits and Always Allowed

To set limits for app usage, tap **App Limits** (⌛) on the Screen Time screen. On the App Limits screen, set the **App Limits** switch to On (◉), and tap **Add Limit** to display the Choose Apps panel. Tap to select the app (J) (✓ changes to), tap **Next** (K), specify the time limit (L), and then tap **Add** (M).

To allow anytime usage of some apps, tap **Always Allowed** (✓) on the Screen Time screen. On the Always Allowed screen, tap **Add** (N, ➕) to move an app from the Choose Apps list to the Allowed Apps list, or tap **Remove** (O, ➖) to remove an app from the Allowed Apps list.

Set Content and Privacy Restrictions

To set limits on the content the user can access and the degree to which the user can expose personal information, tap **Content & Privacy Restrictions** (🚫) on the Screen Time screen. On the Content & Privacy Restrictions screen, set the **Content & Privacy Restrictions** switch (P) to On (◉) to enable the controls. You can then configure the settings. For example, tap **Content Restrictions** (Q) and then use the controls on the Content Restrictions screen to set restrictions on movies (R, S), TV shows (T), books (U), apps (V), and other items.

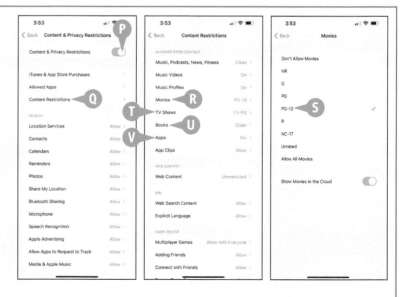

Set Up Family Sharing

Apple's Family Sharing feature enables you to share purchases from Apple's online services with other family members. You can also share photos and calendars, and you can use the Find My iPhone feature to find your iOS devices and Macs when they go missing.

This section assumes that you are the Family organizer, the person who gets to set up Family Sharing; invite others to participate; and pay for the content they buy on Apple Services, such as the iTunes Store, the Apple Book Store, and the App Store.

Access the Family Sharing Controls

To configure Family Sharing, tap **Settings** (⚙) on the Home screen to open the Settings app. Tap **Apple ID** — the button bearing your Apple ID name — at the top of the Settings screen to display the Apple ID screen, and then tap **Family** (A) to display the Family screen.

If you have not yet use Family Sharing, tap **Get Started** to display the Get Started screen, and then follow the prompts to begin specifying your family members and deciding what to share with them.

Once you have added family members, they appear in the list at the top of the Family screen (B). You can tap **Add** (C, ⨁) to start adding another family member.

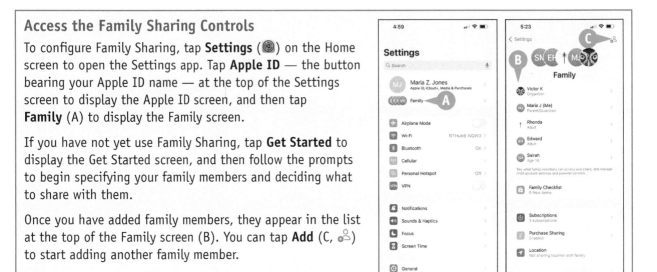

View Information for a Family Member

On the Family screen, tap the button for an existing family member to display a screen showing the member's information, including their Apple ID (D). You can tap **Subscriptions** (E, ⊕) to display a list of their subscriptions (F); tap **Purchases** (G, ⓟ) to determine whether they are sharing their purchases; or look at the **Location** button (H, ➤) to learn whether they are sharing their location with you.

For a child, you can view and configure other information, including Parents/Guardians (I, 👪), Screen Time (J, ⌛), Ask To Buy (K, 💬), and Apple Cash (L, ⬤).

Complete the Family Checklist

The Family Checklist feature rounds up disparate but helpful family-sharing features you may want to implement for your family. Tap **Family Checklist** () to display the Family Checklist screen, and then work your way through those items that will benefit you and your family. The list varies, because it excludes those Family Sharing features you have already implemented, but the example here is fairly typical.

Add Family to Medical ID (✳). Tap **Update Medical ID** (M) to open your Medical ID record for editing so you can add your family members to the Emergency Contacts section.

Share Your Location with Family (●). Tap **Share My Location** (N) to display the Share Your Location with Family screen. If you want to share your location with all the family members, tap **Share Location with Family** (O); if you want to pick specific family members, tap **Customize** (P), and then set the switch for each of those members to On (●). On this screen, you can also set the **Share Location Automatically** switch to On (●) to have iOS automatically share your location with each family member you add from now on.

Share iCloud+ with Your Family (●). Tap this button (Q) to display the iCloud+ screen, which enables you to see how much space of your iCloud+ space each family member is using.

Add a Recovery Contact (●). Tap **Set Up a Recovery Contact** (R) to display the Account Recovery screen, on which you can start the process of specifying the person you want to help you when you lock yourself out of your account.

Configure Exposure Notifications

iOS includes an Exposure Notifications feature that helps you to track, report, and manage your exposure to infectious diseases, such as COVID-19. The Exposure Notifications feature uses Bluetooth to track nearby smartphones running iOS or Android that also have Exposure Notifications turned on and to exchange identifiers with them. When someone reports a positive diagnosis, their phone can report it, enabling public health authorities to notify those people who have been exposed to them and who may need testing.

Configure Exposure Notifications

On the Home screen, tap **Settings** (⚙) to open the Settings app, and then tap **Exposure Notifications** (A, ☀) to display the Exposure Notifications screen. Set the **Availability Alerts** switch (B) to On (◯) to receive notifications when Exposure Notifications are available in your current region.

If the Availability Alerts switch is dimmed and unavailable, you probably need to turn on Location Services for Location-Based Alerts. From the Exposure Notifications screen, tap **Settings** (C, ‹) to display the Settings screen. Next, tap **Privacy & Security** (✋) to display the Privacy & Security screen, and then tap **Location Services** (➤) to display the Location Services screen. Tap **System Services** (⚙) to display the System Services screen, and then set the **Location-Based Alerts** switch to On (◯).

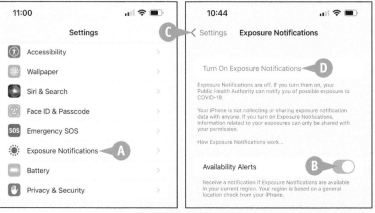

On the Exposure Notifications screen, tap **Turn On Exposure Notifications** (D) to display the COVID-19 Exposure Notifications screen.

On the COVID-19 Exposure Notifications screen, you can tap **How Exposure Notifications Work** (E) to see more information on how the notifications work.

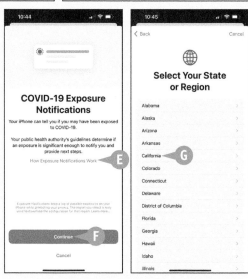

Tap **Continue** (F) to display the Select Your Country or Region screen, and then tap your country or region. If you follow this example, which uses **United States**, the Select Your State or Region screen appears. Tap your state (G) or region to display a screen with terms for that state or region's public heath department, and then follow the prompts to enable and configure notifications.

Choose Date, Time, and International Settings

To keep yourself on time and your data accurate, you need to make sure not only that the iPhone is using the correct date and time but also that it knows which time zone you are currently occupying. The easiest approach, and usually the best, is to set your iPhone to retrieve the time, date, and location from online sources; but sometimes you may need to set these items manually instead.

To make dates, times, and other data appear in the formats you prefer, you may need to change the iPhone's International settings.

Choose Date & Time Settings

On the Home screen, tap **Settings** (⚙) to display the Settings screen, and then tap **General** (⚙). On the General screen, tap **Date & Time** to display the Date & Time screen.

Set the **24-Hour Time** switch (A) to On (⬤) if you want to use 24-hour times.

If you want to set the date and time manually, set the **Set Automatically** switch (B) to Off ( ), and then tap the bar (C) that shows the current date and time. iOS displays controls for setting the date and time. On the calendar panel, navigate to and then tap the appropriate date (D). Next, tap the time readout (E) and use the pop-up panel to set the time.

Tap **Time Zone** (F) to display the Time Zone screen. Tap **Search** (G, 🔍), and then start typing the time zone or a location in it. Tap the result (H) you want to use.

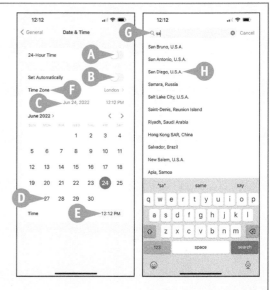

Choose International Settings

On the Home screen, tap **Settings** (⚙) to display the Settings screen, and then tap **General** (⚙). On the General screen, tap **Language & Region** to display the Language & Region screen. Here, the Region Format Example area (I) shows examples of the time, date, currency, and number formats for the current region.

To change the region, tap **Region** (J), and then tap the region on the Select Region screen.

To add a language, tap **Add Language** (K). On the Select Language screen, tap the language (L). In the dialog that opens at the bottom of the screen, tap **Use** (M) for the appropriate language.

CHAPTER 3

Using Voice, Accessibility, and Continuity

Your iPhone includes the Siri personal assistant, helpful accessibility features, and integration with your Mac and Apple Watch via the Continuity feature.

Give Commands and Get Information with Siri

Your iPhone's powerful Siri feature enables you to take essential actions by using your voice. Siri processes your spoken input directly on your iPhone, so you can give commands when the iPhone does not have an Internet connection. However, Siri does require an Internet connection to look up information.

You can use Siri either with the iPhone's built-in microphone or with the microphone on a headset. The built-in microphone works well in a quiet environment or if you hold your iPhone close to your face, but in noisy situations you will do better with a headset microphone.

Open Siri

You can open Siri from the Home screen or any app. Press and hold **Side** for several seconds. If you have connected a headset with a clicker button, you can also press and hold the headset clicker button for several seconds to invoke Siri. If you have chosen to allow Siri access when your iPhone is locked, you can also activate Siri while the lock screen is displayed.

The Siri icon appears. A tone or a prompt such as "Hm?" or "Yes?" indicates that Siri is ready to take your commands. If you enable the "Hey Siri" feature in the Settings app, you can also activate Siri by saying "Hey Siri."

Send an E-Mail Message

Say "E-mail" and the contact's name, followed by the message. Siri creates an e-mail message to the contact and enters the text. Review the message, and then tap **Send** to send it.

If you prefer, you can start the message by saying "E-mail" and the contact's name and then pausing. Siri then prompts you for the subject and text of the message in turn.

> **Mail**
>
> To: Mark Ernst
> Subject: Keynote speaker
>
> Please see if you can get Grant Smith as the Keynote speaker for next week's conference. Let me know how you get on.
>
> Cancel   Send

Set an Alarm

Say "Set an alarm for 4:30 a.m." and check the alarm that Siri displays.

You can turn the alarm off by tapping its switch (changes to).

You can ask a question such as "Which alarms do I have set?" to make Siri display a list of your alarms.

> 7:26
>
> Clock
> **4:30 AM**
> Alarm

Set a Reminder for Yourself

Say "Remind me" and the details of what you want Siri to remind you of. For example, say "Remind me to take my iPad to work tomorrow morning." Siri listens to what you say and creates a reminder. Check what Siri has written. If the reminder is correct, simply leave it; if not, tap **Change** and edit it.

> **Reminders**
>
> Take my iPad to work
> Tomorrow
>
> Change

Send a Text Message

Say "Tell" and the contact's name. When Siri responds, say the message you want to send. For example, say "Tell Victor Kemp" and then "I'm stuck in traffic, so I'll be about 10 minutes late to the meeting. Please start without me." Siri creates a text message to the contact, enters the text, and sends the message when you say "Send" or tap **Send**.

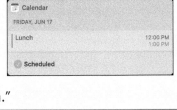

You can also say "Tell" and the contact's name followed immediately by the message. For example, "Tell Bill Sykes the package will arrive at 10 a.m."

Set Up a Meeting

Say "Meet with" and the contact's name, followed by brief details of the appointment. For example, say "Meet with Don Williamson at noon on Friday for lunch." Siri listens and warns you of any scheduling conflict. Siri then sends a meeting invitation to the contact if it finds an e-mail address and adds the meeting to your calendar after you tap **Confirm** or say "Confirm."

Look Up Information

Launch Siri and ask for the type of information you want. Here are three examples:

- "Siri, when's the next White Sox game?"

- "Siri, where is the movie *Avatar: The Way of Water* playing in Indianapolis this weekend?"

- "Hey, Siri, is there a brewpub in Minneapolis?"

Get Directions

Launch Siri, and then say "Get directions," followed by the start place and the end place. For example, say "Get directions from O'Hare to Lollapalooza."

Find Out What Music You Are Listening To

Launch Siri and ask a question such as "What song is this?" or "Do you know what this music is called?" Siri monitors the microphone's input, consults the Shazam music-recognition service, and returns a result if there is a match.

Dictate Text Using Siri

Siri can transcribe your speech quickly and accurately into correctly spelled and punctuated text. You can dictate into any app that supports the keyboard, which means you can dictate e-mail messages, notes, documents, and more. To dictate, tap the microphone icon (🎤), speak after Siri beeps, and then tap **Done** or **Keyboard** (⌨).

Siri automatically inserts punctuation where it is clearly required and capitalizes the first letter of each paragraph, sentence, and proper noun. But to get the most out of dictation, you will likely want to dictate some punctuation, capitalization, symbols, layout, and formatting.

Insert Punctuation, Standard Symbols, and Currency Symbols

To insert punctuation, standard symbols, and currency symbols, use the terms shown in Table 3-1.

Table 3-1:   Dictating Punctuation, Standard Symbols, and Currency Symbols

Term	Character	Term	Character
Punctuation			
comma	,	hyphen	-
period *or* full stop	.	dash	–
exclamation point *or* exclamation mark	!	em dash	—
question mark	?	open parenthesis	(
semicolon	;	close parenthesis	)
colon	:	open bracket	[
asterisk	*	close bracket	]
ampersand	&	open brace	{
underscore	_	close brace	}
Standard Symbols			
at sign	@	percent	%
greater than	>	less than	<
forward slash	/	backslash	\
registered sign	®	copyright sign	©
Currency Symbols			
dollar sign	$	euro sign	€
cent sign	¢	pound sterling sign	£
yen sign	¥		

Control Layout

You can control text layout by creating new lines and new paragraphs as needed. A new paragraph enters two line breaks, creating a blank line between paragraphs. To create a new line, say "New line." To create a new paragraph, say "New paragraph."

For example, say "Dear Anna comma new paragraph thank you for the parrot period new paragraph it's the most amazing gift I've ever had period" to enter the text shown here.

> 10:26
>
> Cancel
>
> **New Message**
>
> To:
>
> Cc/Bcc, From: maria_z_jones@icloud.com
>
> Subject:
>
> Dear Anna,
>
> Thank you for the parrot.
>
> It's the most amazing gift I've ever had.

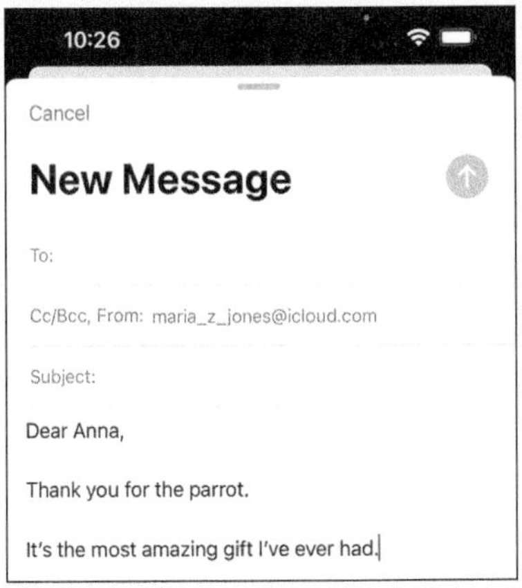

Control Capitalization

You can apply capitalization to the first letter of a word or to a whole word. You can also switch capitalization off temporarily to force lowercase:

> 10:28
>
> ‹ Notes   Done
>
> **Ongoing Notes**
>
> Give the Head Dining Table a french polish.

- Say "Cap" to capitalize the first letter of the next word.

- Say "Caps on" to capitalize all the words until you say "Caps off."

- Say "No caps" to prevent automatic capitalization of the next word — for example, "No caps Monday" produces "monday" instead of "Monday."

- Say "No caps on" to force lowercase of all words until you say "No caps off."

For example, say "Give the cap head cap dining cap table a no caps french polish period" to enter the text shown here.

Insert Quotes and Emoticons

To insert double quotes, say "Open quotes" and "Close quotes." To insert single quotes, say "Open single quotes" and "Close single quotes." To enter standard emoticons, say "Smiley face," "Frown face," and "Wink face."

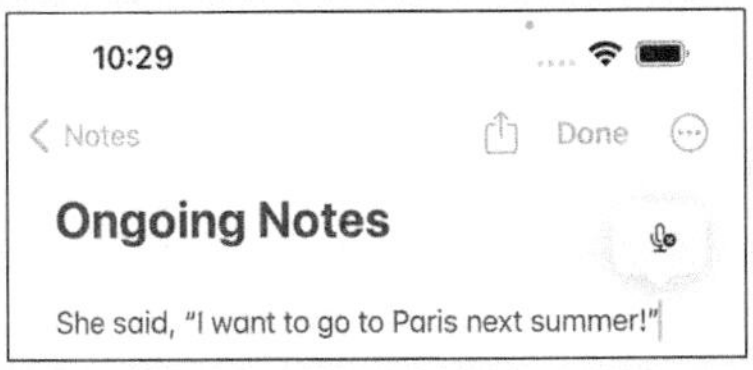

> 10:29
>
> ‹ Notes   Done
>
> **Ongoing Notes**
>
> She said, "I want to go to Paris next summer!"

For example, say "She said comma open quotes I want to go to Paris next summer exclamation point close quotes" to enter the text shown here.

Configure Siri to Work Your Way

To get the most out of Siri, spend a few minutes configuring Siri. You can set the language Siri uses and choose when Siri should give you voice feedback. You can also decide whether to use the Raise to Speak option, which activates Siri when you raise your iPhone to your face, and whether Siri displays its interpretation of your speech on the screen.

Most important, you can tell Siri which contact record contains your information so that Siri knows your name, address, phone numbers, e-mail address, and other essential information.

Configure Siri to Work Your Way

1 On the Home screen, tap **Settings** (⚙).

The Settings screen appears.

2 Tap **Siri & Search** (🔍).

The Siri & Search screen appears.

3 Set the **Listen for "Hey Siri"** switch to On (🔘) if you want to be able to activate Siri by saying "Hey Siri!"

4 Set the **Press Side Button for Siri** switch to On (🔘) if you want to be able to summon Siri by pressing and holding the Side button.

5 Set the **Allow Siri When Locked** switch to On (🔘) if you want to use Siri from the lock screen.

6 Tap **Language**.

The Language screen appears.

7 Tap the language you want to use.

8 Tap **Siri & Search** (<).

The Siri & Search screen appears again.

9 Tap **Siri Voice**.

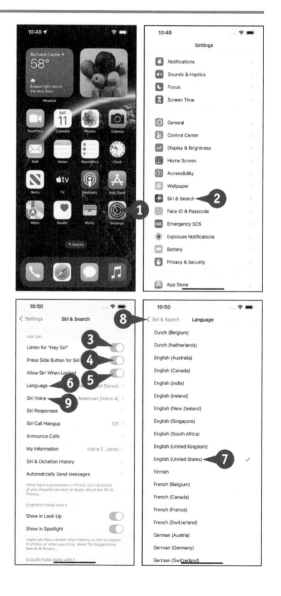

74

The Siri Voice screen appears.

10 In the Variety box, tap the accent you want Siri to use. For example, for English (United States), you can tap **American**, **Australian**, **British**, **Indian**, **Irish**, or **South African**.

11 In the Voice box, tap a voice, such as **Voice 1** or **Voice 2**.

12 Tap **Siri & Search** (<).

The Siri & Search screen appears again.

13 Tap **Siri Responses**.

The Siri Responses screen appears.

14 In the Spoken Responses box, tap **Automatic** or **Prefer Spoken Responses**, as appropriate.

15 Set the **Always Show Siri Captions** switch to On (●) if you want to see Siri's responses to you as text.

16 Set the **Always Show Speech** switch to On (●) if you want Siri to display its interpretation of what you say.

17 Tap **Siri & Search** (<).

The Siri & Search screen appears again.

18 Tap **My Information**.

The Contacts screen appears, showing either the All Contacts list or the lists you have selected.

Note: If necessary, tap **Lists** to display the Lists screen, select the lists you need, and then tap **Done**.

19 Tap the contact record that contains your information.

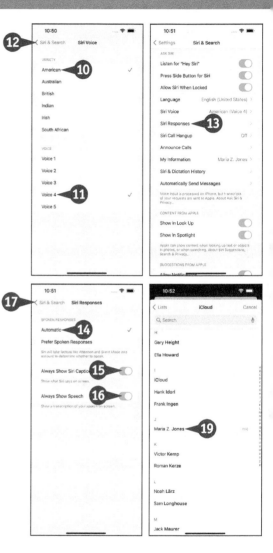

TIP

Does Apple store the details of what I ask Siri?

Apple stores some details, but you can delete them. When you use Siri, your iPhone processes your vocal input and consults the Siri servers in Apple's data center in North Carolina, USA, when it needs assistance. The data center stores the details of your request and may analyze them to determine what people use Siri for and work out ways of making Siri more effective. You can delete your Siri and dictation history by tapping **Siri & Dictation History** on the Siri & Search screen, tapping **Delete Siri & Dictation History** on the Siri & Dictation History screen, and then tapping **Delete Siri & Dictation History** in the Delete Siri & Dictation History dialog.

Set Up VoiceOver and Key Accessibility Features

Your iPhone provides a wide range of accessibility features designed to make the device easier to use for people with vision problems, hearing problems, and physical and motor problems. To enable and configure these features, you open the Settings app and display the Accessibility screen.

If you have trouble identifying the iPhone's controls on-screen, you can use the VoiceOver feature to read them to you. VoiceOver changes your iPhone's standard finger gestures so that you tap to select the item whose name you want it to speak, double-tap to activate an item, and flick three fingers to scroll.

Display the Accessibility Screen

To display the Accessibility screen, tap **Settings** (⚙) on the Home screen, and then tap **Accessibility** (🔵).

The Accessibility screen, shown here, contains four sections. The Vision section (A) gives you access to features such as VoiceOver, Zoom, and Magnifier. The Physical and Motor section (B) presents features such as Touch, Switch Control, and Voice Control. The Hearing section (C) includes the Hearing Devices, Sound Recognition, and Subtitles & Captioning features. Lastly, the General section (D) contains the Guided Access, Siri, Accessibility Shortcut, and Per-App Settings features.

Set Up VoiceOver to Identify Items On-Screen

On the Accessibility screen, tap **VoiceOver** (🔵) to display the VoiceOver screen. Set the **VoiceOver** switch (E) to On (🔵); if a warning dialog opens, read its contents, and then dismiss it. You then need to use VoiceOver gestures to navigate. Start by tapping **VoiceOver Practice** (F) to select the button, putting a black selection border around it; then double-tap **VoiceOver Practice** to "click" the button. The VoiceOver Practice screen appears, on which you can practice tapping, double-tapping, triple-tapping, swiping, and flicking. VoiceOver identifies each gesture it recognizes and displays an explanation (G). Tap **Done** (H), and then double-tap **Done**, when you finish practicing.

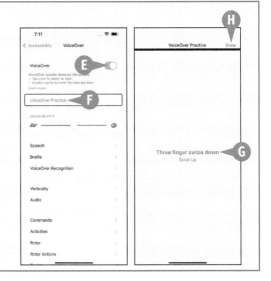

If you use VoiceOver, experiment with its many settings to find which suit you best. Drag the **Speaking Rate** slider (I) to set the speed at which VoiceOver speaks. Tap **Speech** (J) to display the Speech screen, where you can select the voice to use (K), set custom pronunciations, and adjust the pitch. Tap **Braille** (L) to display the Braille screen, on which you can configure Braille input and output. Tap **Verbosity** (M) to display the Verbosity screen, where you can control what items VoiceOver announces. Tap **Typing** (N) to display the Typing screen, and there choose what typing feedback you want.

Configure Zoom Settings

The Zoom feature enables you to zoom in and out easily to improve your view of the screen's contents. On the Accessibility screen, tap **Zoom** (⊚) to display the Zoom screen, shown here, and then set the **Zoom** switch (O) to On (◯) to enable Zoom.

Set the **Follow Focus** switch (P) to On (◯) to make the zoom area follow the part of the screen that is currently active. Set the **Smart Typing** switch (Q) to On (◯) to use Window Zoom when the on-screen keyboard is displayed and to have Zoom avoid the keyboard. Tap **Keyboard Shortcuts** (R) to display Keyboard Shortcuts screen, set the **Keyboard Shortcuts** switch (S) to On (◯), and then set the individual switches to On (◯) or Off ( ) to specify which shortcuts to use.

continued ▶

To help you see the screen's contents, you can turn on the Zoom feature; you can then double-tap the screen with three fingers to zoom in, drag with three fingers to pan the zoomed view, and double-tap with three fingers again to zoom out. You can also display the Zoom Controller for easy control of zoom; set the maximum zoom level; and specify which type of zoom region to use, either a movable window or the full screen.

In the Display & Text Size category, you can adjust display brightness and contrast, invert the colors, and change the text size.

Configure Zoom Settings (continued)

On the Zoom screen, tap **Zoom Controller** (T) to display the Zoom Controller screen, and then set the **Show Controller** switch (U) to On (◯) to display the Zoom Controller (V), which gives quick access to Zoom commands. Tap the Zoom Controller to display the Zoom dialog (W), which provides additional commands.

On the Zoom screen, tap **Zoom Region** (X) to display the Zoom Region screen, and then tap **Full Screen Zoom** or **Window Zoom**, as appropriate. Windows Zoom displays a frame (Y) that you can reposition by dragging the handle (Z) at the bottom.

Configure Display and Text Size Settings

To adjust your iPhone's display brightness and contrast, invert the colors, or change the text size and weight, tap **Display & Text Size** on the Accessibility screen. On the Display & Text Size screen, set the **Bold Text** switch (AA) to On (◯) if you want to make text bold, and then tap **Larger Text** (AB) to display the Larger Text screen. Set the **Larger Accessibility Sizes** switch (AC) to On (◯), and then drag the slider (AD) to set the text size in apps that support the Dynamic Type feature.

Set the **Button Shapes** switch (AE) to On (◯) to display "button shapes" such as the underline (AF) on the Back button. Set the **On/Off Labels** switch (AG) to On (◯) to display an *I* on an On switch and an *O* on an Off switch.

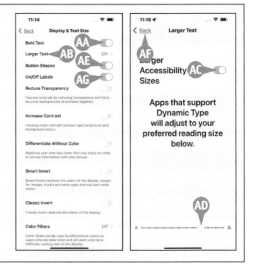

To make text more readable, you can set the **Reduce Transparency** switch (AH) to On (⬤). You can set the Increase Contrast switch (AI) to On (⬤) to boost contrast; set the **Differentiate Without Color** switch (AJ) to On (⬤) to use visual differentiations other than color; set the **Smart Invert** switch (AK) to On (⬤) to invert most colors except for those in images and media; or set the **Classic Invert** switch (AL) to On (⬤) to invert all colors.

If you have color blindness, tap **Color Filters** (AM), and then work on the Color Filters screen (AN).

If the iPhone's screen looks too intense, try setting the **Reduce White Point** switch (AO) to On (⬤).

To set screen brightness manually, set the **Auto-Brightness** switch (AP) to Off ( ).

Configure Touch Features

Tap **Touch** (✋) to display the Touch screen.

To use the AssistiveTouch feature, which is designed to help with difficulty touching the screen accurately, tap **AssistiveTouch** (AQ). On the AssistiveTouch screen, set the **AssistiveTouch** switch (AR) to On (⬤). You can then tap **Customize Top Level Menu** (AS) and work on the resulting screen to customize the AssistiveTouch menu (AT). In the Custom Actions box (AU), choose custom actions for single-tap, double-tap, and long press. Further down the AssistiveTouch screen, choose other options as needed.

On the Touch screen, set the **Reachability** switch (AV) to On (⬤) if you want to be able to bring the top of the screen down to about halfway by swiping down on the bottom edge of the screen. To configure the duration for haptic touch, tap **Haptic Touch** (AW) and use the controls on the Haptic Touch screen.

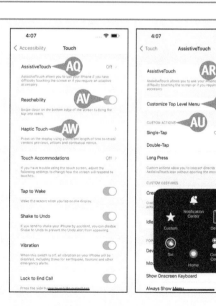

continued ▶

Your iPhone includes various features designed to make it easier for you to interact with the touch screen and other hardware. Changes you can make include setting the tap-and-hold duration and the repeat interval, adjusting the pressure needed for 3D Touch, and configuring the double- and triple-click speed for the Side button. You can also choose your default audio device for call audio.

You can configure the Spoken Content settings to control what on-screen content your iPhone reads to you. And you can set up the Accessibility Shortcut to give quick access to your key Accessibility settings.

Configure Touch Features (continued)

Tap **Haptic Touch** (AX) to display the Haptic Touch screen, and then tap **Fast** (✓ appears) or **Slow** (✓ appears), as necessary.

To adjust how iOS interprets your touching the screen, tap **Touch Accommodations** (AY) to display the Touch Accommodations screen. Set the **Touch Accommodations** switch (AZ) to On (⬤), and then use the other controls to configure touch accommodations. For example, to adjust the length of time you must touch the screen before iOS registers a touch, set the **Hold Duration** switch (BA) to On (⬤), and then tap + and − to set the delay.

Set the **Tap to Wake** switch (BB) to On (⬤) to wake your iPhone by tapping the screen. Set the **Shake to Undo** switch (BC) to On (⬤) to undo the last action by shaking the iPhone. Set the **Vibration** switch (BD) to Off ( ) to disable all vibration.

Set the **Lock to End Call** switch (BE) to On (⬤) to enable yourself to end a call by pressing **Side**. Tap **Call Audio Routing** (BF) to display the Call Audio Routing screen. Tap **Automatic** (✓), **Bluetooth Headset** (✓), or **Speaker** (✓) to specify the audio routing for phone calls and FaceTime audio. Tap **Auto-Answer Calls** (BG) to display the Auto-Answer Calls screen, and then set the **Auto-Answer Calls** switch to On (⬤) if you want the iPhone to answer calls automatically after a delay.

Tap **Back Tap** (BH) to display the Back Tap screen. Here, you can tap **Double Tap** or **Triple Tap** to set up the gestures you want to give by double- or triple-tapping the back of the iPhone.

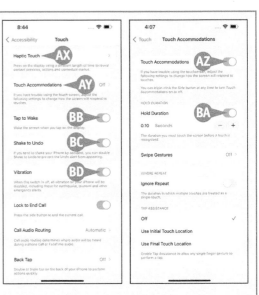

Configure Spoken Content Settings

Tap **Spoken Content** () on the Accessibility screen and then set the **Speak Selection** switch (BI) or the **Speak Screen** switch (BJ) to On (⬤). Set the **Speak Screen** switch to On (⬤) to enable swiping down the screen with two fingers to make your iPhone speak all the text on-screen. To have your iPhone speak what you type, tap **Typing Feedback** (BK) and then choose settings on the Typing Feedback screen. Tap **Voices** (BL) to display the Voices screen, where you can select the speaking voices you want (✓); back on the Spoken Content screen, drag the **Speaking Rate** slider (BM) to set the speaking speed.

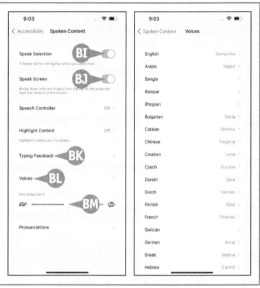

Configure the Accessibility Shortcut

To get quick access to your preferred Accessibility features, tap **Accessibility Shortcut** in the General section at the bottom of the Accessibility screen. On the Accessibility Shortcut screen, tap each feature (✓, BN) you want to access via the Shortcut.

To invoke the Accessibility Shortcut, triple-click the Side button. If you selected a single item, iOS toggles that feature on or off; for example, if you selected Smart Invert, iOS applies the smart inversion if it is off or removes it if it is on. If you selected multiple items, the Accessibility Shortcuts dialog opens (BO), and you can tap the feature you want to enable or disable.

Using Your iPhone with Your Mac

If you have a Mac, you can enjoy the impressive integration that Apple has built into iOS, iPadOS, and the Mac's operating system, macOS. Apple calls this integration Continuity. Continuity involves several features, including Handoff, which enables you to pick up your work or play seamlessly on one device exactly where you have left it on another device. For example, you can start writing an e-mail message on your Mac, continue it on your iPad, and then complete it on your iPhone.

Enable Handoff on Your iPhone

To enable your iPhone to communicate with your Mac, you need to enable the Handoff feature. On the Home screen, tap **Settings** (⚙) to open the Settings app, tap **General** (⚙) to display the General screen, and then tap **AirPlay & Handoff** (A). On the AirPlay & Handoff screen, set the **Handoff** switch (B) to On (⬤). If you want to use Continuity Camera, set the **Continuity Camera Webcam** switch (C) to On (⬤).

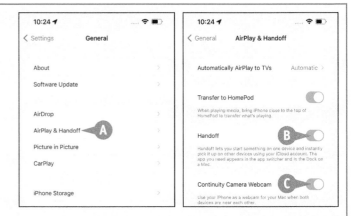

Enable Handoff on Your Mac

You also need to enable Handoff on your Mac. To do so, click on the menu bar and then click **System Settings** to open the System Settings window. Click **General** (⚙) to display the General pane. Set the **Allow Handoff between this Mac and your iCloud devices** switch (D) to On (⬤). You can then click **System Settings** on the menu bar and click **Quit System Settings** to quit System Settings.

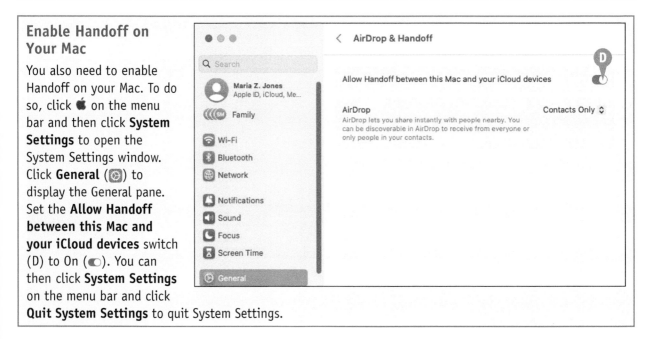

Make and Take Phone Calls on Your Mac

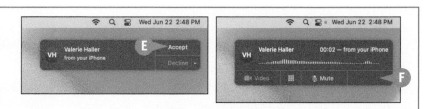

When you are using your Mac within Bluetooth range of your iPhone, Continuity enables you to make and take phone calls on your Mac instead of your iPhone. For example, when someone calls you on your iPhone, your Mac displays a call window automatically, and you can click **Accept** (E) to pick up the call on your Mac. Click **End** (F) when you want to end the call.

Send and Receive Text Messages from Your Mac

Your Mac can already send and receive messages via Apple's iMessage service, but when your iPhone's connection is available, your Mac can send and receive messages directly via Short Message Service (SMS) and Multimedia Messaging Service (MMS). This capability enables you to manage your messaging smoothly and tightly from your Mac.

Using Your iPhone with Your Apple Watch

Apple Watch puts timekeeping, notifications, and other essential information directly on your wrist. Apple Watch is an accessory for the iPhone — it requires an iPhone to set it up, to provide apps and data, and to give full access to the cellular network and the Internet.

Apple Watch works with iPhone 5 and later models.

Pair Your Apple Watch with Your iPhone

You must pair Apple Watch with your iPhone before you can use the devices together. Press and hold the **side button** on Apple Watch until the Apple logo appears, and then wait while Apple Watch finishes starting up.

Bring your iPhone close to Apple Watch, and the Apple Watch dialog (A) opens automatically. Tap **Continue** (B) to display the Set Up Apple Watch screen, and then tap **Set Up for Myself** (C) or **Set Up for a Family Member** (D), as appropriate. Follow the resulting prompts, which walk you through the setup process.

Configure Your Apple Watch Using Your iPhone

The Watch app on your iPhone enables you to configure your Apple Watch. On your iPhone, display the Home screen, tap **Watch** (◉) to open the Watch app, and then tap **My Watch** (E, ◉) to display the My Watch screen.

From here, you can choose a wide range of settings. For example, you can tap **Notifications** (F, ▣) to choose which notifications you receive on your Apple Watch, or you can tap **App View** (G, ▦) to configure the layout of the apps on your Apple Watch's screen.

Install Apps on Your Apple Watch

The Watch app on your iPhone enables you to install apps on your Apple Watch — and remove them if necessary.

When you install an iPhone app that has a companion app for Apple Watch, the app's name appears on the My Watch screen. Tap the app's name (H) to display the app's screen. You can then set the **Show App on Apple Watch** switch (I) to On () to install the app.

Receive Notifications on Your Apple Watch

When you receive a notification from an app you have permitted to raise notifications, your Apple Watch displays an icon showing the app and other information, such as the sender of an e-mail message. You can tap the notification to view its details.

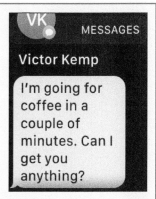

Receive Calls on Your Apple Watch

When you receive a phone call, it rings on both your Apple Watch and your iPhone. You can tap **Accept** (J, ) to pick up the call on Apple Watch or tap **Decline** (K, ) to decline the call, sending it to voicemail.

Setting Up Communications

In this chapter, you learn how to add your e-mail accounts to the Mail app and control how Mail displays your messages. This chapter also shows you how to control the way your iPhone displays your contacts; browse, search, create, and import contacts; choose options for your calendars; set up Wallet and Apple Pay; and set up and use eSIMs, virtual SIM cards.

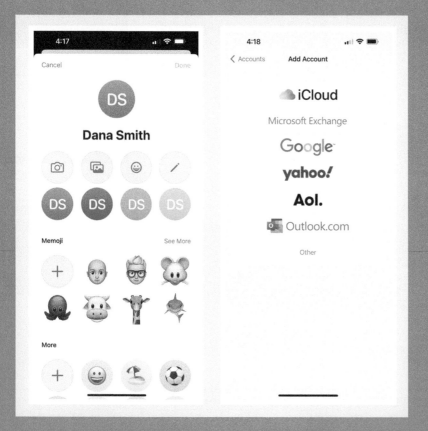

Set Up Your Mail Accounts

Usually, you set up your iCloud account while going through the initial setup routine for your iPhone. You can set up other e-mail accounts as explained here.

To set up an e-mail account, you need to know the e-mail address, the password, and the e-mail provider. You may also need to know the addresses of the mail servers the account uses. For Microsoft Exchange, including Microsoft 365, you may need the domain name as well; consult the system's administrator to find out. Alternatively, set up your Exchange account using a configuration profile file that the administrator provides.

Set Up Your Mail Accounts

1 On the Home screen, tap **Settings** (⚙).

The Settings screen appears.

Note: If you have not yet set up an e-mail account on the iPhone, you can also display the Add Account screen by tapping **Mail** on the Home screen.

Note: For Microsoft Exchange or Microsoft 365, you can use the iPhone's Mail app, but you might also try Microsoft's Outlook mail app, which integrates tightly with these services.

2 Tap **Mail** (✉).

The Mail screen appears.

3 Tap **Accounts**.

The Accounts screen appears.

4 Tap **Add Account**.

The Add Account screen appears.

5 Tap the kind of account you want to set up. For example, tap **Google**.

Note: Some account types have fields other than those shown here. For example, some accounts include a field for entering your name the way you want it to appear on outgoing messages. Some include a field for changing the description displayed for the account.

The screen for setting up that type of account appears.

 You can tap **Create account** to create a new account.

 Tap **Email or phone** and type the e-mail address or phone number.

Note: For a Google e-mail address ending gmail.com, you need not type *gmail.com*.

 Tap **Next**.

The Password screen appears.

8 Type your password.

 You can tap **Show password** (☐ changes to ☑) to display the password you have typed.

9 Tap **Next**.

Note: If another security screen appears, such as the 2-Step Verification screen, enter the required information and tap **Next**.

The configuration screen for the account appears.

10 Make sure the **Mail** switch is set to On (◉).

11 Set the **Contacts** switch, **Calendars** switch, **Notes** switch, and any other switches to On (◉) or Off (○), as needed.

12 Tap **Save**.

 The account appears on the Accounts screen.

TIP

How do I add my Hotmail account to my iPhone?

Hotmail is one of the services that Microsoft has integrated into its Outlook.com service. Tap **Outlook.com** on the Add Account screen, enter your e-mail address on the Outlook screen that appears, and tap **Next**. On the Enter Password screen, type your password and tap **Sign In**. After Mail verifies the account, set the **Mail** switch, **Contacts** switch, **Calendars** switch, and **Reminders** switch to On (◉) or Off (○), as needed, and then tap **Save**.

Control E-Mail Display and Default Account

In the Mail app, you can choose how many lines to include in message previews, decide whether to display the To and Cc labels, and control whether Mail prompts you before deleting a message. You can enable the Privacy Protection feature; choose whether to mark e-mail addresses outside a particular domain, such as that of your company or organization; and specify the default account, the account Mail uses to send messages when you start creating a message from another app. For example, if you open the Photos app and share a photo via Mail, Mail uses your default account.

Control E-Mail Display and Default Account

1 On the Home screen, tap **Settings** (⚙️).

The Settings screen appears.

2 Tap **Mail** (✉️).

The Mail screen appears.

3 Set the **Cellular Data** switch to On (⬤) if you want to allow Mail to transfer data across the cellular connection. This is good for synchronization but increases use of data and battery power.

4 Tap **Preview**.

The Preview screen appears.

5 Tap the number of preview lines you want.

6 Tap **Mail** (‹).

The Mail screen appears again.

7 Set the **Show To/Cc Labels** switch to On (⬤) or Off ( ), as needed.

8 Set the **Ask Before Deleting** switch to On (⬤) or Off ( ), as needed.

9 Tap **Privacy Protection** to display the Privacy Protection screen; make sure the **Protect Mail Activity** switch is set to On (⬤); and then tap **Mail** (‹). See the first tip for more information.

10 Tap **Swipe Options**.

The Swipe Options screen appears.

11 Tap **Swipe Left** to display the Swipe Left screen; tap **None**, **Mark as Read**, **Flag**, or **Move Message** to specify the action for when you swipe left on a message; and then tap **Swipe Options** (<) to return to the Swipe Options screen.

12 Tap **Swipe Right** to display the Swipe Right screen; tap **None**, **Mark as Read**, **Flag**, **Move Message**, or **Archive** to specify the action for when you swipe right on a message; and then tap **Swipe Options** (<) to return to the Swipe Options screen.

13 Tap **Mail** (<).

The Mail screen appears again.

14 Tap **Mark Addresses**.

The Mark Addresses screen appears.

15 In the Mark Addresses Not Ending With box, type the domain name of your company or organization, such as firstinformedchurch.net.

16 Tap **Mail** (<).

The Mail screen appears again.

17 Tap **Default Account**.

The Default Account screen appears.

18 Tap the account you want to use as the default account (✓ appears).

TIP

What does the Protect Mail Activity feature do?
When you set the Protect Mail Activity switch on the Privacy Protection screen to On (⬤), Mail hides your iPhone's IP address while retrieving the content of messages, including images stored remotely. Hiding the IP address prevents a message's sender from using a remote image to learn that you have read the message, the date and time you read it, and the IP address of the Internet connection used, which can reveal your approximate location.

Configure Private Relay and Hide My Email

Your iCloud account provides two privacy features that help reduce your exposure to online threats. The Private Relay feature hides your iPhone's IP address and your browsing activity, preventing anyone from following your actions or determining your exact location. You can choose to have Private Relay either maintain your general location or simply use your current country and time zone. The Hide My Email feature enables you to create unique, random e-mail addresses that forward to your real e-mail address. You can use these addresses for services you do not want to trust with your real e-mail address.

Configure Private Relay and Hide My Email

① On the Home screen, tap **Settings** (⚙).

The Settings screen appears.

② Tap **Apple ID**, the button at the top that bears your iCloud name.

The Apple ID screen appears.

③ Tap **iCloud** (☁).

The iCloud screen appears.

④ In the iCloud+ box, tap **Private Relay** (🌐).

The Private Relay screen appears.

⑤ Set the **Private Relay** switch to On (🔘).

⑥ Tap **IP Address Location**.

The IP Address Location screen appears.

⑦ Tap **Maintain general location** (✓) or **Use country and time zone** (✓).

⑧ Tap **Back** (‹).

The Private Relay screen appears again.

⑨ Tap **iCloud** (‹).

The iCloud screen appears again.

⑩ Tap **Hide My Email** (✉).

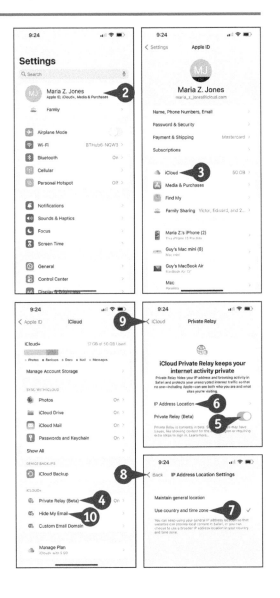

The Hide My Email screen appears.

Ⓐ The Main Relay Address button shows your main relay address for Hide My Email. You can tap **Main relay address** to edit or deactivate this address.

⑪ Tap **Create New Address**.

A Hide My Email panel opens.

Ⓑ A new random e-mail address appears.

Ⓒ You can tap **Use Different Address** to change to a different random address.

⑫ Tap **Label Your Address** and type a descriptive label for the address.

⑬ Optionally, tap **Make a Note** and type a note.

⑭ Tap **Next**.

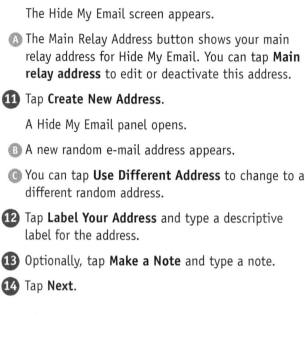

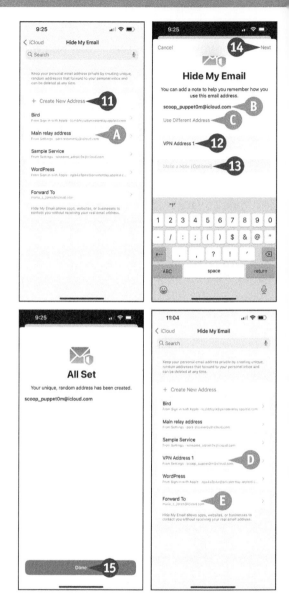

The All Set screen appears.

⑮ Tap **Done**.

The Hide My Email screen appears again.

Ⓓ The new address appears, listed alphabetically by its label.

Ⓔ You can tap **Forward To** to change the address to which Hide My Email is forwarding your messages.

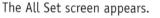

What does the Custom Email Domain feature do?

The Custom Email Domain feature enables you to set up a custom domain of your own to work with iCloud Mail. You can either use a domain you already have or set up a new domain. To get started, tap **Custom Email Domain** (✉) in the iCloud+ box on the iCloud screen in the Settings app, tap **Continue**, and then follow the prompts.

Organize and Read Your E-Mail by Threads

The Mail app gives you two ways to view e-mail messages. You can view the messages as a simple list, or you can view them with related messages organized into *threads*, which are sometimes called *conversations*.

Having Mail display your messages as threads can help you navigate your Inbox quickly and find related messages easily. You may find threading useful if you tend to have long e-mail conversations, because threading reduces the number of messages you see at once.

Organize and Read Your E-Mail by Threads

Set Mail to Organize Your Messages by Thread

1 On the Home screen, tap **Settings** (⚙️).

The Settings screen appears.

2 Tap **Mail** (✉️).

The Mail screen appears.

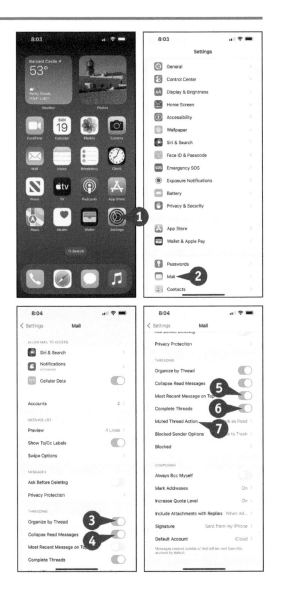

3 In the Threading section, set the **Organize by Thread** switch to On (⬤).

4 Set the **Collapse Read Messages** switch to On (⬤) to save space by collapsing messages you have read.

5 Set the **Most Recent Message on Top** switch to On (⬤) to make the newest message in each thread appear at the top of the screen. This option is often helpful for keeping up with your messages.

6 Set the **Complete Threads** switch to On (⬤) to have each thread show all its messages, even if you have moved some messages to other mailboxes. This option is usually helpful.

7 Tap **Muted Thread Action** to display the Muted Thread Action screen, and then tap **Mark as Read** or **Archive or Delete** to specify which action Mail should take when you mute a thread.

Read Messages Organized into Threads

1 On the Home screen, tap **Mail** ().

The Mailboxes screen appears.

Note: If Mail displays the contents of a mailbox, tap **Back** (‹) to return to the Mailboxes screen.

2 Tap the mailbox you want to open.

The Inbox for the account appears.

The Expand Thread icon on the right, a right-pointing arrow in a circle (⊙), indicates a thread.

3 Tap **Expand Thread** (⊙ changes to ⊙).

The thread expands, showing the messages it contains from other people.

You can get an overview of the thread's contents.

4 Tap the message you want to view.

The thread opens.

A The bar at the top of the screen shows the number of messages in the thread.

5 Tap the message you want to display.

TIP

Is there a quick way to enter my name and information at the end of a message?
Yes. You can create one or more e-mail signatures, which are sections of predefined text that Mail can insert at the end of messages. From the Home screen, tap **Settings** (⚙), and then tap **Mail** (✉). Scroll down to the Composing section and tap **Signature** to display the Signature screen. Tap **All Accounts** to use the same signature for each account, or tap **Per Account** to use a different signature for each account. Then type the text to use for the signature or signatures.

Browse or Search for Contacts

Your iPhone's Contacts app enables you to store contact data that you sync from your computer or online accounts or that you enter directly on your iPhone. You can access the contacts either via the Contacts app itself or through the Contacts tab in the Phone app.

To locate a particular contact, you can browse through the list of contacts or through selected lists, such as your friends, or use the Search feature.

Browse or Search for Contacts

Browse Your Contacts

 On the Home screen, tap **Contacts** (⊙).

The Contacts screen appears, showing either all contacts or your currently selected lists.

Note: You can also access your contacts by displaying the Home screen, tapping **Phone** (📞), and then tapping **Contacts** (⊙ changes to ⊙).

Ⓐ The top card, which bears your name and the text My Card, is the card that Contacts is using for your information.

Ⓑ To navigate the screen of contacts quickly, tap the letter on the right that you want to jump to. To navigate more slowly, scroll up or down.

② Tap the contact whose information you want to view.

The contact's screen appears.

Note: From the contact's screen, you can quickly phone the contact by tapping the phone number you want to use.

③ If necessary, swipe or drag up to scroll down the screen to display more information.

Ⓒ You can tap **Edit** to open the contact record for editing.

④ Tap **Contacts** (<) or the name of the current list, such as **iCloud** (<) in this example, when you want to return to the Contacts screen.

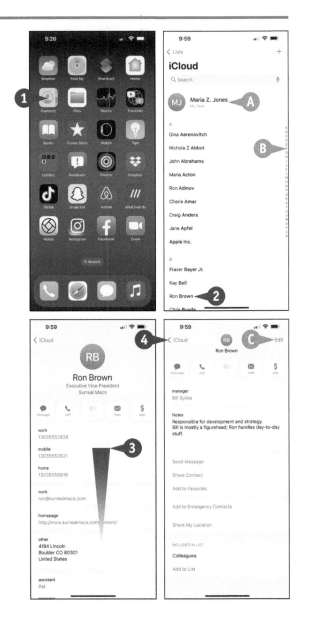

Choose Which Lists of Contacts to Display

1 From the Contacts screen or the screen showing the current list, tap **Lists**.

The Lists screen appears.

D You can tap **Edit** to change or remove the existing lists.

E You can tap **Add List** to add another list.

F If the Lists screen includes lists from multiple accounts, such as iCloud and Gmail, you can tap **All Contacts** (⚇) to display all the contacts.

G You can tap the All button for an account, such as **All iCloud** (also ⚇), to display all the contacts in that account.

H You can tap a list, such as **Friends** (⚇), to display just that list.

Search for Contacts

1 From the Contacts screen, tap **Search** (Q).

The Search screen appears.

The on-screen keyboard appears.

2 Start typing the name you want to search for.

3 From the list of matches, tap the contact you want to view.

The contact's information appears.

TIP

What is a linked contact?

A *linked contact* is a contact record that the Contacts app has created by combining contact records from two or more separate sources. For example, if your iCloud account and your Gmail account each contain a contact called Ron Brown, Contacts creates a linked contact called Ron Brown. To unlink a linked contact, tap **Edit** at the top of the screen for a contact. In the Linked Contacts area, tap **Remove** (⊖) for the appropriate contact record, and then tap **Unlink**. Alternatively, tap **Edit** and then tap **link contacts** (⊕) in the Linked Contacts area to link another contact record to the current record.

Create a New Contact

As well as syncing your existing contacts via cloud services such as iCloud or Yahoo!, you can create new contact records directly on your iPhone. For example, if you meet someone you want to remember, you can create a contact record for that person — and take a photo using the iPhone's camera. You can then sync that contact record online, adding it to your other contacts.

Create a New Contact

1 On the Home screen, tap **Phone** ().

The Phone app opens.

2 Tap **Contacts** (changes to).

The Contacts screen appears.

Note: You can also access the Contacts app by tapping **Contacts** () on the Home screen.

3 Tap **Add** (+).

The New Contact screen appears.

4 Tap **First name** and type the first name.

5 Tap **Last name** and type the last name.

6 Fill in other information, such as a company or phone numbers.

7 Tap **Add Photo**.

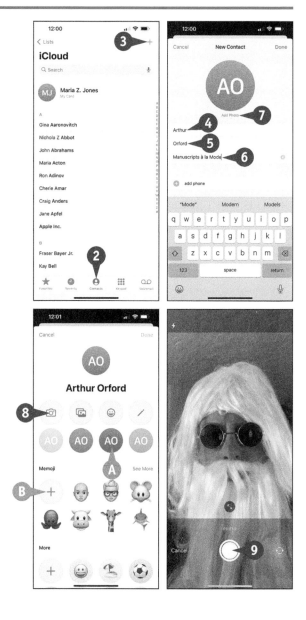

The Add Photo screen appears.

A You can tap a suggested logo or photo to use instead of taking a photo.

B You can tap a suggested memoji or tap **New** (+) to create a new memoji.

8 Tap **Take Photo** ( ).

The Take Photo screen appears.

9 Compose the photo, and then tap **Take Photo** ().

The Move and Scale screen appears.

10 Position the part of the photo you want to use in the middle.

Note: Pinch in with two fingers to zoom the photo out. Pinch out with two fingers to zoom the photo in.

C You can tap **Retake** to take another photo.

11 Tap **Use Photo**.

The Select a Filter screen appears.

12 Tap the filter you want to apply.

D To remove a filter you have applied, tap the upper-left thumbnail, which shows the original photo.

13 Tap **Done**.

The photo appears on the Add Photo screen.

14 Tap **Done**.

The photo appears in the contact record.

15 Tap **Done**.

The contact record closes.

The contact appears in your Contacts list.

TIP

How do I assign my new contact an existing photo?

On the Add Photo screen, tap **Photos** (⌕) to display the Photos screen. You can then tap a photo container, such as an album, to display its contents. Tap the photo you want to use, and it appears on the Move and Scale screen. Position and scale the photo as needed within the frame, and then tap **Choose**.

Control How Your Contacts Appear

To swiftly and easily find the contacts you need, you can make your iPhone sort and display the contacts in your preferred order. Your iPhone can sort contacts either by first name, putting Abby Brown before Bill Andrews, or by last name, putting Bill Andrews before Abby Brown. Your iPhone can display contacts either as first name followed by last name or as last name followed by first name. You can also specify how you want your iPhone to display short names for contacts.

Control How Your Contacts Appear

1 On the Home screen, tap **Settings** (⚙️).

The Settings screen appears.

2 Tap **Contacts** (👤).

The Contacts screen appears.

3 Tap **Sort Order**.

The Sort Order screen appears.

4 Tap **First, Last** or **Last, First**, as needed.

5 Tap **Contacts** (<).

The Contacts screen appears again.

6 Tap **Display Order**.

The Display Order screen appears.

7 Tap **First, Last** or **Last, First**, as needed.

8 Tap **Contacts** (<).

The Contacts screen appears again.

9 Tap **Short Name**.

The Short Name screen appears.

10 Set the **Short Name** switch to On (⬤).

11 Tap **First Name & Last Initial**, **First Initial & Last Name**, **First Name Only**, or **Last Name Only** to specify the format for short names.

12 Set the **Prefer Nicknames** switch to On (⬤) or Off (◯), as needed.

Choose Default Alert Options for Calendar Events

Your iPhone enables you to sync your calendars via iCloud and other online services. To help keep on schedule, you can set default alert times for calendar events. You can set a different alert time for each type of event — for example, 15 minutes' notice for a regular event and a week's notice for a birthday. You can also turn on the Time to Leave feature to make the Calendar app allow travel time based on your location and current traffic.

Choose Default Alert Options for Calendar Events

1 On the Home screen, tap **Settings** ().

The Settings screen appears.

2 Tap **Calendar** (📅).

The Calendar screen appears.

A If you want your iPhone to suggest creating events from apparent event data found in apps such as Mail and Messages, tap **Siri & Search** (🔍) to display the Siri & Search screen, and then set the **Show in App** switch to On (⬤).

B Set the **Location Suggestions** switch to On (⬤) if you want Calendar to suggest locations for events.

3 Tap **Default Alert Times**.

The Default Alert Times screen appears.

4 Tap the event type for which you want to set the default alert time. For example, tap **Events**.

The Events screen, Birthdays screen, or All-Day Events screen appears.

5 Tap the amount of time for the alert.

6 Tap **Default Alert Times** (<).

The Default Alert Times screen appears again.

7 Set default alert times for other event types by repeating steps **4** to **6**.

8 Set the **Time to Leave** switch to On (⬤) if you want Calendar to suggest leave times based on your location and current traffic information.

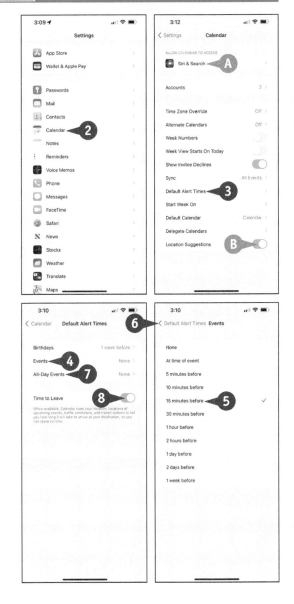

Set Up and Use Wallet and Apple Pay

Your iPhone enables you to make payments using the Apple Pay system and the Wallet app on your iPhone. Apple Pay can be faster and more convenient than paying with cash. It can also be more secure than paying with a credit card or debit card.

Understanding Apple Pay and Wallet

Apple Pay is Apple's electronic-payment and digital-wallet service. After setting up Apple Pay with one or more credit cards or debit cards, you can make payments using your iPhone either at contactless payment terminals or online. If you have an Apple Watch, you can use Apple Pay on that device as well. You can also set up the Apple Cash service and use it to make peer-to-peer payments via apps such as Messages.

Wallet is the app you use on your iPhone to manage Apple Pay and the digital documents you want to carry with you, such as airline tickets or store rewards cards.

On the Home screen, tap **Wallet** (A, 📇) to open the Wallet app.

Set Up Wallet

If you have not yet set up a credit card or debit card, tap **Add** (B, ➕) at the top of the Wallet screen. Follow the prompts to add a card to Wallet. You can add the card either by lining it up within an on-screen frame and using the camera to recognize it or by typing in the details manually; if the card is one you already use with Apple, you may need to provide only the card verification code, or CVV.

Complete the card registration by selecting the correct billing address. For some cards, you may need to contact the card provider to confirm you are setting up Apple Pay.

After you add cards, they appear at the top of the Wallet screen.

Set Apple Pay to Use Face ID

After setting up Apple Pay, you can set your iPhone to use Face ID instead of your Apple ID password for buying items. Face ID enables you to authenticate yourself and approve a purchase by looking at your iPhone. This is much more convenient than typing a password, especially when you are shopping in the physical world rather than online.

To set your iPhone to use Face ID for Apple Pay, swipe up from the bottom of the screen to display the Home screen, and then tap **Settings** (⚙️) to display the Settings screen. Tap **Face ID & Passcode** (C, 😐), and then type your passcode when prompted, to display the Face ID & Passcode screen. Then go to the Use Face ID For section and set the **Wallet & Apple Pay** switch (D) to On ( ).

While in the Settings app, you may want to tap **Wallet & Apple Pay** (E, 📧) to display the Wallet & Apple Pay screen. Here, you can set the **Double-Click Side Button** switch to On ( ) to give yourself instant access to your cards and passes.

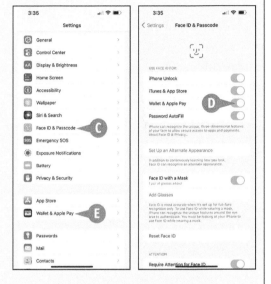

Make a Payment with Apple Pay

Now that you have set up Apple Pay and configured your iPhone to use it, you can make payments by bringing your iPhone close to the contact area on a payment terminal.

When the Near Field Communication (NFC) chips on the two devices make contact, a tone sounds. Your iPhone then displays details of the transaction and prompts you to confirm it using Face ID.

Set Up and Use eSIMs

SIM is the acronym for subscriber identity module, a container that holds unique information used to identify a phone to cellular providers and to specify what it is allowed to do through their networks. A SIM can be either a physical SIM card or an electronic SIM, which is entirely virtual.

The iPhone 14 models sold in the United States use only electronic SIMs — they have no slot for a physical SIM card. iPhone 14 models sold in some other markets contain a slot for a single physical SIM card — specifically, a nano-SIM. All earlier iPhone models have a slot for a single physical SIM card. But as well as this SIM card, or instead of it, you can use one or more eSIMs, which enables you to use different cellular plans on the same phone. Before using an eSIM, you must add it to your iPhone and configure it. Only one eSIM can be active at a time, but you can easily switch back and forth between eSIMs.

Determine Whether You Can Use eSIMs

First, determine whether you can use eSIMs with your iPhone.

If your iPhone is an unlocked model — one that is not bound to a particular carrier — you should be able to use eSIMs freely. But if your iPhone is locked to a carrier, you will only be able to use eSIMs from that carrier. If that carrier does not support eSIMs, you will not be able to use eSIMs with your iPhone. Similarly, some corporate policies restrict eSIM use on managed phones.

The simplest way to find out whether your carrier supports eSIMs in your region is to check the Apple website. Alternatively, consult your carrier.

Get and Add an eSIM

Once you have determined that you can use eSIMs with your iPhone, evaluate your options for getting an eSIM.

If your iPhone is locked to a particular carrier, you must use that carrier's method of adding an eSIM. But if your iPhone is unlocked, you may have multiple options for adding an eSIM. In this case, your next step is to identify the eSIM plan you want to buy. Go to Apple's website and look at the list of carriers per region that support eSIM to determine your choice of carriers, and then explore the eSIM plans they offer.

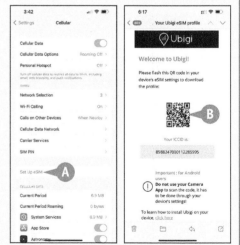

After choosing your plan, you need to add it to your iPhone. You can add an eSIM to your iPhone in four different ways, depending on your carrier and how it handles eSIMs:

- If the carrier tells you to enter the eSIM details manually, tap **Settings** (⚙) on the Home screen, tap **Cellular** (📶) on the Settings screen, and then tap **Set Up eSIM** (A) on the Cellular screen. Next, tap **Enter Details Manually** at the bottom of the Add Cellular Plan screen.

Get and Add an eSIM (continued)

- If the carrier provides a card or sends an e-mail with a QR code (B), scan or flash the QR code. A Cellular Plan Detected notification appears. Tap the notification, tap **Continue**, and then tap **Add Cellular Plan**.

- If the carrier provides an app, tap **App Store** () on the Home screen. In the App Store app, search for the carrier's app, and then download and install it. Tap the app's icon on the Home screen, and then follow the prompts to buy a cellular plan.

- If the carrier assigns cellular plans "over the air," your iPhone will display a Carrier Cellular Plan Ready to Be Installed notification. Tap this notification to open the Settings app, and then tap **Carrier Cellular Plan Ready to Be Installed**. Tap **Continue**, and follow the prompts.

If the Activate eSIM screen appears, tap **Activate eSIM** (C) and follow the prompts. You may need to turn off your iPhone's Wi-Fi (D) and enable the eSIM's "phone line" (E) to force the iPhone to connect via the eSIM so that you can finish activating the eSIM and create an account for it.

Configure an eSIM

After installing an eSIM, you can choose what roles the iPhone uses it for. You can assign a descriptive label to each SIM to make them easy to identify.

To control which number is used for calling or messaging anyone not in your contacts, you set the default line. On the Cellular screen, tap **Default Voice Line** (F) to display the Default Voice Line screen, and then tap **Primary** (✓) or **Secondary** (✓), as needed.

For each contact, you can configure the Preferred Line setting between Last Used (G, ✓) and the two SIMs, the SIM card (H) and the active eSIM (I). This feature lets you continue using the number with which a contact is familiar so that the contact can see who the call is coming from.

CHAPTER 5

Making Calls and Messaging

You can make calls by holding your iPhone to your face, by using the speakerphone, or by using a headset or your car's audio system. You can also make calls using Favorites and recent numbers, send and receive text and multimedia messages, and make chat and video calls via FaceTime.

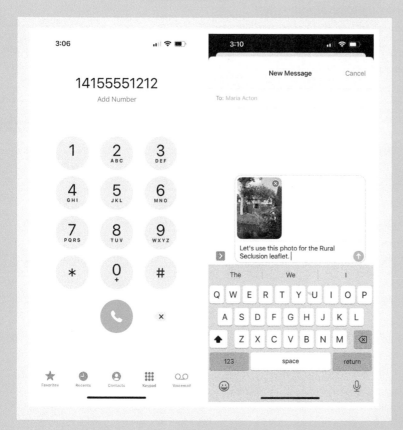

Make Phone Calls and FaceTime Audio Calls

W ith your iPhone, you can make cellular phone calls anywhere you have a connection to the cellular network; you can make audio or video calls via FaceTime across either Wi-Fi or cellular connections. You can dial a phone number using the iPhone's keypad, but you can place calls more easily by tapping the appropriate phone number for a contact, using the Phone app's Recents screen, using the Favorites list, or using Siri. When other people near you need to be able to hear the call, you can switch on your iPhone's speaker; otherwise, you can use a headset for privacy.

Make Phone Calls and FaceTime Audio Calls

Open the Phone App

1 On the Home screen, tap **Phone** (📞).

The Phone app opens and displays the screen you used last — for example, the Contacts screen.

Ⓐ Your contact card appears at the top of the Contacts list for quick reference. You can tap it to see your phone number and other details.

Note: You can dial a call by activating Siri and speaking the contact's name or the number. See Chapter 3 for instructions on using Siri.

Dial a Call Using the Keypad

1 Tap **Keypad** (⠿ changes to ⠿).

The Keypad screen appears.

Note: On the Keypad screen, you can tap **Call** (📞) without dialing a number to display the last number dialed.

2 Tap the number keys to dial the number.

Note: You can tap **Add to Contacts** (⊕) to add this number to your Contacts list.

Ⓑ If you dial a contact's number, the contact's name and phone type appear.

3 Tap **Call** (📞).

Your iPhone makes the call.

4 Tap **End** (📞) when you are ready to end the call.

Place a Call to a Contact

1 Tap **Contacts** (👤 changes to 👤).

The Contacts list appears.

2 Tap the contact you want to call.

The contact's info appears.

3 If FaceTime (☏) appears, tap **FaceTime Audio** (☏) to place a FaceTime Audio call. Otherwise, tap **Call** (📞).

Ⓒ You can tap a number to place a phone call to that number.

Note: You can also place a call to a phone number that the iPhone has identified — for example, by tapping an underlined phone number on a web page or in an e-mail message.

Your iPhone places the call.

Ⓓ In a FaceTime Audio call, you can tap **FaceTime** (📹) to switch to a FaceTime Video call.

4 Tap blank space in the call dialog.

iOS switches the call to full screen.

5 When you are ready to end the call, tap **End** (📞).

Your iPhone ends the call.

The Call Ended screen appears for a moment.

The screen from which you placed the call appears — for example, the Contacts screen.

Note: To end a call for which you are using the headset, press the clicker button.

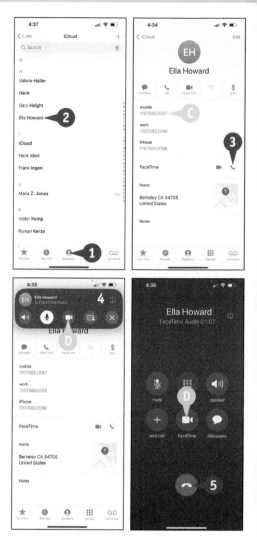

TIPS

Can I use the iPhone as a speaker phone?
Yes. Tap **speaker** (🔊 changes to 🔊) on the screen that appears while you are making a phone call; if you are using an audio device, tap **Audio** (🔊), and then tap **speaker** (🔊 changes to 🔊). The iPhone starts playing the phone call through the speaker on the bottom instead of the small speaker at the top. Tap **speaker** (🔊 changes to 🔊) to switch off the speaker.

What is Dial Assist?
Dial Assist is a feature that automatically determines the correct local prefix or international prefix when you place a call. To turn Dial Assist on or off, tap **Settings** (⚙️) on the Home screen, tap **Phone** (📞), and then set the **Dial Assist** switch to On (🔵) or Off ( ).

Make a Conference Call

As well as making phone calls to one other phone at a time, your iPhone can make calls to multiple phones at once, making either cellular calls or FaceTime audio calls, but not mixing the two. To make a conference call, you call the first participant and then add each other participant in turn. During a conference call, you can talk in private to individual participants. You can also drop a participant from the call.

Make a Conference Call

1 On the Home screen, tap **Phone** (📞).

The Phone app opens.

2 Tap **Contacts** (👤 changes to 👤).

The Contacts screen appears.

3 Tap the contact you want to call first.

The contact's record appears.

4 Tap **Call** (📞) on the phone number to use.

Note: You can also add a contact to the call by using Favorites, Recents, or Keypad.

Your iPhone establishes the call.

5 Tap **add call** (➕).

The Contacts screen appears.

Ⓐ The time readout takes on a green background (such as 5:19) to indicate that a call is active.

6 Tap the contact you want to add.

The contact's record appears.

7 Tap **Call** (📞). This button may have a different label, such as iPhone.

Ⓑ Your iPhone places the first call on hold and makes the new call.

8 Tap **merge calls** (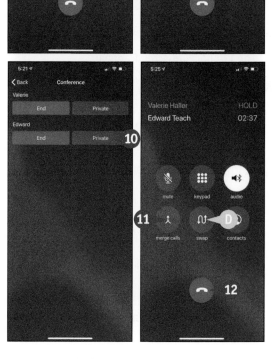).

The iPhone merges the calls and displays the participants' names at the top of the screen. You can now speak to both participants.

C You can add more participants by tapping **add call** (⊕), specifying the contact or number, and then merging the calls.

9 To speak privately to a participant, tap **Information** (ⓘ).

The Conference screen appears, showing a list of the participants.

10 Tap **Private** next to the participant.

The iPhone places the other caller or callers on hold.

D You can tap **swap** (↺) to swap the caller on hold and the active caller.

11 When you are ready to resume the conference call, tap **merge calls** (⋏).

The iPhone merges the calls, and all participants can hear each other again.

12 When you finish the call, tap **End** (☎).

The iPhone ends the call.

How do I drop a participant from a conference call?
Tap **Information** (ⓘ) to display the Conference screen, and then tap **End** for the participant you want to drop.

How many people can I add to a conference call?
This depends on your carrier, not on your iPhone. Ask your carrier what the maximum number of participants can be.

Make Video Calls Using FaceTime

By using your iPhone's FaceTime feature, you can enjoy video chats with any of your contacts who have an iPhone, an iPad, or a Mac. To make a FaceTime call, you and your contact must both have Apple IDs. Your iPhone must be connected to either a Wi-Fi network or the cellular network. Using a Wi-Fi network is preferable because you typically get better performance and do not use up your cellular data allowance.

After starting a FaceTime call, you can use the SharePlay feature to enjoy a movie, a TV show, or songs with the call's participants who are using Apple devices.

Make Video Calls Using FaceTime

Receive a FaceTime Call

1. When your iPhone receives a FaceTime request and the screen shows who is calling, aim the camera at your face, and then tap **Video Call** (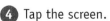).

   The Connecting screen appears.

2. Tap **Join**.

   When the connection is established, your iPhone displays the caller full-screen, with your video inset.

3. Start your conversation.

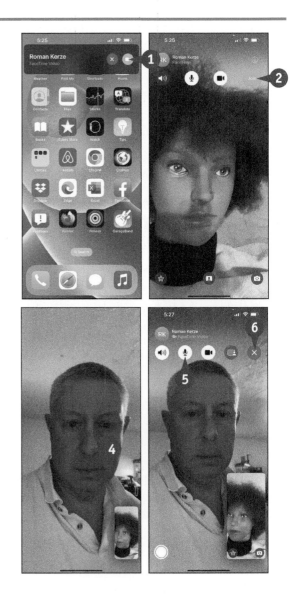

4. Tap the screen.

   The controls appear.

5. If you need to mute your microphone, tap **Mute** (changes to). Tap **Mute** again (changes to) when you want to turn muting off.

6. Tap **End** (×) when you are ready to end the FaceTime call.

Make a FaceTime Call

1 On the Home screen, tap **FaceTime** (📷).

The FaceTime app opens.

Ⓐ You can tap **Create Link** to create a link to send to someone who does not have an iPhone, an iPad, or a Mac — for example, a Windows user — to let them join a FaceTime call via a web browser.

2 Tap the contact you want to call.

The FaceTime app starts a video call.

3 When your contact answers, smile and speak.

Ⓑ If you need to show your contact something using the rear-facing camera, tap **flip** (📷).

Ⓒ Tap **Effects** (⭐) to access a variety of visual effects, such as replacing your head with a cartoon animal's head or motion-tracking animated stickers to a location on the screen.

Ⓓ You can share your screen by tapping **Share My Screen** (🖥) and then tapping **Share My Screen** (🖥).

4 When you are ready to end the call, tap **End**.

TIP

Are there other ways of starting a FaceTime call?
Yes. Here are two easy ways to start a FaceTime call:

- Ask Siri to call a contact via FaceTime. For example, press and hold **Side** to summon Siri, and then say "FaceTime John Smith."
- During a phone call, tap **FaceTime** (📷).

Save Time with Call Favorites and Recents

You can dial phone numbers easily from your Contacts list, but you can save time and effort by using the Favorites and Recents features built into the Phone app.

Favorites are phone numbers that you mark as being especially important to you. Recents are phone numbers you have called and received calls from recently.

Save Time with Call Favorites and Recents

Add a Contact to Your Favorites List

1 On the Home screen, tap **Phone** ().

The Phone app opens.

2 Tap **Contacts** (changes to).

The Contacts list appears.

3 Tap the contact you want to add.

The contact's record appears.

4 Tap **Add to Favorites**.

The Add to Favorites dialog opens.

5 Tap the heading for the type of favorite you want to add. This example uses **Call**.

The list of phone numbers for the contact appears.

6 Tap the phone number you want to add to your Favorites list.

The Add to Favorites dialog closes, and the iPhone creates a favorite for the contact.

Call a Favorite

1 In the Phone app, tap **Favorites** (⭐ changes to ⭐).

The Favorites list appears.

2 Tap the Favorite you want to call.

Your iPhone places the call.

Ⓐ To display the contact's record, tap **Information** (ⓘ) instead of tapping the contact's button. You can then tap a different phone number for the contact if necessary.

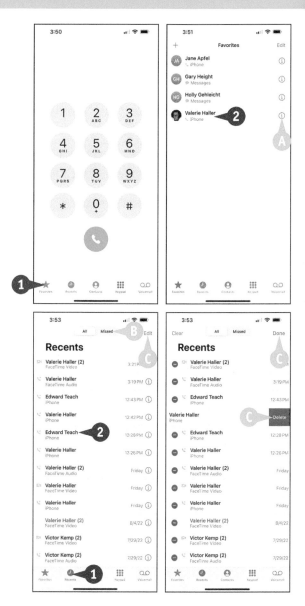

Call a Recent

1 In the Phone app, tap **Recents** (🕐 changes to 🕐).

The Recents screen appears. Red entries indicate calls you missed.

Ⓑ Tap **Missed** if you want to see only recent calls you missed.

Ⓒ To delete some recents, tap **Edit**; tap **Delete** (➖) to the left of the recent, and then tap the textual **Delete** button; and finally tap **Done**.

2 Tap the recent you want to call.

Your iPhone places the call.

Note: If you want to clear the Recents list, tap **Edit** and then tap **Clear**. In the dialog that opens, tap **Clear All Recents**.

TIP

How do I remove a contact from my Favorites?
Tap **Favorites** (⭐ changes to ⭐) to display the Favorites list, and then tap **Edit**. Tap **Delete** (➖) next to the contact, and then tap the textual **Delete** button. You can also rearrange your favorites by tapping the handle (≡) and dragging up or down. Tap **Done** when you have finished changing your favorites.

Send Text and Multimedia Messages

Your iPhone can send instant messages using the Short Message Service, abbreviated SMS; the Multimedia Messaging Service, MMS; or Apple's iMessage service. An SMS message consists of only text, whereas an MMS message can contain text, videos, photos, sounds, or other data. An iMessage can contain text, multimedia content, emoji, animations, handwriting, and other features. The Messages app automatically chooses the appropriate type — SMS, MMS, or iMessage — for the messages you create and the ways you send them.

Send Text and Multimedia Messages

 On the Home screen, tap **Messages** (○).

The Messages screen appears.

2 Tap **New Message** (✏️).

Note: Before sending an SMS or MMS message, make sure the recipient's phone number can receive such messages. Typically, you do not receive an alert if the message cannot be delivered.

Note: The iMessage service can send messages via Wi-Fi rather than the cellular network, but it is restricted to Apple devices and Macs.

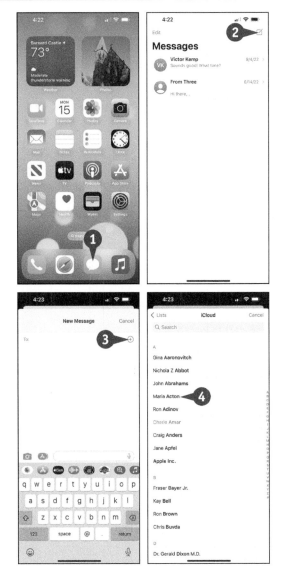

The New Message screen appears.

3 Tap **Add Contact** (⊕).

The Contacts list appears.

4 Tap the contact to whose phone you want to send the message.

Note: If the contact's record contains multiple phone numbers, Messages displays the contact record. Tap the phone number to use.

Note: iMessage is available only for communicating with other users of Apple devices using their Apple IDs. SMS and MMS work with any device but may use up your messaging allowance from your carrier. Keep in mind that sending group texts to a mix of devices does not always work entirely as it should.

The contact's name appears in the To field of the New Message screen.

 Tap the text field.

 Type your message.

The More button appears.

 Tap **More** ( ).

The other buttons reappear.

Ⓐ To take a photo and add it, tap **Photo** ( ).

Note: Messages from contacts sent via iMessage appear in blue balloons. Messages from contacts sent via SMS or MMS appear in green balloons.

 Tap **Apps** ( ) to display the Apps bar.

9 Tap **Photos** ( ).

The Photos list appears, showing your Recents photo album with the most recent photos first.

Note: You can swipe the handle at the top of the Photos list up to expand the list. You can then navigate to other photo albums. Swipe the handle back down to return to the message.

10 Tap the photo you want to add.

Ⓑ The photo appears in the message.

Ⓒ You can tap **Remove** ( ) to remove the photo from the message.

 Tap **Send** ( ).

Messages sends the message and the photo.

TIPS

How can I respond quickly to an instant message?
When Messages displays a notification for an instant message, tap and hold the notification to display the Quick Reply box. You can then type a reply and tap **Send** to send it.

Is there another way to send a photo or video?
Yes. You can start from the Camera app or the Photos app. Select the photo or video you want to share, and then tap **Share** ( ). On the Share sheet, tap **Message**. Your iPhone starts a new message containing the photo or video. You can then address and send the message.

Undo Sending a Message

As you likely know, it is all too easy to send an incomplete or ill-advised message when using text messaging. To help reduce misunderstandings, embarrassment, and worse, the Messages app in iOS 16 provides two new features. First, you can undo sending a message, as explained in this section. Second, you can edit a message you have sent and then send it again, as explained in the next section, "Edit a Sent Message."

Both undoing a message's sending and editing a sent message work only within Apple's iMessage system and only for a limited time after sending the original message.

Undo Sending a Message

1 In a conversation in the Messages app, type or dictate a message, and then tap **Send** (⬆).

Note: The conversation must be with another iMessage user. It cannot be an SMS or MMS conversation.

2 Tap and hold the bubble of the message you want to undo sending.

The contextual menu opens.

3 Tap **Undo Send** (↺).

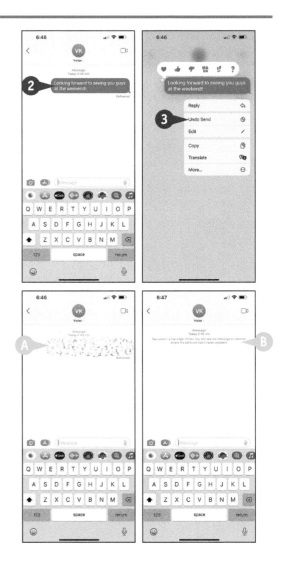

A The message balloon swells, bursts, and vanishes.

B Messages displays information telling you that you unsent the message and warning you that the recipient may still see the message on devices whose software hasn't been updated.

118

Edit a Sent Message

The Messages app enables you to edit a sent message soon after you send it. This feature works only for messages on Apple's iMessage service, not for SMS messages or MMS messages. The recipient sees a notification that the message has been edited.

As of this writing, a message is available for editing only for two minutes after you send it; after that, you cannot edit the message. Assuming you do start editing the message within two minutes, you can edit the message up to five times.

 In a conversation in the Messages app, type or dictate a message, and then tap **Send** (⬆).

Note: The conversation must be with another iMessage user. It cannot be an SMS or MMS conversation.

 Tap and hold the bubble of the message you want to edit.

The contextual menu opens.

 Tap **Edit** (✏).

Messages retrieves the message, if possible.

Messages opens the message for editing.

Ⓐ The *Delivered* status shows that the message was delivered.

 Type your corrections.

Note: You can move the insertion point quickly and precisely by tapping and holding the spacebar until iOS blanks out the keys, and then sliding your finger on the keyboard area like a trackpad to move the insertion point.

⑤ Tap **Send** (✓).

Messages sends the edited message.

Ⓑ The *Delivered – Edited* status shows that the message has been edited.

Note: The recipient sees the edited message as *Edited to* followed by the message in quotes.

Using Emoji and iMessage Features

The Messages app makes it easy to include *emoji* — graphical characters — in your messages. You can send emoji to users of most instant-messaging services, not just to iMessage users.

When you are sending a message to another user of the iMessage service, you can also use a wide range of features that are not available for SMS messages and text messages. These features include stickers, handwriting and sketches, animations, and Digital Touch, which enables you to send a pattern of taps or your heartbeat. You can also respond quickly to a message by using the Tapback feature.

Add Emoji to Messages

The Messages app makes it easy to add emoji to your messages. After typing text (A), tap **Emoji** (B, 😃) on the keyboard. Messages highlights with color any words in the message that you can replace with emoji; tap a word to insert the corresponding emoji icon, such as 👀 for "look" (C). If multiple emoji are available, as for "great" in the example, tap the emoji you want — such as 👍 (D) — on the pop-up panel.

You can also insert other emoji manually by tapping them on the emoji keyboard. Tap the buttons at the bottom of the screen, or simply scroll the emoji panel left or right, to browse the available emoji.

Some emoji offer different skin tones. Tap and hold an emoji, such as the Clapping icon, to display a pop-up panel showing the skin tones available, and then tap the tone you want.

Send a Handwritten Message or Sketch

To send a handwritten message or sketch in a message to an iMessage user, tap **Apps** (🅰), and then tap **Digital Touch** (E, ⬤) to display the Digital Touch controls.

Tap or drag **Expand** (F, —) to expand the panel to full screen, tap the color (G) you want, and then write or draw (H) what you want to send. Tap **Send** (I, ⬆) to send the message.

Send Heartbeats or Taps

To send heartbeats or taps in a message to an iMessage user, tap **Apps** (🅰), and then tap **Digital Touch** (J, ⬤) to display the Digital Touch controls.

To send a fireball (K), tap with one finger. To send a heartbeat, tap and hold with two fingers. Messages displays the graphic and sends it automatically; you do not need to tap Send (⬆).

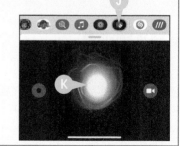

Send a Message with Effect

To send a message with effect, write the text for the message, and then tap and hold **Send** (⬆). The Send with Effect screen appears. At the top of the screen, tap **Bubble** (L) if you want to send a bubble with an effect such as Slam (M) or Invisible Ink (N), and then tap the button for the effect; a preview then plays. To send text with a full-screen effect, tap **Screen** (O) at the top of the screen, and then swipe left or right to reach the effect you want; again, a preview plays (P). When you are ready to send the message, tap **Send** (⬆).

Respond Quickly Using the Tapback Feature

iMessage enables you to respond quickly to an incoming message by tapping and holding it (Q). The Tapback panel opens, and you can tap the icon (R) you want to send as an instant response. The icon appears on the message (S).

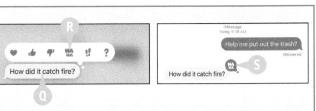

Share the Music You Are Listening To

With iMessage, you can quickly share links to the music you are enjoying on Apple Music. In a message to an iMessage user, tap **Apps** (Ⓐ) to display the Apps panel. Swipe left or right if necessary to display the Music panel, and then tap the item you want to share. A button for the item appears in the message box. Type any explanatory or exhortatory text needed, and then tap **Send** (⬆).

Send a Payment or Request a Payment

With iMessage, you can send a payment to a contact; you can also request a payment from a contact. In a message to an iMessage user, tap **Apps** (Ⓐ) to display the Apps panel. Swipe left or right if necessary to display the Apple Cash button, and then tap **Apple Cash** (T, ⬤). Use the controls (U) to specify the amount — tap **Show Keypad** (V) to type in an amount — and then tap **Send** (W) to send the recipient the amount or tap **Request** (X) to request payment. The payment ticket or request ticket appears in the message box. Tap **Send** (⬆) to send it.

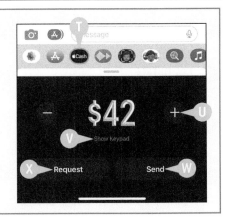

Manage Your Instant Messages

essages is great for communicating quickly and frequently with your nearest and dearest and with your colleagues, so it may not take long before the interface is so full of messages that it becomes hard to navigate.

To keep your messages under control, you can forward messages to others and delete messages you do not need to keep. You can either delete messages from a conversation, leaving the conversation's other messages, or delete the entire conversation.

Manage Your Instant Messages

Delete an Entire Conversation

A To take action quickly on a single conversation, swipe it to the left.

B You can then tap **Delete** (🗑) to delete the conversation.

C You can then tap **Hide Alerts** (🔕) to suppress alerts from the conversation's contact.

Note: To recover a deleted conversation, tap **Recently Deleted** (🗑) on the Messages screen. The Recently Deleted folder keeps deleted items for up to 40 days.

1 To affect multiple conversations, tap **Edit**.

A pop-up panel opens.

2 Tap **Select Messages** (⊘).

The Messages screen switches to Edit Mode.

3 Tap each message you want to delete (changes to ⊘).

Note: You can tap either the message preview or the selection circle ( ).

The Delete button appears.

4 Tap **Delete**.

A confirmation dialog opens.

5 Tap **Delete**.

Messages deletes the conversation.

6 When you finish deleting conversations, tap **Done**.

Messages turns off Edit Mode.

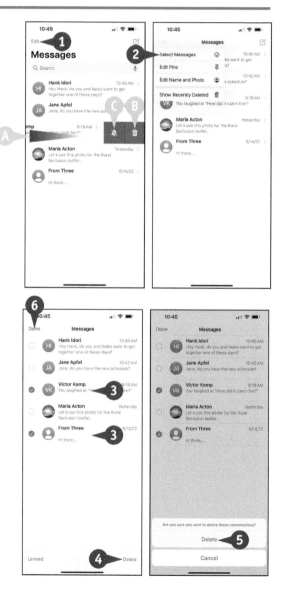

Forward or Delete One or More Messages from a Conversation

 On the Messages screen, tap the conversation that contains the message or messages you will forward.

The conversation appears.

Note: You can tap in a conversation and slide your finger left to display the time of each message.

 Tap and hold a message.

A pop-up panel appears.

③ Tap **More** (⊙).

A selection button ( ) appears to the left of each message.

④ Tap each message you want to affect (changes to ✓).

Note: You can tap either the message bubble or the selection circle ( ).

Ⓓ You can tap **Delete** (🗑) to delete the selected messages from the conversation.

⑤ Tap **Forward** (↪).

Messages starts a new message containing the message or messages you selected.

 Address the message.

 Type any extra text needed.

 Tap **Send** (⬆) to send the message.

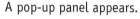

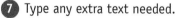

TIP

Can I resend a message?
Yes, you can resend a message in either of these ways:

- If a red icon with an exclamation point appears next to the message, the message has not been sent. Tap the icon to try sending the message again.

- If the message has been sent, you can forward it as described in this section. Alternatively, tap and hold the message text, and then tap **Copy** to copy it. Tap and hold in the message text field, and then tap **Paste** to paste the text. Tap **Send** to send the message.

Choose Settings for Messages

Messages includes many settings that you can configure to control the way the app looks and behaves. These settings include whether to send messages as SMS if the iMessage service is unavailable, whether to use MMS messaging, how long to keep messages, and whether to send low-quality images to reduce the amount of data transferred.

A key setting is whether to send read receipts for the messages you receive. You can turn read receipts on or off for Messages as a whole, but you can also make exceptions for individual contacts.

Choose Settings for Messages

① On the Home screen, tap **Settings** (⚙️).

The Settings screen appears.

② Tap **Messages** (◯) to display the Messages screen.

③ In the Allow Messages to Access section, choose which features Messages may access.

Ⓐ For example, set the **Focus** switch to On (◯) to allow Messages to interact with the Focus feature.

④ Set the **iMessage** switch to On (◯) to use the iMessage service.

⑤ Set the **Show Contact Photos** switch to On (◯) to display contact photos.

⑥ Set the **Send Read Receipts** switch to On (◯) or Off ( ) to control whether Messages sends read receipts for all messages.

⑦ Tap **Send & Receive** to display the iMessage screen.

⑧ Verify that this list shows the correct phone number and address.

Note: Messages may be set to use only your iPhone's phone number for iMessage. If so, tap **Use Your Apple ID for iMessage**, and then tap **Sign In** in the confirmation dialog that opens.

⑨ Tap the phone number or e-mail address from which to start new conversations.

⑩ Tap **Messages** (‹) to return to the Messages screen.

⑪ Set the **Send as SMS** switch to On (◯) to send iMessage messages as SMS or MMS messages when iMessage is unavailable.

⑫ Tap **Text Message Forwarding**.

The Text Message Forwarding screen appears.

13 Set the switch to On (⬤) for each Mac or device you want to allow to send text messages via the iPhone.

14 Tap **Back** (‹) to return to the Messages screen.

15 Set the **MMS Messaging** switch to On (⬤) to enable MMS messaging.

16 Set the **Show Subject Field** switch to On (⬤) or Off ( ), as needed.

17 Set the **Character Count** switch to On (⬤) or Off ( ), as needed.

18 Tap **Keep Messages**.

The Keep Messages screen appears.

19 Tap **30 Days**, **1 Year**, or **Forever**, as needed.

20 Tap **Messages** (‹) to return to the Messages screen.

21 Set the **Filter Unknown Senders** switch to On (⬤) if you want to keep messages from unknown senders separate.

22 Tap **Expire** and choose **After 2 Minutes** or **Never** for audio messages.

23 Set the **Raise to Listen** switch to On (⬤) or Off ( ), as needed.

24 Set the **Low Quality Image Mode** switch to On (⬤) or Off ( ), as needed.

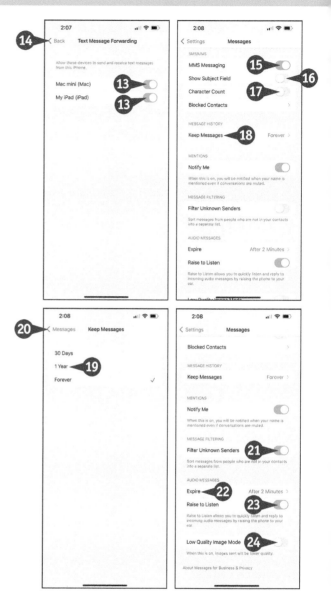

TIP

How do I control read receipts for individual contacts?

First, on the Messages screen in the Settings app, set the **Send Read Receipts** switch to On (⬤) or Off ( ) to control whether Messages sends read receipts by default.

Next, in the Messages app, open a message to or from the appropriate contact. Tap the contact's icon to display the Details screen for the contact. Set the **Send Read Receipts** switch to On (⬤) or Off ( ), as needed, and then tap **Done**.

Block and Unblock Senders

Messages enables you to block any sender from whom you do not want to receive communications. You can implement blocking from the Messages app or from the Phone app. Whichever app you start from, blocking the contact prevents you from receiving notifications when the contact phones or messages you.

You can review your list of blocked senders and unblock any sender from whom you want to receive messages again. You can also unblock one means of communication while leaving others blocked for the same sender — for example, you might unblock a particular phone.

Block and Unblock Senders

Block a Sender from the Messages App

1. In a conversation with the contact you want to block, tap the contact's icon.

   The Details screen for the contact appears.

2. Tap **Info** (ⓘ).

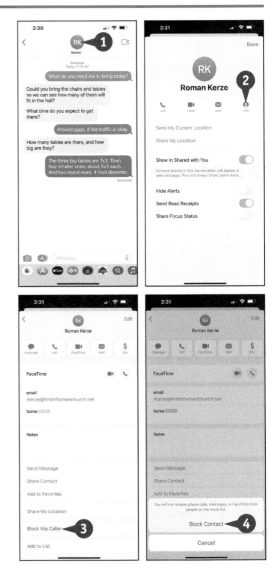

The contact record opens.

3. Toward the bottom of the screen, tap **Block this Caller**.

   A confirmation dialog opens.

4. Tap **Block Contact**.

View Your Blocked List and Unblock Senders

1 On the Home screen, tap **Settings** (⚙️).

The Settings screen appears.

2 Tap **Messages** (💬).

The Messages screen appears.

3 In the SMS/MMS section, tap **Blocked Contacts**.

The Blocked Contacts screen appears, showing the list of contacts you have blocked.

Ⓐ You can tap **Add New** to display the Contacts screen and then tap the contact you want to block. Blocking the contact blocks all the means of contact, but you can then unblock any means of contact you want to allow.

4 To unblock a means of contact, swipe its button to the left.

The Unblock button appears.

5 Tap **Unblock**.

TIP

How do I block a contact in the Phone app?

In the Phone app, tap **Contacts** (👤 changes to 👤), tap the contact to display the contact record, and then tap **Block This Caller**. In the confirmation dialog that opens, tap **Block Contact**.

Set Up and Use the Emergency SOS Feature

Your iPhone's Emergency SOS feature can either display the Emergency SOS screen or dial emergency services automatically when you give the Emergency SOS shortcut, five quick presses on the Side button. Emergency SOS can also automatically text a group of emergency contacts to tell them you have dialed emergency services.

To be ready for an emergency, enable the Emergency SOS feature, configure its settings, and then set up your emergency contacts in the Health app.

Set Up and Use the Emergency SOS Feature

Set Up the Emergency SOS Feature

1. On the Home screen, tap **Settings** (⚙) to display the Settings screen.

2. Tap **Emergency SOS** (🆘).

   The Emergency SOS screen appears.

3. Set the **Call with Hold** switch to On (◯) if you want to make an emergency call by holding down **Side** and either **Volume Up** or **Volume Down**.

4. Set the **Call with 5 Presses** switch to On (◯) if you want to make an emergency call by pressing **Side** five times in quick succession.

5. If you set either the Call with Hold switch or the Call with 5 Presses switch to On (◯), or you set both switches to On (◯), set the **Countdown Sound** switch to On (◯) to receive a three-second countdown before your iPhone dials emergency services.

6. Tap **Set up Emergency Contacts in Health**.

   The Medical ID screen in the Health app appears.

7. Tap **Edit**.

   The Medical ID screen opens for editing.

A. Set the **Show When Locked** switch to On (◯) if you want your iPhone to display your medical ID when it is locked.

B. Set the **Show During Emergency Call** switch to On (◯) if you want your iPhone to share your medical ID during an emergency call.

8. Tap **add emergency contact** (➕).

128

The Contacts screen appears.

C If the contact you want does not appear, tap **Lists** (<), and then tap the appropriate list.

9 Tap the contact you want to designate an emergency contact.

The Relationship screen appears.

10 Tap the button for the term that describes the contact's relationship to you, such as **mother**, **sister**, or **partner**.

The Medical ID screen appears again.

You can add other contacts by repeating steps **7** to **10**.

11 Tap **Done**.

Using the Emergency SOS Feature

1 When you need to place an emergency call, give the emergency keypress:

To use Call with Hold, press and hold **Side** and either **Volume Up** or **Volume Down**.

To use Call with 5 Presses, press **Side** five times in quick succession.

D Your iPhone displays a countdown timer before calling emergency services.

If you set the **Countdown Sound** switch to On (⬤), a countdown alarm plays.

E You can tap **Stop** (✕) to stop the call. In the dialog that opens, tap **Stop Calling**.

F If the screen shown to the right appears, you can swipe **Emergency SOS** (sos) right to place the emergency call.

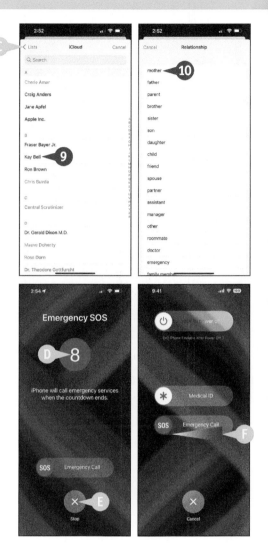

How can I quickly disable Face ID to prevent someone from forcing me to unlock my iPhone?
You can temporarily disable Face ID by pressing and holding either **Side** and **Volume Up** or **Side** and **Volume Down** for two seconds. The Power Off screen appears. At this point, Face ID is disabled, and you will need to enter your passcode to enable it again.

CHAPTER 6

Networking Your iPhone

You can control which cellular and wireless networks your iPhone uses, connect Bluetooth devices, and share the iPhone's Internet connection via the Personal Hotspot feature.

Using Airplane Mode

Normally, you will want to keep your iPhone connected to the cellular network so that you can make or receive phone calls and access the Internet. But when you do not need or may not use the cellular network, you can turn on the iPhone's Airplane Mode feature to cut off all connections.

Turning on Airplane Mode initially turns off Wi-Fi as well, but you can turn Wi-Fi on and off separately when you need to — for example, when you need to connect to in-flight Wi-Fi services.

Using Airplane Mode

1 Swipe down from the upper-right corner of the screen to open Control Center.

Note: You can open Control Center from within most apps. If an app blocks you opening Control Center, first display the Home screen, and then open Control Center. If all apps block you opening Control Center, tap **Settings** (⚙️), tap **Control Center** (🔲), and then set the **Access Within Apps** switch to On (⬤).

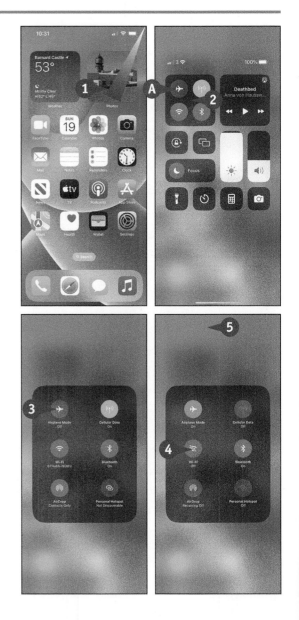

A You can tap **Airplane Mode** (✈️ changes to ✈️) to turn Airplane Mode on quickly.

2 Tap and hold the upper-left box.

The pop-up panel opens.

3 Tap **Airplane Mode** (✈️ changes to ✈️).

Your iPhone turns off all cellular and wireless connections.

4 To turn on Wi-Fi, tap **Wi-Fi** (📶 changes to 📶).

5 Tap the screen above the pop-up panel.

The pop-up panel closes.

6 Tap the screen at the top of Control Center.

Control Center closes.

Note: When your iPhone has a wireless network connection, it uses that connection instead of the cellular connection. This helps minimize your cellular network usage and often gives a faster connection.

Monitor Your Cellular Network Usage

I f you use your iPhone extensively, you may need to monitor your usage of the cellular network to avoid incurring extra charges beyond your data allowance. You can check your current data usage and roaming data usage in the Cellular Data Usage area of the Cellular screen in the Settings app. However, you should also see if your carrier provides an app for monitoring data usage, because such apps frequently offer extra features, such as warning you when your phone is using data quickly.

Monitor Your Cellular Network Usage

1 On the Home screen, tap and hold **Settings** (⚙).

The pop-up panel opens.

2 Tap **Cellular Data** (📶).

The Cellular screen appears.

Note: You can also display the Cellular screen by tapping **Settings** (⚙) on the Home screen and then tapping **Cellular** (📶) on the Settings screen.

3 Set the **Cellular Data** switch to On (⚪) to enable cellular data.

A To control data roaming, tap **Cellular Data Options**. On the Cellular Data Options screen, set the **Data Roaming** switch to On (⚪). Tap **Cellular** (<) to return to the Cellular screen.

B The readouts in the Cellular Data area show your cellular data usage since last resetting the statistics and how much roaming data you have used.

C The readouts in the Call Time area show the amount of time you have spent making calls since last resetting the statistics and during your phone's lifetime.

D You can reset your usage statistics by tapping **Reset Statistics** at the bottom of the Cellular screen.

E You can set the **Wi-Fi Assist** switch to On (⚪) to make your iPhone automatically use cellular data when the phone's Wi-Fi connection is poor. This switch may be set to On (⚪) by default. The readout shows the amount of cellular data used.

Control Cellular Data and Background Refresh

To control your iPhone's use of cellular data, you can turn cellular data on and off, and you can specify which apps can use cellular data. You can determine which apps and services use the most data and then turn off greedy apps.

You can also use the Background App Refresh feature to control which apps refresh their content via Wi-Fi or cellular connections when running in the background rather than the foreground.

Control Cellular Data and Background Refresh

1 On the Home screen, tap and hold **Settings** (⚙).

The pop-up panel opens.

2 Tap **Cellular Data** ((ᵗᵖ)).

The Cellular screen appears.

Note: Turning off cellular data does not affect cellular voice services: You can still make phone calls, and GPS tracking still works.

3 If you need to turn cellular data off altogether, set the **Cellular Data** switch to Off (🔘 changes to ◯).

4 Tap **Cellular Data Options** to display the Cellular Data Options screen.

5 Tap **Voice & Data** to display the Voice & Data screen.

Note: The options on the Voice & Data screen vary depending on your carrier and region.

6 Tap the appropriate button (✓). In the example, you might tap **5G On** to turn 5G on all the time or tap **5G Auto** to have iOS switch to 5G for data-heavy activities.

7 Tap **Back** (<) to display the Cellular Data Options screen again.

8 Tap **Data Mode** to display the Data Mode screen.

9 Tap the appropriate button (✓). In the example, the choices are **Allow More Data on 5G**, **Standard**, and **Low Data Mode**.

10 Tap **Back** (<) to display the Cellular Data Options screen again.

11 Set the **Limit IP Address Tracking** switch to On (🔘) to have iOS hide your iPhone's IP address from known trackers in Safari and Mail.

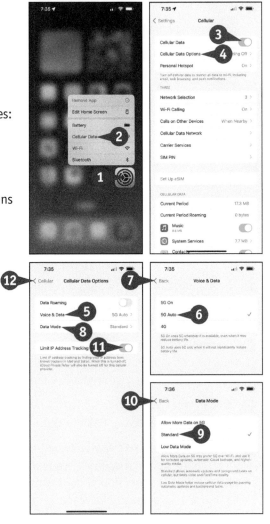

12 Tap **Cellular** (<).

The Cellular screen appears again.

13 If cellular data is enabled, set each app's switch to On (●) or Off ( ), as needed.

14 To see which system services have been using cellular data, tap **System Services**.

The System Services screen appears.

15 Browse the list to identify any services that hog cellular data.

16 Tap **Cellular** (<).

The Cellular screen appears.

17 Tap **Settings** (<).

The Settings screen appears.

18 Tap **General** (⚙).

The General screen appears.

19 Tap **Background App Refresh**.

The Background App Refresh screen appears.

20 Tap **Background App Refresh**; tap **Off**, **Wi-Fi**, or **Wi-Fi & Cellular Data**, as needed; and then tap **Background App Refresh** (<).

21 Assuming you chose Wi-Fi or Wi-Fi & Cellular Data, set each individual app switch to On (●) or Off ( ), as needed.

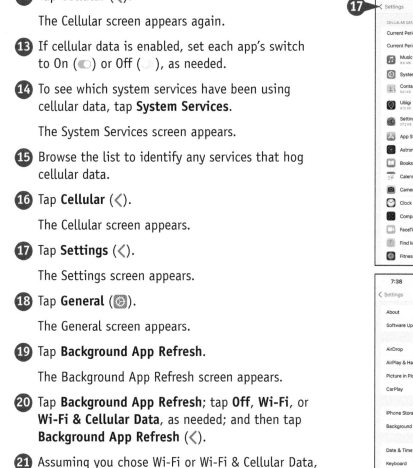

TIP

Which apps should I allow to use Background App Refresh?
Normally, you should restrict Background App Refresh to those apps for which it is important to have updated information immediately available each time you access the app. For example, if you use your iPhone for navigation, getting updated map and GPS information in the background is vital, whereas updating magazine subscriptions is usually a waste of cellular data.

Using Bluetooth Devices with Your iPhone

To extend your iPhone's functionality, you can connect devices to it that communicate using the wireless Bluetooth technology. For example, you can connect a Bluetooth headset and microphone so that you can listen to music and make and take phone calls. Or you can connect a Bluetooth keyboard so that you can quickly type e-mail messages, notes, or documents.

Before you can use a Bluetooth device, you must *pair* it with your iPhone, establishing a formal relationship between the two. After pairing the device and the iPhone, you can quickly connect and disconnect the device, as needed.

Using Bluetooth Devices with Your iPhone

Pair a Bluetooth Device with Your iPhone

1. On the Home screen, tap and hold **Settings** (⚙).

   The pop-up panel opens.

2. Tap **Bluetooth** (✳).

   The Bluetooth screen appears.

3. Make sure the **Bluetooth** switch is set to On (⬤).

   Your iPhone searches for Bluetooth devices.

4. Turn on the Bluetooth device, and make it discoverable.

Note: Read the Bluetooth device's instructions to find out how to make the device discoverable via Bluetooth.

Ⓐ Devices in the My Devices list are already paired with your iPhone. You can tap a device to connect it.

Note: A paired device may connect automatically when it is powered on and within range.

5. Tap the device's button.

Note: The Other Devices list may show multiple entries for a single device. In this example, both of the Keyboard K780 entries represent the same keyboard. One entry works, whereas the other gives a timeout error.

B For a device such as a keyboard or a computer, the Bluetooth Pairing Request dialog opens.

6 Type the pairing code on the device.

The iPhone pairs with the device and then connects to it.

C The My Devices list shows the device as *Connected*. You can start using the device.

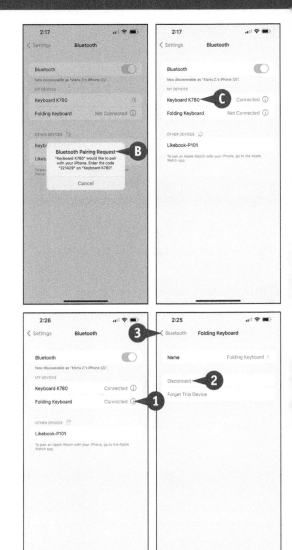

Disconnect and Reconnect a Bluetooth Device

1 On the Bluetooth screen, when the device is marked *Connected* in the My Devices list, tap **Info** ((i)).

The Info screen for the device appears, showing the device's name at the top.

2 Tap **Disconnect**.

Note: If the Disconnect button does not appear on the Info screen, see the following tip.

iOS disconnects the device.

3 Tap **Bluetooth** (<).

TIP

How do I disconnect a Bluetooth device if the Disconnect button does not appear?
If the Disconnect button does not appear on the Info screen for the Bluetooth device, you will need to use controls on the Bluetooth device to disconnect it. For example, with the foldable Bluetooth keyboard shown in the examples, folding the keyboard shut disconnects it automatically. Depending on the device, you may need to press a button to disconnect the device or power it down.

continued ▶

$\mathcal{S}$ome Bluetooth devices display straightforward descriptive names, such as "Apple Watch 7," but others display only cryptic model numbers, such as "OE-P211." Fortunately, you can rename many — but not all — Bluetooth devices from the Info screen for a device. For an audio device, you can usually also specify its type: car stereo, headphone, hearing aid, speaker, or other.

When you no longer need to use a Bluetooth device with your iPhone, you make iOS forget the device. You can also use the Forget Device command as preparation for reestablishing the pairing between your iPhone and a device.

Using Bluetooth Devices with Your iPhone (continued)

The Bluetooth screen appears again.

D The My Devices list shows the device's status as *Not Connected*.

4 To connect the device again, tap the main part of the button — not the Info (ⓘ) icon.

iOS reconnects the device.

E The device's status appears as *Connected* again.

You can start using the device again.

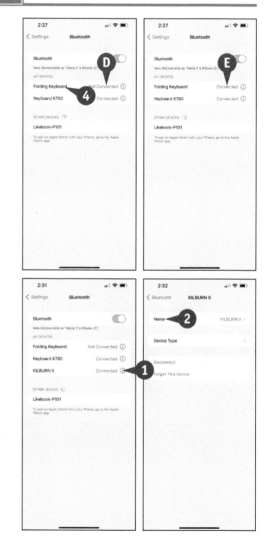

Rename a Bluetooth Device

Note: You can rename some Bluetooth devices but not others. Whether you can rename a device depends on how the manufacturer has configured it.

1 On the Bluetooth screen, when the device is marked *Connected* in the My Devices list, tap **Info** (ⓘ).

The Info screen for the device appears, showing the device's name at the top.

2 Tap **Name**.

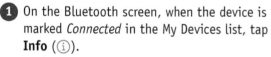

The Name screen appears.

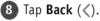 You can tap **Delete** (×) to delete the existing name.

3 Type the new name.

4 Tap **done**.

5 Tap **Back** (〈).

The Info screen appears again, now showing the new name.

6 If the device is an audio output device, tap **Device Type**.

The Device Type screen appears.

7 Tap **Car Stereo**, **Headphone**, **Hearing Aid**, **Speaker**, or **Other**, as needed.

8 Tap **Back** (〈).

The Info screen appears again.

Make Your iPhone Forget a Bluetooth Device

1 On the Bluetooth screen, tap **Info** (ⓘ) for the device.

The Info screen appears, showing the device's name at the top.

2 Tap **Forget This Device**.

A confirmation dialog opens.

3 Tap **Forget Device**.

The Bluetooth screen appears again.

The device you removed no longer appears in the My Devices list.

TIP

How can I increase the range of my Bluetooth headphones?

You cannot directly increase the range of Bluetooth headphones — for example, you cannot turn up the power of Bluetooth transmissions on your iPhone.

You could get a *Bluetooth repeater* or *Bluetooth extender,* a hardware device that amplifies the Bluetooth signal. However, most such devices are better suited for use with larger, stationary devices, such as a desktop PC or a TV, than with an iPhone.

Otherwise, position the iPhone as centrally as possible in the location you want to cover, and remove as many obstacles as possible. Alternatively, if you wear an Apple Watch, pair it with the Bluetooth headphones and use it, instead of the iPhone, to play back audio.

Share Items via AirDrop

AirDrop enables you to share files quickly and easily with iOS devices and Macs near your iPhone. For example, you can use AirDrop to share a photo, a contact record, or an item from Wallet. You can use AirDrop in any app that displays a Share button (⬆).

You can turn AirDrop on when you need it and off when you do not. When AirDrop is on, you can choose between accepting items only from your contacts — usually the better choice — or from everyone.

Share Items via AirDrop

Turn AirDrop On or Off

1 Swipe down from the upper-right corner of the screen.

Control Center opens.

2 Tap and hold the upper-left box.

The pop-up panel opens.

A The readout shows AirDrop's status: *AirDrop: Receiving Off; AirDrop: Contacts Only;* or *AirDrop: Everyone.*

3 Tap **AirDrop** (◉).

Note: AirDrop uses Wi-Fi or Bluetooth to transfer files wirelessly without the devices having to be on the same wireless network.

The AirDrop panel opens.

4 Tap **Receiving Off**, **Contacts Only**, or **Everyone**, as needed.

The AirDrop panel closes.

B The AirDrop readout shows the AirDrop setting you chose.

5 Tap the screen above the pop-up panel.

The pop-up panel closes.

6 Tap the screen at the top of Control Center.

Control Center closes.

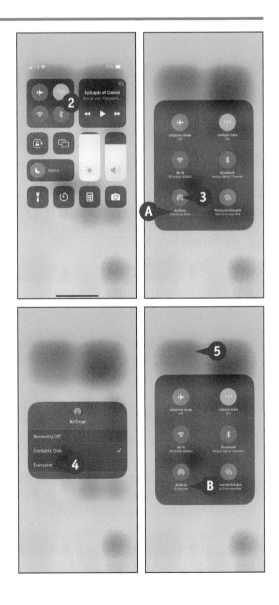

Share an Item via AirDrop

1 In the appropriate app, navigate to the item you want to share. For example, in Photos, tap a photo to open it.

2 Tap **Share** (⬆) to display the Share sheet.

C In some apps, you can select other items to share at the same time. For example, in Photos, you can select other photos.

D The banner shows the number of photos selected and which information is included, such as the location.

3 Tap **Options** (>).

The Options screen appears.

4 In the Send As box, tap **Automatic** to have iOS choose the best format when you are sending via Messages. Tap **Individual Photo** to send the photo as a file. Tap **iCloud Link** to send a link to download the photo from iCloud.

5 Set the **Location** switch to On (⬤) or Off ( ), as needed.

6 Set the **All Photos Data** switch to On (⬤) or Off ( ), as needed.

Note: Setting the All Photos Data switch to On (⬤) disables the Location switch, because All Photos Data includes Location.

7 Tap **Done**.

8 In the AirDrop area, tap **AirDrop** (◉).

The AirDrop panel opens.

9 Tap the icon for the device to which you want to send the item.

AirDrop sends the item.

The *Sent* readout appears below the icon for the device.

10 Tap **Done**. The app and the share sheet appear again.

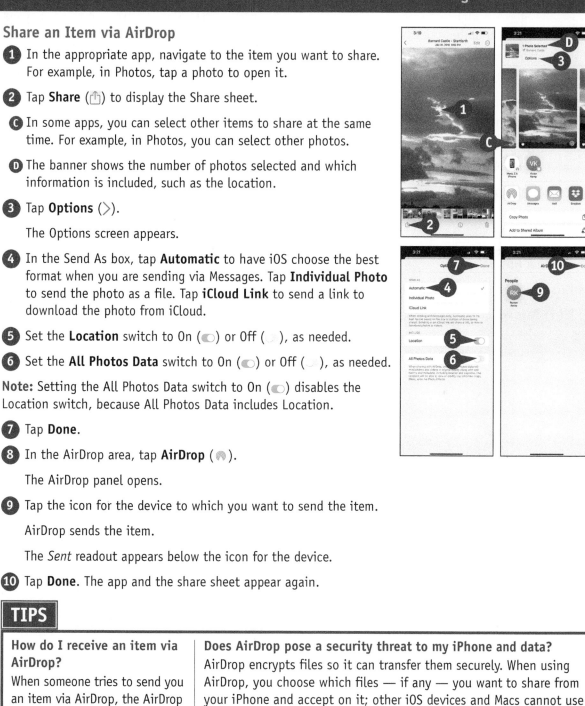

TIPS

How do I receive an item via AirDrop?	Does AirDrop pose a security threat to my iPhone and data?
When someone tries to send you an item via AirDrop, the AirDrop dialog opens. Tap **Accept** if you want to receive the item; otherwise, tap **Decline**.	AirDrop encrypts files so it can transfer them securely. When using AirDrop, you choose which files — if any — you want to share from your iPhone and accept on it; other iOS devices and Macs cannot use AirDrop to grab files from your iPhone. For security, however, it is best to turn off AirDrop until you need to use it — and then turn off AirDrop again as soon as you finish using it.

Share Internet Access via Personal Hotspot

Not only can your iPhone access the Internet itself from anywhere it has a suitable connection to the cellular network, but it can also share that Internet access with your computer and other devices. This feature is called *Personal Hotspot*.

For you to use Personal Hotspot, your iPhone's carrier must permit you to use it. Some carriers charge an extra fee per month on top of the standard data plan charge.

Share Internet Access via Personal Hotspot

Set Up Personal Hotspot

1 On the Home screen, tap **Settings** (⚙).

The Settings screen appears.

2 Tap **Personal Hotspot** (📶).

The Personal Hotspot screen appears.

3 Tap **Wi-Fi Password**.

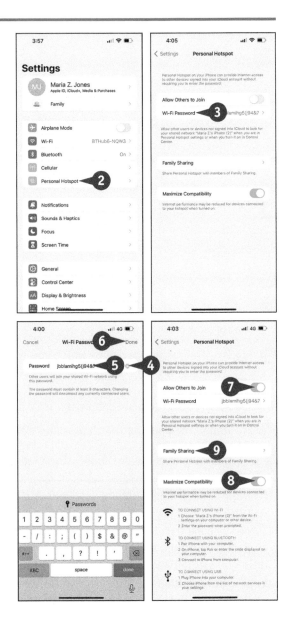

The Wi-Fi Password screen appears.

4 Tap **Delete** (×) to delete the default password.

5 Type the password you want to use.

6 Tap **Done**.

The Personal Hotspot screen appears again.

7 Set the **Allow Others to Join** switch to On (⚪) if you want to allow people other than Family Sharing members to use the hotspot.

8 Set the **Maximize Compatibility** switch to On (⚪) if you want to make the hotspot accessible to all types of devices.

9 Tap **Family Sharing**.

The Family Sharing screen appears.

10 Set the **Family Sharing** switch to On (⬤) if you want to let Family Sharing members use the hotspot.

11 Tap the family member whose access you want to configure.

The screen for that family member appears.

12 Tap **Ask for Approval** or **Automatic**, as appropriate.

13 Tap **Back** (‹).

The Family Sharing screen appears again.

14 Tap **Back** (‹).

The Personal Hotspot screen appears again.

You can now connect your computer or other devices.

Stop Using Personal Hotspot

A The contrasting background for the clock readout indicates that Personal Hotspot is active and has one or more connections.

1 Tap the clock readout with the contrasting background.

The Personal Hotspot screen appears.

2 Set the **Allow Others to Join** switch to Off (⬤ changes to ◯).

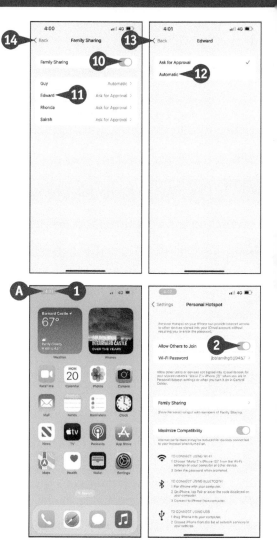

How else can I connect a PC or Mac to Personal Hotspot?

Usually, you can connect a PC to Personal Hotspot by simply connecting your iPhone to the PC via USB. Windows automatically detects the iPhone's Internet connection as a new network connection and installs any software needed.

Similarly, you can connect a Mac via USB, but you may need to configure the network connection. Press `Control`+click or right-click **System Settings** (⚙) or **System Preferences** (⚙) on the Dock; click **Network** on the contextual menu to open the Network pane; and then click **iPhone USB**, and work with the controls that appear.

If you cannot get USB to work, connect the computer via Wi-Fi or Bluetooth, if your computer has either of those features.

Connect to Wi-Fi Networks and Hotspots

To conserve your data allowance, use a Wi-Fi network instead of the cell phone network whenever you can. Your iPhone can connect both to private Wi-Fi networks and to public Wi-Fi hotspots. Public Wi-Fi hotspots may not be secure, so use them sparingly, with caution, and with a virtual private network, or VPN.

The first time you connect to a Wi-Fi network, you must provide the network's password. After that, the iPhone stores the password, so you can connect to the network without entering the password again.

Connect to Wi-Fi Networks and Hotspots

Connect to a Network Listed on the Wi-Fi Screen

1 On the Home screen, tap and hold **Settings** ( ).

The pop-up panel opens.

2 Tap **Wi-Fi** (🛜).

The Wi-Fi screen appears.

3 If Wi-Fi is off, set the **Wi-Fi** switch to On (⬜ changes to ◯).

The list of networks appears.

Ⓐ A lock icon (🔒) indicates the network uses security such as a password.

4 Tap the network you want to connect to.

Note: If the network does not have a password, your iPhone connects to it without prompting you for a password.

Note: When connecting to a Wi-Fi hotspot, you may need to enter login information in Safari. In this case, Safari usually opens automatically and prompts you to log in.

The Enter Password screen appears.

5 Type the password.

6 Tap **Join**.

Your iPhone connects to the wireless network.

Ⓑ The Wi-Fi screen appears again, showing a check mark (✓) next to the network the iPhone has connected to.

Connect to a Network Not Listed on the Wi-Fi Screen

1 On the Wi-Fi screen, tap **Other**.

The Other Network screen appears.

2 Type the network name.

Note: If the network does not use security, tap **Join**.

C The Wi-Fi signal icons (📶) on the Wi-Fi screen and in the status bar show the strength of the Wi-Fi signals. The more bars that appear in black rather than gray, the stronger a signal is.

3 Tap **Security**.

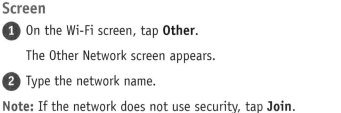

The Security screen appears.

4 Set the **Private Wi-Fi Address** switch to On (⬤) to make your iPhone use a private IP address. This helps reduce tracking of your iPhone across separate Wi-Fi networks.

5 Tap the security type — for example, **WPA2/WPA3**.

6 Tap **Other Network** (‹).

The Other Network screen appears.

7 Type the password.

8 Tap **Join**.

Your iPhone joins the network.

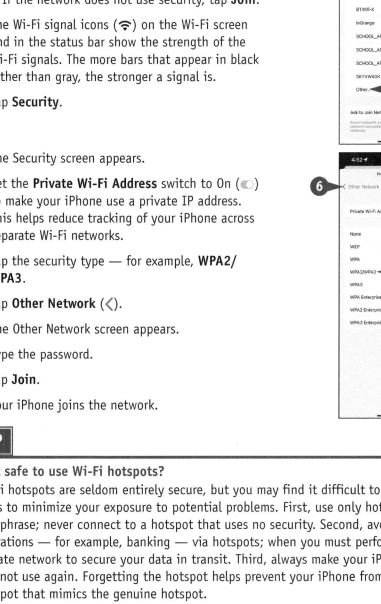

TIP

Is it safe to use Wi-Fi hotspots?

Wi-Fi hotspots are seldom entirely secure, but you may find it difficult to avoid using them. Here are three ways to minimize your exposure to potential problems. First, use only hotspots that use security, such as a passphrase; never connect to a hotspot that uses no security. Second, avoid performing sensitive operations — for example, banking — via hotspots; when you must perform such operations, use a virtual private network to secure your data in transit. Third, always make your iPhone forget a Wi-Fi hotspot you will not use again. Forgetting the hotspot helps prevent your iPhone from connecting to a malevolent hotspot that mimics the genuine hotspot.

Manage Your Wi-Fi Networks

You can manage your Wi-Fi networks to improve performance, increase security, and control which networks your iPhone uses.

You can control whether your iPhone automatically detects available Wi-Fi networks or nearby personal hotspots. For a particular network, you can control whether your iPhone automatically joins that network, whether it uses a private IP address for security on that network, and whether it uses Low Data Mode to reduce the amount of data transferred via that network. When you no longer want to use a particular network, you can make your iPhone forget it.

Manage Your Wi-Fi Networks

Configure Settings for Wi-Fi Networks

1 On the Home screen, tap and hold **Settings** (⚙).

   The pop-up panel opens.

2 Tap **Wi-Fi** (🛜).

   The Wi-Fi screen appears.

3 Tap **Ask to Join Networks**.

   The Ask to Join Networks screen appears.

4 Tap **Off**, **Notify**, or **Ask**, as appropriate.

Note: The Ask to Join Networks settings take effect when no known Wi-Fi network is available. Tap **Ask** to have iOS ask your permission before it joins a new network. Tap **Notify** to have iOS notify you of available networks. Tap **Off** to receive neither permission request nor notification.

5 Tap **Wi-Fi** (<).

   The Wi-Fi screen appears again.

6 Tap **Auto-Join Hotspot**.

   The Auto-Join Hotspot screen appears.

7 Tap **Never**, **Ask to Join**, or **Automatic**, as needed.

   Tap **Wi-Fi** (<).

   The Wi-Fi screen appears once more.

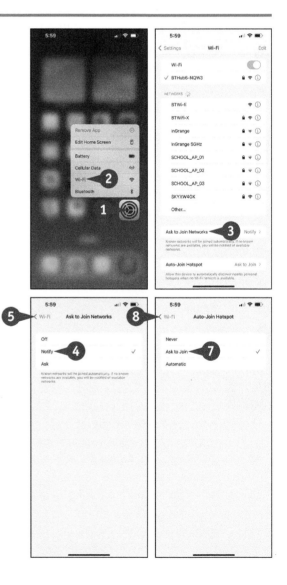

Configure Settings for a Wi-Fi Network

1 On the Wi-Fi screen, tap **Info** (ⓘ) for the Wi-Fi network you want to configure.

The Info screen for the network appears.

2 Set the **Auto-Join** switch to On (◯) if you want your iPhone to join this network automatically.

3 Set the **Low Data Mode** switch to On (◯) if you want to use Low Data Mode — for example, because this is a metered network.

4 Set the **Private Wi-Fi Address** switch to On (◯) if you want the iPhone to use a private IP address.

5 Set the **Limit IP Address Tracking** switch to On (◯) to have iOS hide your iPhone's IP address from known trackers in Safari and Mail.

A Further down the Info screen, you can tap **Configure DNS** to configure networking settings.

Forget a Wi-Fi Network

1 On the Wi-Fi screen, tap **Info** (ⓘ) for the Wi-Fi network you want to forget.

The Info screen for the network appears.

2 Tap **Forget This Network**.

The Forget Wi-Fi Network? dialog opens.

3 Tap **Forget**.

iOS forgets the network.

The Wi-Fi screen appears again.

TIP

How do I set an order of preference for Wi-Fi networks?

There is no way to set an order of preference explicitly. iOS chooses among available Wi-Fi networks based on four factors: first, your "most preferred" network; second, the private network your iPhone joined most recently; third, private networks ranked by security method — highest first; and fourth, public networks ranked by security method — again, highest first.

To help guide iOS to your preferred networks, enable Auto-Join for them. When connected to a network, tap **Info** (ⓘ) for the Wi-Fi network to display the Info screen, and then set the **Auto-Join** switch to On (◯).

After that, review the list of Wi-Fi networks and make iOS forget any you no longer want to use.

CHAPTER 7

Working with Apps

iOS enables you to customize the Home screen, putting the icons you need most at your fingertips and organizing the icons into folders and the App Library. You can switch instantly among the apps you are running, find the apps you need on Apple's App Store, and update and remove apps. You can also work easily with text and take notes.

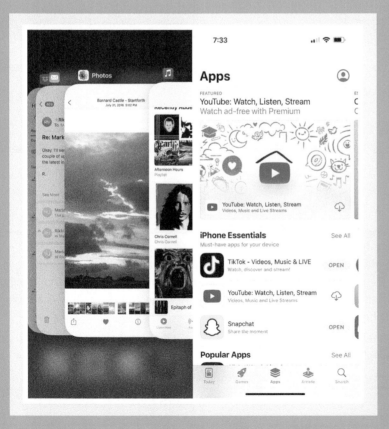

Customize the Home Screen

From the Home screen, you run the apps on your iPhone. You can customize the Home screen to put the apps you use most frequently within easy reach. You can create additional Home screen pages as needed and move the app icons among them so that the app icons are arranged in the way you find fastest and most convenient to use.

Customize the Home Screen

Unlock the Icons for Customization

1. On the Home screen, swipe left or right to display the page you want to customize.

2. Tap and hold any app's icon on that Home screen page.

   The pop-up menu opens.

3. Tap **Edit Home Screen** (🗒).

   The Home screen enters Jiggle Mode. In this mode, the icons jiggle, indicating that you can move them.

Move an Icon Within a Home Screen Page

1. After unlocking the icons, drag the icon to where you want it.

   The other icons move out of the way.

2. When the icon is in the right place, drop it.

   Ⓐ The icon snaps to the grid and then stays in its new position.

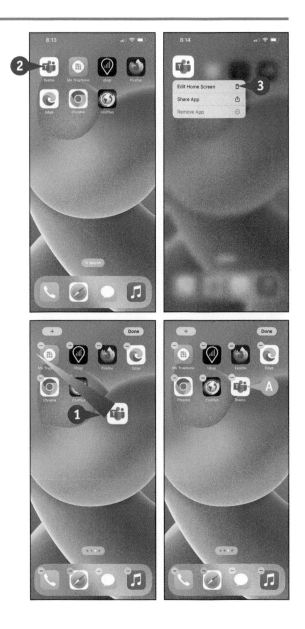

Move an Icon to a Different Home Screen Page

 After unlocking the icons, drag the icon to the left edge of the screen to display the previous Home screen page or to the right edge to display the next page.

The previous page or next page appears.

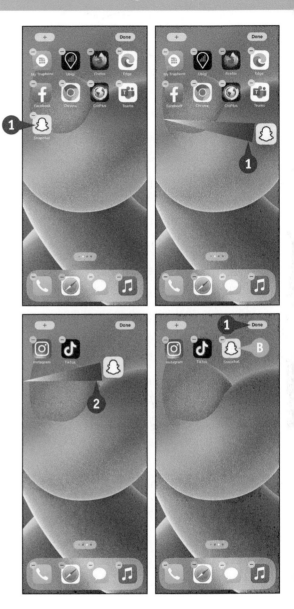

 Drag the icon to where you want it.

If the page contains other icons, they move out of the way as needed.

3 Drop the icon.

B The icon snaps to the grid and stays in its new position.

Stop Customizing the Home Screen

1 Tap **Done**.

The Home screen exits Jiggle Mode.

The icons stop jiggling.

Note: You can also simply tap the screen to exit Jiggle Mode.

TIP

How can I put the default apps back into their original Home screen locations?
On the Home screen, tap **Settings** (⚙), and then tap **General** (⚙). At the bottom of the General screen, tap **Transfer or Reset iPhone**. On the Transfer or Reset iPhone screen, tap **Reset**, and then tap **Reset Home Screen Layout** in the dialog that opens. In the confirmation dialog, tap **Reset Home Screen**. Swipe up from the bottom of the screen to return to the Home screen.

Organize Apps with Folders

To organize the Home screen pages, you can arrange the items into folders. The iPhone's default Home screen layout includes a folder named Utilities, which contains items such as the Calculator app and the Compass app, but you can create as many other folders as you need. Like the Home screen, each folder can have multiple pages, with up to nine apps on each page, so you can put many apps in a folder.

Organize Apps with Folders

Create a Folder

1 On the appropriate Home screen page, tap and hold an icon.

The pop-up menu opens.

2 Tap **Edit Home Screen** (▣).

The Home screen enters Jiggle Mode. The icons jiggle, indicating that you can move them.

Note: When creating a folder, you may find it easiest to first put both items you will add to the folder on the same page.

3 Drag the icon to the other icon you want to place in the folder you create.

The iPhone creates a folder, puts both icons in it, and assigns a default name based on the genre, if it can identify a genre.

4 Tap and hold the folder.

The pop-up menu opens.

5 Tap **Rename** (✏).

The folder opens in Jiggle Mode, with its name selected.

6 Tap **Delete** (ⓧ) to delete the folder name.

The keyboard appears.

7 Type the new name for the folder.

8 Tap **done** on the keyboard.

The iPhone applies the name to the folder.

9 Tap outside the folder.

The folder closes.

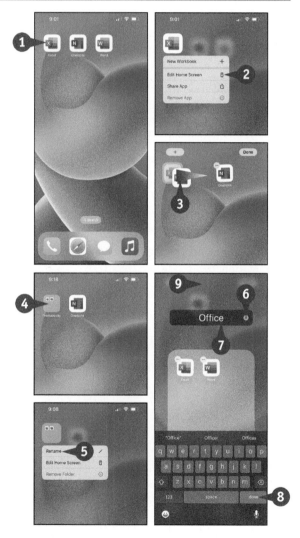

10 Tap **Done**.

The Home screen exits Jiggle Mode.

Open an Item in a Folder

 Tap the folder's icon.

The folder's contents appear, and the items outside the folder fade and blur.

 If necessary, swipe left or right or tap to the left or right of the dots to navigate to another page in the folder.

 Tap the item you want to open.

The item opens.

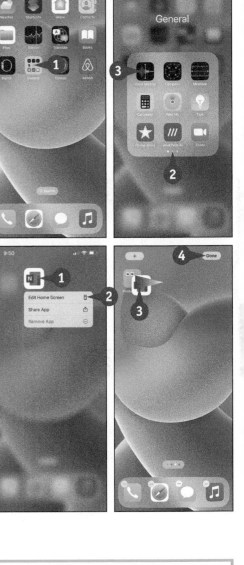

Add an Item to a Folder

 Tap and hold the item.

The pop-up menu opens.

 Tap **Edit Home Screen** (▣).

The Home screen enters Jiggle Mode. The icons jiggle, indicating that you can move them.

3 Drag the icon on top of the folder and drop it there.

Note: If the folder is on a different Home screen page from the icon, drag the icon to the left edge to display the previous page or to the right edge to display the next page.

The item goes into the folder.

4 Tap **Done**.

The Home screen exits Jiggle Mode.

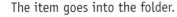
TIPS

How do I take an item out of a folder?
Tap the folder to display its contents, and then tap and hold an icon until the pop-up menu opens. Tap **Edit Home Screen** (▣). The Home screen enters Jiggle Mode. Drag the icon out of the folder and drop it where you want it on the Home screen. When you remove the last icon, iOS deletes the folder automatically.

How do I create another page in a folder?
Open the folder, and then tap and hold an icon until the pop-up menu opens. Tap **Edit Home Screen** (▣). The Home screen enters Jiggle Mode. Drag the icon to the right side of the current page. A new page appears automatically.

Place Widgets on the Home Screen

OS enables you to place widgets on the Home screen pages. This capability lets you mix widgets and app icons in whatever way you find most helpful.

iOS provides a wide section of widgets. For example, the Calendar app's Up Next widget shows your upcoming events; the Stocks app's Watchlist widget displays the prices and status of your chosen stocks and indices; and the Reminders app's List widget shows your next task. Third-party developers provide other widgets. Widgets come in various sizes and shapes, typically taking up the space of 4, 8, or 16 app icons.

Place Widgets on the Home Screen

1 Display the Home screen page to which you want to add a widget.

2 Tap and hold open space on the Home screen page.

The Home screen enters Jiggle Mode.

Note: You can also switch the Home screen to Jiggle Mode by tapping and holding an icon and then tapping **Edit Home Screen** (▣).

3 Tap **Add** (✚).

The Widgets panel opens.

Ⓐ You can tap **Search Widgets** (🔍) and type a search term.

Note: You can scroll up and down the Widgets panel to browse the available widgets.

4 Tap the widget you want to add.

The Details pane for that widget appears.

Ⓑ Dots indicate that different widgets of this type are available. The darker dot indicates the widget displayed.

5 If more widgets are available, swipe left or right, as needed. To follow this example, you would swipe left.

154

The next widget appears.

6 When you locate the widget you want to add, tap **Add Widget** (⊕).

The Widgets panel closes.

The widget appears on the Home screen.

7 Tap the widget, hold for a moment, and then drag it to where you want it.

The widget appears in its new position.

8 Tap **Done**.

The Home screen exits Jiggle Mode.

You can start using the widget.

TIP

How do I remove a widget from a Home screen page?

Tap and hold the widget's icon to display the contextual menu, and then tap **Remove Widget** (⊖). The Remove Widget dialog opens, identifying the widget by name and explaining that removing the widget will not delete any apps or data. Tap **Remove**. iOS removes the widget from the Home screen page.

Hide Home Screen Pages

As well as enabling you to customize your Home screen pages with apps and widgets in your preferred layout, iOS also enables you to hide Home screen pages temporarily.

You may find hiding Home screen pages helpful when sharing your iPhone's screen with others who you would prefer not to see certain apps or widgets. Or you may simply want to reduce temptation by hiding your Home screen pages of entertainment and social-networking apps until you complete your work.

Hide Home Screen Pages

1 On any Home screen page, tap and hold open space.

The Home screen enters Jiggle Mode.

Note: You can also switch the Home screen to Jiggle Mode by tapping and holding an icon and then tapping **Edit Home Screen** (▣).

2 Tap the dots that represent the Home screen pages.

The Edit Pages screen appears.

3 Deselect (◉) the check circle for each Home screen page you want to hide.

4 Tap **Done**.

The Edit Pages screen closes, returning you to the active Home screen page, which is still open for customization.

Note: If you have hidden the Home screen page that was active, the nearest page that you have not hidden appears.

5 Tap **Done**.

The Home screen exits Jiggle Mode.

Work with the App Library

To help you manage your apps, iOS provides the App Library, a special Home screen page that appears after all your other pages. The App Library contains groups of app icons organized by categories including Suggestions, Recently Added, Utilities, and Entertainment.

The Suggestions group displays four full-size app icons. Each other group displays three full-size app icons; if the group contains further apps, a fourth icon appears, showing thumbnails of the icons for some of those apps. You can tap this fourth icon to display the full list of apps and then tap an app's icon to open the app.

Work with the App Library

1 From any regular Home screen page, swipe left until the App Library screen appears.

A The Suggestions group contains apps based on your recent usage.

B The Recently Added group contains apps you have added recently.

C Other groups contain apps organized by purpose, such as Productivity & Finance.

D You can tap **Search** (🔍) to search by app name.

E You can tap a full-size app icon to launch that app.

2 To view other apps in a group, tap the thumbnails icon.

The screen for that group appears, such as the Productivity & Finance screen.

3 Tap the app you want to open.

The app opens.

Note: To move an app icon from the App Library to a Home screen page, tap and hold open space on the App Library screen until the Home screen enters Jiggle Mode. Tap and drag an app icon a short way. iOS displays the last Home page screen, and you can place the app icon as usual.

Note: You cannot reorganize the apps in the App Library.

Switch Quickly from One App to Another

You can run many apps on your iPhone at the same time, switching from one app to another as needed.

You can switch apps by displaying the Home screen and then tapping the icon for the next app. But the iPhone also has an app-switching screen that enables you to switch quickly from one running app to another running app. From the app-switching screen, you can also easily close one or more running apps.

Switch Quickly from One App to Another

1 On the Home screen, tap the app you want to launch. This example uses **Maps** ().

The app's screen appears.

2 Start using the app as usual.

Note: You can also switch quickly from one app to another by swiping left or right on the invisible bar at the bottom of the screen.

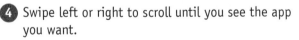

3 Swipe up from the bottom of the screen to the middle, and then pause momentarily.

A The app-switching screen appears, showing a carousel of thumbnails of the open apps.

B The icons identify the app thumbnails.

4 Swipe left or right to scroll until you see the app you want.

Note: The last app you used appears on the right side of the app-switching screen. To its left are the apps you have used most recently.

Note: To display the Home screen, tap above or below the carousel.

5 Tap the app.

The app appears, and you can work in it as usual.

6 When you are ready to switch back, display the app-switching screen again. Swipe up from the bottom of the screen to the middle, and then pause momentarily.

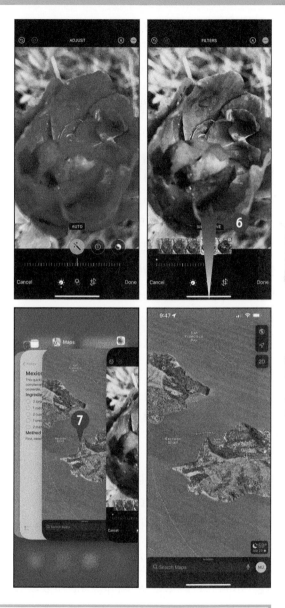

7 Scroll left or right as needed, and then tap the app to which you want to return.

The app appears, ready to resume from where you stopped using it.

Find Apps on the App Store

The iPhone comes with essential apps, such as Safari for surfing the web, Mail for e-mail, and Calendar for keeping track of your schedule. But to get the most out of your iPhone, you will likely need to add other apps. For example, if you use Google Mail, you may prefer the Gmail app; if you use Microsoft's Outlook or Hotmail, you may prefer the Outlook app.

To get apps, you use the App Store, which provides apps that Apple has approved as correctly programmed, suitable for purpose, and free of malevolent code.

Find Apps on the App Store

Note: Before you can download any apps, including free apps, you must create an App Store account.

1 On the Home screen, tap **App Store** ().

The App Store screen appears.

Usually, the Today screen appears at first.

2 Tap **Apps** (≋ changes to ≋).

A You can tap **Games** (🚀 changes to 🚀) or **Arcade** (🕹 changes to 🕹) if you want to browse games or arcade games instead of apps. Arcade is a subscription service; you can pay monthly or yearly.

The Apps screen appears.

B You can tap **See All** for a list to see the whole list.

3 Swipe up to scroll down until the Top Categories list appears.

Note: The Top Categories list shows the free apps that App Store users are downloading. The Top Paid Apps list shows the apps that App Store users are buying.

4 Tap **See All** in the Top Categories section.

The Categories screen appears.

⑤ Tap the category you want to see. This example uses the **Business** category.

The category's screen appears.

ⓒ You can tap **See All** to view the full list.

⑥ Tap the app you want to view.

Note: To understand what an app does and how well it does it, look at the app's rating, read the description, and read the user reviews. Swipe the images to see screen captures from the app.

The app's screen appears.

⑦ Tap the price button or the **Get** button.

Note: If the iPhone prompts you to sign in, type your password, and then tap **OK**.

Note: If you have not created an App Store account already, the iPhone prompts you to create one now.

The iPhone downloads and installs the app.

⑧ Tap **Open**.

Note: If you switch to another app while the new app downloads and installs, launch the new app from the Home screen or the App Library instead.

The app opens, and you can start using it.

TIP

Why does App Store not appear on the Home screen or when I search for it?
If App Store (🅰) does not appear on the Home screen and if searching for it does not show a result, the iPhone has restrictions applied that prevent you from installing apps. You can remove these restrictions if you know the restrictions passcode. Swipe up from the bottom of the screen to display the Home screen, tap **Settings** (⚙), and then tap **Screen Time** (⏳). On the Screen Time screen, tap **Content & Privacy Restrictions** (🚫), and then tap **iTunes & App Store Purchases**. Tap **Installing Apps**, and then tap **Allow**.

Update and Remove Apps

To keep your iPhone's apps running smoothly, you should install app updates when they become available. Most minor updates for paid apps are free, but you must often pay to upgrade to a new version of the app.

When you no longer need an app you have installed on your iPhone, you can remove it, thus recovering the space it occupied. You can remove some but not all of the built-in apps.

Update and Remove Apps

Update One or More Apps

 The badge on the App Store icon shows the number of available updates.

1 Tap **App Store** ( ).

The App Store screen appears.

2 Tap **Account** (or your chosen picture).

Note: You can go straight to the Updates screen by tapping and holding **App Store** ( ) on the Home screen and then tapping **Updates** ( ) on the pop-up panel.

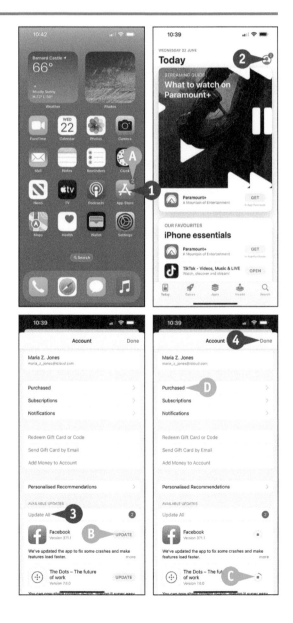

The Account screen appears.

3 Tap **Update All** to apply all the available updates now.

B You can tap **Update** to update a single app.

C A readout shows the progress of each update.

D You can tap **Purchased** to display the Purchased screen, from which you can install apps you have bought previously but not yet installed on this iPhone.

4 Tap **Done**.

Remove an App from the iPhone

1 Tap and hold the app you want to delete.

The pop-up menu appears.

2 Tap **Remove App** (⊖).

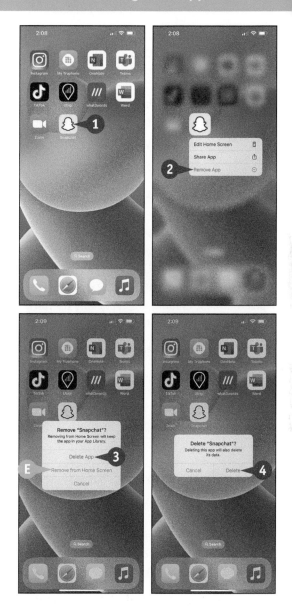

The Remove? dialog opens.

E You can tap **Remove from Home Screen** to move the app to the App Library, keeping the app and its data for future use.

3 Tap **Delete App**.

The Delete? dialog appears.

4 Tap **Delete**.

The iPhone deletes the app, and the app's icon disappears.

TIP

Can I set my iPhone to update its apps automatically?
Yes. On the Home screen, tap **Settings** (⚙) to open the Settings app. Tap **App Store** (🅐) to display the App Store screen, go to the Automatic Downloads section, and then set the **App Updates** switch to On (🔘).

Using App Clips

Millions of apps are available for the iPhone, but you can, of course, install only some of those millions on your own iPhone. To give you access to the app functionality you need without you having to install an entire app, iOS provides a feature called app clips.

An *app clip* is a small, discrete section of an app. The app clip enables you to perform a particular task without having to install the whole app. For example, an app clip might enable you to place an order at a particular online store or to pay for parking.

Understanding App Clips and Where You Find Them

An app clip is usually 5MB to 10MB in size, much smaller than a complete app, so it loads quickly. Small size and fast loading are especially useful when your iPhone is using a metered cellular connection rather than an unlimited connection.

App clips appear automatically in various apps, including the Safari web browser, the Maps app, and the Messages app.

You can also launch an app clip manually in either of two ways. The first way is by scanning a QR code with the iPhone's camera. The second is by tapping an NFC tag, a physical object that uses the Near-Field Communications protocols for short-range wireless communication.

Using an App Clip from Safari

When you are browsing the web with Safari and you load a web page from which an app clip is available, a panel offering the app clip appears at the top of the page, as in the left image here.

Tap **Open** (A). Your iPhone downloads the app clip and launches it as a separate app. The first screen of the app clip appears, as in the middle image here, where you can tap **Open** (B). You can then start using the app clip's functionality, as in the right image here.

Using an App Clip from Maps

When you are using the Maps app and you select a place that has an app clip, a button appears in the Location panel to give you access to the functionality that the app clip offers. For example, when you select a restaurant that offers takeout or delivery, the Location panel may include a button for ordering food, such as the Order Food button (C) in the middle screen.

Tap the button to download and launch the app clip. The first screen of the app clip appears, as in the right image here, and you can use the clip's functionality — for example, to assemble an order of food and pay for it. The final screen of the app clip enables you to get the full app.

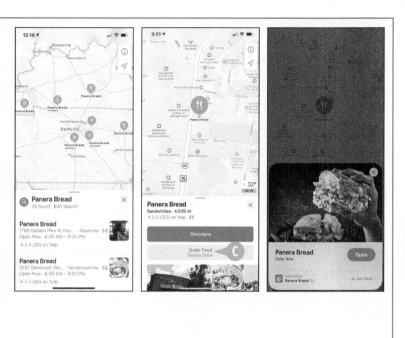

Using an App Clip from a QR Code

When you encounter a QR code for an app clip, tap **Camera** ( ) on the Home screen to launch the Camera app. Point the lens at the QR code (D), as in the left image here. The Camera app recognizes the QR code, causing iOS to look up the code and display the associated app clip at the bottom of the screen, as in the middle image here. Tap the action button, such as the Play button (E) here, to launch the app clip. You can then use the app clip's functionality, as in the right image here. The final screen of the app clip includes a button (F) enabling you to get the full app.

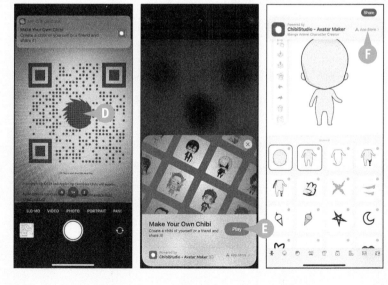

A QR code can direct your browser to almost any web address, including dangerous or unsavory sites, so make sure the QR code is for a wholesome app clip before you scan it.

Type, Cut, Copy, and Paste Text

You can easily type text on your iPhone's keyboard, either by tapping each letter or by sliding your finger from letter to letter, using the QuickPath feature; you can also dictate text using Siri. If the text already exists, you can copy and paste it instead.

If the text is in a document you can edit, you can either copy the text or cut it. If the text is in a document you cannot edit, you can only copy the text.

Type, Cut, Copy, and Paste Text

Type Text

① Open an app that supports text entry. To follow this example, tap **Notes** ( ) on the Home screen, and then tap **New** ( ) to start a new note.

② Type a word by placing your finger on the first letter and then sliding it to each successive letter. Lift your finger off the screen when the word is complete.

Ⓐ If the suggestion bar shows the word you want, tap the word to enter it.

③ Type a word by tapping each letter in turn.

④ Tap **return** to create a new line.

⑤ Type some more text to use for the copy-and-paste example.

Copy Text

① Double-tap in the section of text you want to copy or cut.

The word you double-tap becomes highlighted.

Ⓑ Selection handles appear around the selection.

Ⓒ The formatting bar appears.

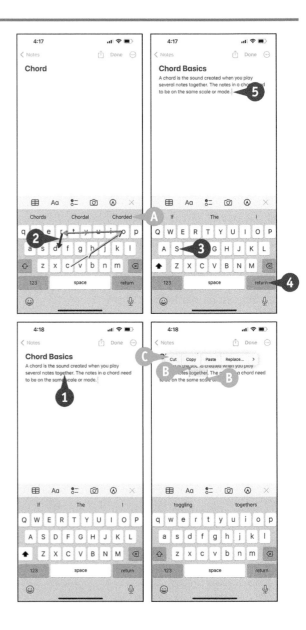

2 Drag the start handle (⌇) to the beginning of the text you want.

3 Drag the end handle (⌇) to the end of the text you want.

4 Tap **Copy**.

D You can tap **Cut** if you want to remove the selected text from the document.

The formatting bar disappears.

Your iPhone places the text on the Clipboard, a hidden storage area.

5 If you no longer need the text to be selected, tap outside the text to deselect it.

Paste the Content You Have Copied or Cut

1 Open the app and document into which you want to paste the text. This example uses a new note in the Notes app.

2 Tap where you want to paste the text.

The formatting bar appears.

3 Tap **Paste**.

E The pasted text appears in the document.

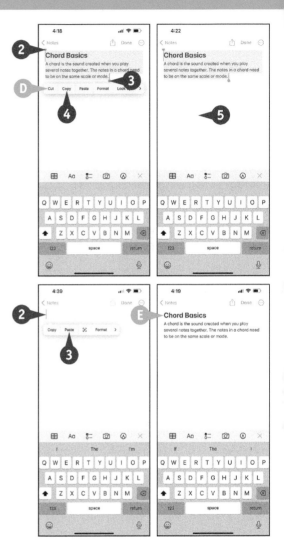

TIPS

How many items can I store on the Clipboard?

You can store only one item on the Clipboard at a time. Each item you cut or copy replaces the existing item on the Clipboard. But until you replace the existing item on the Clipboard, you can paste it as many times as needed.

Can I transfer the contents of the Clipboard to my computer?

If your computer is a Mac, you have enabled the Handoff feature in the General category of System Preferences, and the Mac is signed into the same iCloud account as the iPhone, the Universal Clipboard feature synchronizes Clipboard content across devices automatically. Otherwise, transfer the Clipboard contents indirectly — for example, paste it into an e-mail message and send it to yourself.

Format and Replace Text

Some apps enable you to add text formatting such as boldface, underline, or italics to text to make parts of it stand out. For example, you can apply formatting in e-mail messages you create using the Mail app on some e-mail services and in various apps for creating word-processing documents.

To apply formatting, you first select the text and then choose options from the pop-up formatting bar. Some apps also offer other text commands, such as replacing a word or phrase from a menu of suggestions.

Format and Replace Text

Apply Bold, Italics, or Underline

1 Tap and hold the text to which you want to apply bold, italics, or underline.

Part of the text becomes highlighted, and the selection handles appear.

The formatting bar appears.

2 Drag the start handle (▲) to the beginning of the text you want.

3 Drag the end handle (▼) to the end of the text you want.

4 Tap **More** (**>**).

The next section of the formatting bar appears.

5 Tap **Format** on the formatting bar.

The formatting bar displays formatting options.

6 Tap **Bold**, **Italic**, or **Underline**, as needed.

The text takes on the formatting you chose.

7 Tap outside the selected text to deselect it.

Note: Some apps have their own formatting tools, many of which are more extensive than the standard formatting tools shown here.

Note: Some e-mail services and notes services do not support formatting.

Replace Text with Suggested Words

 Double-tap the word you want to replace.

The word becomes highlighted, and selection handles appear around it.

The formatting bar appears.

2 Tap **Replace**.

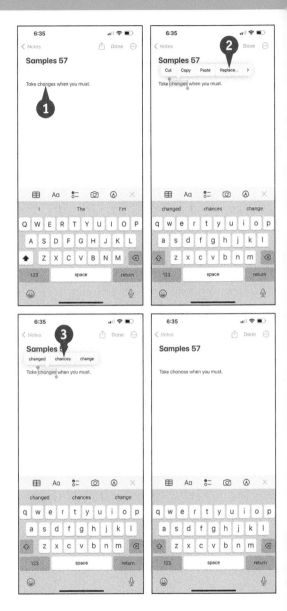

The formatting bar displays suggested replacement words.

3 Tap the word with which you want to replace the selected word.

The word you tapped appears in the text.

Note: Tap **More** (**>**) to display more commands on the formatting bar. For example, in some apps, you can insert photos and videos.

What does the Quote Level button on the pop-up formatting bar in Mail do?
Tap **Quote Level** when you need to increase or decrease the quote level of your selected text. You may need to tap **More** (**>**) to display the Quote Level button. When you tap Quote Level, the formatting bar displays an Increase button and a Decrease button. Tap **Increase** to increase the quote level, indenting the text more and adding a colored bar to its left, or **Decrease** to decrease the quote level, reducing the existing indent and removing a colored bar.

CHAPTER 8

Browsing the Web and E-Mailing

Your iPhone is fully equipped to browse the web and send e-mail via a Wi-Fi connection or via the cellular network.

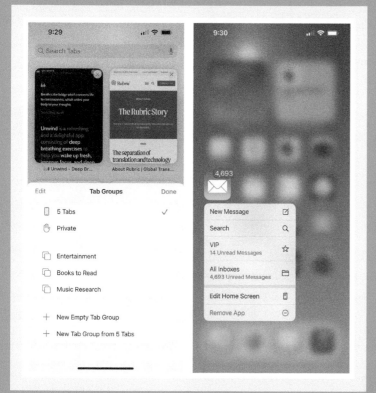

Browse the Web with Safari

Your iPhone comes equipped with the Safari app, which enables you to browse the web. You can quickly go to a web page by entering its address in the Address box or by following a link.

Although you can browse quickly by opening a single web page at a time, you may prefer to open multiple pages and switch back and forth among them. Safari makes this easy to do. You can also install other browsers, such as Google Chrome or Microsoft Edge, from the App Store and use them instead of, or as well as, Safari.

Browse the Web with Safari

Open Safari and Navigate to Web Pages

1 On the Home screen, tap **Safari** ( ).

Safari opens and loads the last web page that was shown.

Note: If no last web page is available, Safari displays the Favorites page. You can tap a thumbnail to display a website.

2 Tap the Address box to activate it, and then tap it again.

Note: You can enter widely used domain extensions, such as .com and .net, by tapping and holding . (the period key) and tapping the extensions on the pop-up panel that appears.

Safari selects the current contents of the Address box, and the on-screen keyboard appears.

3 Tap **Delete** (×) if you need to delete the contents of the Address box.

4 Type the address of the page you want to open.

Ⓐ You can also tap a search result that Safari displays above the Address box.

5 Tap **go**.

Safari displays the page.

6 Tap a link on the page.

Safari displays the linked page.

After going to a new page, tap **Back** ($<$) at the bottom of the screen to display the previous page. You can then tap **Forward** ($>$) to go forward again.

Open Multiple Pages and Navigate Among Them

1 Tap **Tabs** (⟁).

Note: If the controls do not appear at the bottom of the Safari screen, drag the page down a short way to display them.

Safari displays the list of open tabs, each bearing a Close button (✕).

2 Tap **New Tab** (+).

Note: In landscape orientation, a large-screen iPhone displays a tab bar at the top of the screen. Tap the tab you want to view.

Safari opens a new tab and displays your bookmarks.

3 Tap the Address box, and then go to the page you want.

Note: You can also go to a page by using a bookmark, as described in the next section, "Access Websites Quickly with Bookmarks."

The page appears.

4 To switch to another page, tap **Tabs** (⟁).

Safari displays the list of pages.

5 Tap the page you want to see.

B You can tap **Close** (✕) to close a page.

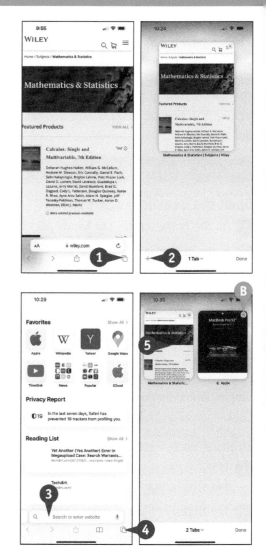

TIPS

How do I search for information?

Tap the Address box to select its current contents, and then type your search terms. Safari searches as you type; you can type further to narrow down the results, and you can stop as soon as you see suitable results. Tap the result you want to see, and then tap a link on the results page that Safari opens. You can change the search engine in Safari settings: Tap **Settings** (⚙), tap **Safari** (🧭), and then tap **Search Engine**.

How can I reopen a tab I closed by mistake?

Tap **Tabs** (⟁) to display the list of open tabs, and then tap and hold **New Tab** (+). In the Recently Closed Tabs list that appears, tap the tab you want to reopen.

Access Websites Quickly with Bookmarks

Typing web addresses can be laborious, even with the help that the iPhone's keyboard provides, so you will probably want to use bookmarks to access websites you visit often.

By syncing your existing bookmarks from your computer or online account, as described in Chapter 1, you can instantly provide your iPhone with quick access to the web pages you want to visit most frequently. You can also create bookmarks on your iPhone, as discussed in the next section, "Create Bookmarks."

Access Websites Quickly with Bookmarks

Open the Bookmarks Screen

1 On the Home screen, tap **Safari** (🧭) to open Safari.

2 If the navigation bar at the bottom is hidden, tap at the top of the screen to display the navigation bar.

Note: You can also scroll up a short distance to display the navigation bar.

3 Tap **Bookmarks** (📖) to display the Bookmarks screen.

Note: You can display the Bookmarks screen quickly from the Home screen by tapping and holding **Safari** (🧭) and then tapping **Show Bookmarks** (📖) on the contextual menu.

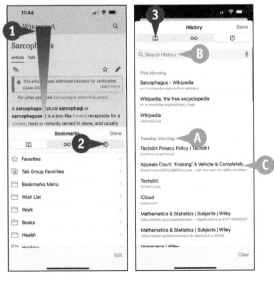

Explore Your History

1 If the Bookmarks screen takes up only the lower half of the screen, drag its title bar up to the top of the screen.

2 Tap **History** (🕐).

The History list appears, showing a list of the web pages you have recently visited.

Ⓐ You can tap a time or a day to display the list of web pages you visited then.

Ⓑ You can tap **Search History** (🔍) and type search terms to search for particular pages.

Note: If the Search History box is hidden, swipe down at the top of the list of pages.

Ⓒ You can tap a page's button to display that page.

3 Tap **Bookmarks** (📖) when you want to return to the Bookmarks screen.

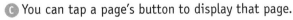

Open a Bookmarked Page

 Tap **Bookmarks** (📖).

The Bookmarks screen appears.

2 If the Bookmarks screen takes up only the lower half of the screen, drag its title bar up to the top of the screen.

3 If the Reading List or the History list appears, tap **Bookmarks** (📖) to display the Bookmarks list.

4 Tap the bookmarks folder or category you want to see. This example uses the **Books** folder.

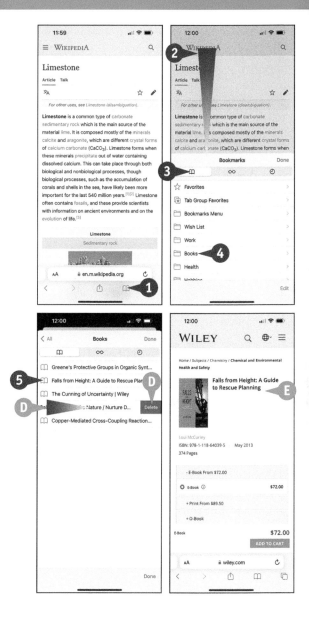

The contents of the folder or category appear. For example, the contents of the Books folder appear.

D You can delete a bookmark by swiping it to the left and then tapping **Delete**.

5 When you find the bookmark for the web page you want to open, tap the bookmark.

E The web page opens.

Create Bookmarks

When you want to access a web page again easily, create a bookmark for it. If you have set your iPhone to sync bookmarks with your iCloud account, the bookmark becomes available on your computer or online account as well when you sync.

If you create many bookmarks, it is usually helpful to create multiple folders in which you can organize the bookmarks. You can create folders easily on the iPhone and choose the folder in which to store each bookmark.

Create Bookmarks

Create a Bookmark

1. On the Home screen, tap **Safari** (🧭).

   Safari opens and displays the last web page you were viewing.

2. Navigate to the web page you want to bookmark.

3. Tap **Share** (📤).

   The Share sheet appears.

4. Swipe the Share sheet's title bar up to the top of the screen.

   The Share sheet expands.

5. Tap **Add Bookmark** (📖).

   The Add Bookmark screen appears.

6. Edit the suggested name, or type a new name, as needed.

7. Tap the current folder under the Location heading.

   The Choose a Folder screen appears.

8. Tap the folder in which to store the bookmark.

   The Add Bookmark screen appears.

9. Tap **Save**.

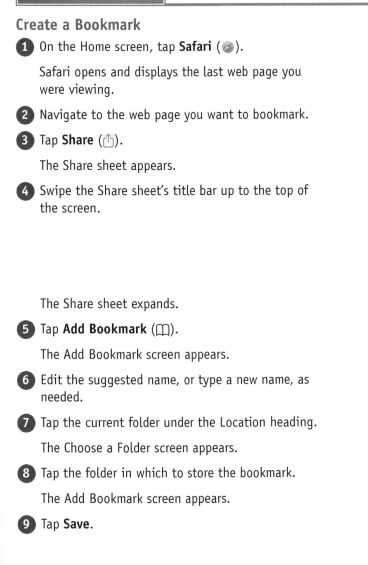

Create a New Folder for Bookmarks

1 In Safari, tap **Bookmarks** (📖).

The Bookmarks screen appears.

2 Swipe the title bar up.

The Bookmarks screen expands.

3 Tap **Edit**.

The editing controls appear.

Ⓐ You can drag a handle (≡) to change the order of the bookmark folders.

Ⓑ You can tap **Delete** (⊖) and then tap the textual **Delete** button to delete a bookmark folder and its contents.

4 Tap **New Folder**.

The Edit Folder screen appears.

5 Type the name for the new folder.

6 Tap the folder under the Location heading.

A screen showing the list of folders appears.

7 Tap the folder in which to store the bookmark folder.

The Edit Folder screen appears again.

8 Tap **All** (〈).

The Bookmarks screen appears, still with editing controls displayed.

9 Tap **Done**.

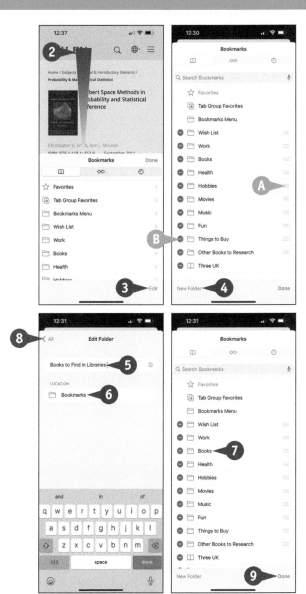

TIP

Can I change a bookmark I have created?

Yes. Tap **Bookmarks** (📖) to display the Bookmarks screen, and then navigate to the bookmark you want to change. Tap **Edit** to switch to Editing Mode. You can then tap a bookmark to open it on the Edit Bookmark screen, where you can change its name, address, or location. In Editing Mode, you can also delete a bookmark by tapping **Delete** (⊖) and then tapping **Delete**, or rearrange your bookmarks by dragging the handle (≡) up or down the list. Tap **Done** when you finish editing bookmarks.

Keep a Reading List of Web Pages

Safari's Reading List feature enables you to save a web page for later without creating a bookmark. You can quickly add the current web page to Reading List by using the Share sheet. Once you have added pages, you access Reading List through the Bookmarks feature. When viewing Reading List, you can display either all the pages it contains or only those you have not read.

If you sync your Safari data through iCloud, Reading List is included, so you can access Reading List on all your iCloud devices.

Keep a Reading List of Web Pages

Add a Web Page to Reading List

1 On the Home screen, tap **Safari** ( ).

Safari opens and displays the last web page you were viewing.

2 Navigate to the web page you want to add to Reading List.

A If the navigation bar is hidden, tap at the top of the screen to display it.

3 Tap **Share** ( ).

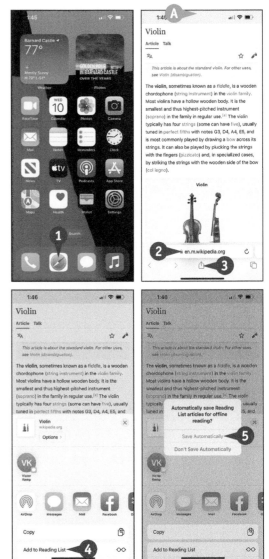

The Share sheet appears.

4 Tap **Add to Reading List** (∞).

The first time you give the Add to Reading List command, the Automatically Save Reading List Articles for Offline Reading? dialog opens.

5 Tap **Save Automatically** if you want to save the articles so you can read them when you do not have an Internet connection, which is usually helpful. If not, tap **Don't Save Automatically**.

Safari adds the web page to Reading List.

Note: To change the Automatically Save Offline setting later, display the Home screen, tap **Settings** ( ), and then tap **Safari** ( ). Scroll down to the Reading List section and set the **Automatically Save Offline** switch to On ( ) or Off ( ), as needed.

Open Reading List and Display a Page

1 In Safari, tap **Bookmarks** (□).

The Bookmarks screen appears.

2 Swipe the title bar up.

The Bookmarks screen expands.

3 Tap **Reading List** (∞).

Note: You can quickly display the Reading List screen from the Home screen by tapping and holding **Safari** (🧭) and then tapping **Show Reading List** on the pop-up panel.

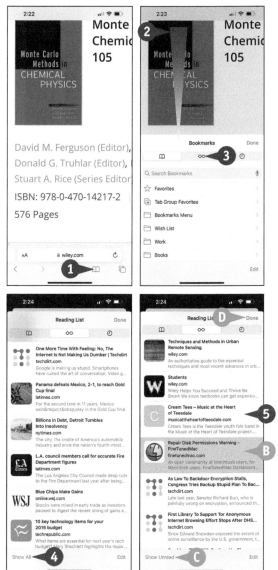

The Reading List screen appears.

4 Tap **Show All**.

Reading List displays all the pages it contains, including those you have read.

B Pages you have read appear with gray shading.

C You can tap **Show Unread** to display only unread pages.

5 Tap the page you want to open.

D If you decide not to open a page from Reading List, tap **Done** to hide the Reading List screen.

TIPS

How do I remove an item from Reading List?

To remove an item from Reading List, swipe it left and then tap the textual **Delete** button that appears.

You can also swipe an item right. When you do so, the Mark Read button also appears if you have not read the item; the Mark Unread button appears if you have read it. You can tap **Mark Read** or **Mark Unread** to switch the item's read status.

Is there another way to add a page to Reading List?

Yes. Tap and hold a link to the page, and then tap **Add to Reading List** (∞) on the pop-up menu that appears under the page's preview.

Navigate Among Open Web Pages Using Tabs

If you browse the web a lot, you will probably need to open many web pages in Safari at the same time. Safari presents your open pages as a list of scrollable tabs, making it easy to navigate from one page to another.

You can change the order of the tabs to suit your needs, and you can quickly close a tab by either tapping its Close button or simply swiping it off the list. You can organize your tabs into tab groups, as explained in the next section, "Create and Use Tab Groups."

Navigate Among Open Web Pages Using Tabs

Open Safari and Display the List of Tabs

 On the Home screen, tap **Safari** ( ).

Safari opens or becomes active.

Note: If Safari has hidden the on-screen controls, tap at the top of the screen to display them. Alternatively, scroll up the screen a short way.

2. Tap **Tabs** ( ).

The list of tabs appears.

Close Tabs You Do Not Need to Keep Open

1. Tap **Close** (✕) on the tab you want to close.

The tab closes and disappears from the list.

2. Alternatively, you can tap a tab and swipe it left off the screen.

The tab closes and disappears from the list.

Note: You can turn a large-screen iPhone to landscape orientation and then tap **Close** (✕) to close the current tab.

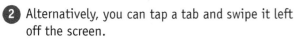

Change the Order of the Tabs

 Tap and hold the tab you want to move.

The tab becomes mobile.

2 Drag the tab to where you want it to appear in the list, and then release it.

The other tabs move out of the way as you drag the tab.

Find a Tab and Display It

 Tap the tab you want to display.

The tab opens.

Note: You can also turn a large-screen iPhone to landscape orientation to display the tab bar at the top of the screen. If the tab bar does not appear at first, place your finger on the screen and pull down a short way to display the tab bar. You can then tap the tab you want to view.

TIP

How do I return from the list of tabs to the tab I was viewing before?

To return to the tab you were viewing before, either tap the tab in the list of tabs or tap **Done** in the lower-right corner of the screen.

Create and Use Tab Groups

Safari enables you to create tab groups, so you can organize your tabs into different sets and quickly switch from one group to another. You can also use a tab group to provide an approved set of websites available in Safari during a Focus that restricts the use of the app.

You can create either an empty tab group or a tab group containing your active open tabs. You can move a tab from one tab group to another, as needed. And when you no longer need a tab group, you can delete it.

Create an Empty Tab Group

In Safari, tap **Tabs** (⬚) to display the Tabs screen, and then tap **Tab Groups** (A, ⌄) to open the Tab Groups screen (B).

At first, the Tab Groups screen takes up only the lower half of the screen, but you can expand it to almost the full screen by dragging its title bar up if you want.

Tap **New Empty Tab Group** (C, +) to display the New Tab Group dialog.

Type the name (D) for the new tab group, and then tap **Save** (E). iOS closes the New Tab Group dialog, creates the tab group, and displays the Start Page for the Tab Group. Tap **Add** (F, +) to start adding a tab to the tab group. Tap **Done** (G) when you finish adding tabs to the tab group.

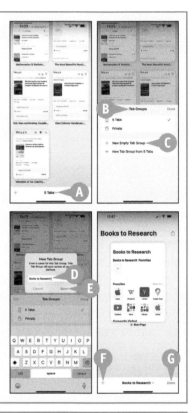

Create a Tab Group Containing Existing Tabs

If you have already opened several tabs in Safari, you can create a new tab group containing those tabs.

First, if the tabs are not currently active, make them active. Tap **Tabs** (⬚) to display the Tabs screen, and then tap **Tab Groups** (⌄) to open the Tab Groups screen. In the top box, tap the unnamed group that gives the number of tabs, such as **5 Tabs**. The tabs become active.

With the tabs active, tap **Tab Groups** (⌄) to open the Tab Groups screen, and then tap **New Tab Group from N Tabs**. In the New Tab Group dialog, type the name for the new tab group, and then tap **Save**. iOS closes the New Tab Group dialog, creates the tab group and assigns the tabs to it, and displays the Start Page for the Tab Group. Tap **Done**.

Move a Tab to a Tab Group

To move a tab to a tab group, tap **Tabs** (⬚) to display the Tabs screen. Tap and hold the tab (H) you want to move until the contextual menu opens. Tap **Move to Tab Group** (I, ⬚) to expand the Move to Tab Group submenu, and then tap the tab group (J, ⬚).

Open a Tab Group

After creating a tab group, you can open the group and all the tabs it contains. Tap **Tabs** (⬚) to display the Tabs screen, tap **Tab Groups** (⌄) to open the Tab Groups screen, and then tap the tab group in the list. The tab group opens, showing a thumbnail of each tab it contains. Tap the tab you want to display, and it appears full screen.

Delete a Tab Group

When you no longer need a tab group, you can delete it. Tap **Tabs** (⬚) to display the Tabs screen, and then tap **Tab Groups** (⌄) to open the Tab Groups screen. In the list of tab groups, swipe left on the tab group (K) you want to delete, and then tap **Delete** (L, 🗑).

Using Zoom and Reader View

Many web pages have small text and complex layouts that can be hard to read on a small screen. To make reading easier, Safari offers two features: First, you can zoom in or out, as needed, to improve the view. Second, you can use Reader View, which simplifies the layout of a web page and enlarges its text and images.

You can quickly switch a page to Reader View to see if it improves readability. In Reader View, you can change the font size, the font, and the background to make further improvements.

Using Zoom and Reader View

1 On the Home screen, tap **Safari** (🧭).

Safari opens or becomes active.

2 Navigate to the web page you want to read.

A The Show Reader View icon (📄) and the *Reader Available* readout appear briefly if Reader View is available for the page. After a few seconds, the Reader View button (AA) and the address appear in their place.

B You can tap **Show Reader View** (📄) to switch the page to Reader View (📄 changes to **AA**).

3 Tap **Reader View** (AA).

The toolbar opens.

C You can tap **Smaller** (A) to zoom out.

D You can tap **Larger** (A) to zoom in.

E You can tap the zoom percentage to return to 100% zoom.

4 Tap **Show Reader** (📄 changes to **AA**).

Safari displays the page in Reader View.

F Element size and positioning may change.

Note: The font may change to a serif font for greater readability.

G Text alignment and margins may change.

5 Tap **Reader View** (⒜⒜).

The toolbar opens.

Ⓗ You can tap **Smaller** (A) to zoom out.

Ⓘ You can tap **Larger** (A) to zoom in.

6 Tap the background color you want to apply.

7 To change the font, tap **Font**.

The Font toolbar appears.

8 Tap the font you want to apply.

9 Tap **Back** (**<**).

10 Tap outside the toolbar.

The toolbar closes.

You can now read the web page using your customized Reader View.

11 When you want to exit Reader View, tap **Reader View** (⒜⒜).

The toolbar appears.

12 Tap **Hide Reader** (⊘).

Safari displays the page in the normal view.

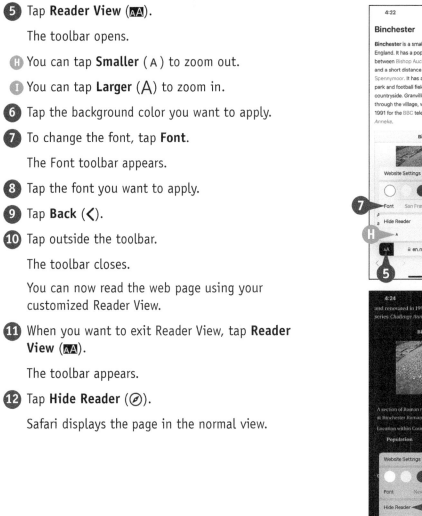

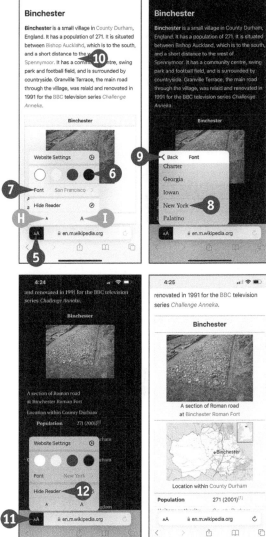

Why is Reader View available for only some web pages?

Whether Reader View is available for a particular web page depends on how the web page is constructed and encoded. As a result, you may find that Reader View is available for some web pages on a particular website but not for other pages.

Generally speaking, Reader View is more likely to be available on web pages that contain a lot of text than on web pages that contain only a small amount of text, but the quantity of text does not directly determine whether Reader View is available.

Switch Between Mobile Sites and Desktop Sites

Many websites provide a mobile version of pages optimized for small screens, such as those on phones, and a "desktop" version for larger screens. When a device requests a page, the website detects the web browser and operating system and then delivers the mobile version or desktop version accordingly.

This means your iPhone normally displays the mobile version of each website you visit. The mobile version is usually best, but you may sometimes want to switch to the desktop version to see more information or to navigate the site. Safari enables you to switch easily between mobile and desktop versions.

Switch Between Mobile Sites and Desktop Sites

① In Safari, navigate to the web page you want to view.

② Tap **Reader View** (ᴀA).

The toolbar appears.

③ Tap **Request Desktop Website** (🖥).

Note: Some websites do not honor requests to display specific versions.

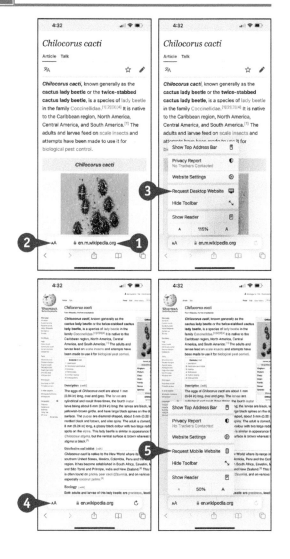

Safari displays the desktop version of the web page.

Note: The mobile version and desktop version of web pages may look almost identical on the iPhone.

Note: If you navigate to another page using the same tab, the desktop version of that page appears.

④ When you want to switch back to the mobile version, tap **Reader View** (ᴀA).

The toolbar appears.

⑤ Tap **Request Mobile Website** (▢).

Safari displays the mobile version of the web page.

Control Settings for a Website

Safari enables you to configure several settings for each particular website. First, you can set Safari to request a site's desktop version by default instead of the mobile version. Second, you can set Safari to use Reader View for a website, saving you the trouble of switching to Reader View manually. Third, you can control whether a website can access your iPhone's camera features, its microphone, and location data.

You can configure these settings either preemptively or after Safari has set them automatically when you accessed the site and allowed or denied it access permission.

Allow a Website to Use the Camera, Microphone, or Location Temporarily

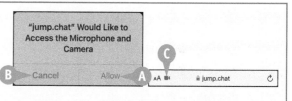

When you go to a web page that requests access to your iPhone's camera, microphone, or location data, Safari displays a dialog whose title tells you the access requested — for example, "jump.chat" Would Like to Access the Microphone and Camera. Tap **Allow** (A) to allow the access this time; tap **Cancel** (B) to deny access this time.

Safari displays Camera On (C, ◼◀) or Microphone On (🎤) at the left end of the address box to show you when the site is using the camera or the microphone. Tap the icon to toggle the feature off (◼◀ changes to 🚫◀ or 🎤 changes to 🚫).

The choice you make in the Would Like to Access dialog lasts only for your current visit to the site. The next time you visit the site and it requests access, Safari displays the dialog again.

Choose Whether a Website Can Use the Camera, Microphone, or Location

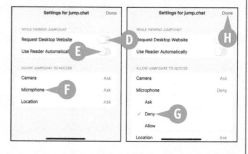

If you visit a site frequently, you can open the Settings page for the site and specify access permissions for the camera, microphone, and location. Go to the site, tap **Reader View** (ᴀA) to display the toolbar, and then tap **Website Settings** (⚙) to display the Settings page.

In the While Viewing [Site] section, set the **Request Desktop Website** switch (D) to On (◯) if you want Safari to display the desktop version of this website by default. Set the **Use Reader Automatically** switch (E) to On (◯) if you want Safari to use Reader View for this site.

In the Allow [Site] to Access section, tap the feature for which you want to set permission, such as **Microphone** (F); and then tap **Ask**, **Deny** (G), or **Allow** in the expanded section that appears. Ask is the default setting. For security, grant the Allow setting sparingly.

The Allow [Site] to Access features are available only for secure websites, meaning those that use Hypertext Transfer Protocol Secure, HTTPS, rather than nonsecure Hypertext Transfer Protocol, HTTP.

When you finish making choices on the Settings page, tap **Done** (H).

View Safari's Privacy Report

Safari's Privacy Report feature enables you to learn which websites and web trackers have been trying to track your movements around the web. A *web tracker* is a script that tries to glean data about your preferences and identity. The Privacy Report screen shows you how many trackers Safari has prevented from profiling you, the percentage of websites you visited that contained trackers, and the most contacted tracker, all for the last 30 days. You can browse the list of websites to see which trackers they use or browse the list of trackers to see which websites use them.

View Safari's Privacy Report

1 In Safari, navigate to a web page.

2 Tap **Reader View** (ᴀА).

The toolbar appears.

Ⓐ The Privacy Report button shows the number of trackers prevented on the active page.

3 Tap **Privacy Report** (◗).

The Privacy Report screen appears.

Ⓑ The *Last 30 Days* readouts show the number of trackers Safari has prevented from profiling you and the percentage of websites that contained trackers.

Ⓒ The *Most Contacted Tracker* readout shows the tracker most often contacted by websites you visited.

Ⓓ The Websites tab lists the websites that have contacted trackers. This tab is displayed at first.

4 Tap **Trackers**.

The Trackers tab appears, listing the trackers that websites have contacted.

5 Tap a tracker.

The screen for the tracker appears, listing the websites that contacted the tracker.

6 Tap **Back** (‹).

The Privacy Report screen appears again.

7 Tap **Done**.

The web page appears again.

Using Private Browsing Mode

S afari's Private Browsing Mode reduces the amount of information Safari retains about the sites you visit and what you do while visiting them. In Private Browsing Mode, Safari does not add the pages you visit to your search history; it does not retain text you enter in form fields, which it might otherwise store as Autofill data; and it deletes cookie files generated during Private Browsing Mode.

Private Browsing Mode offers you a modest privacy boost, but it does not anonymize your identity, and the actions you take online can still be tied to you by your Internet Service Provider.

Switch to Private Browsing Mode

In Safari, tap **Tabs** (⊡) to display your currently open tabs, tap **Tab Groups** (⌄) to display the Tab Groups screen, and then tap **Private** (A, 🖐). The Private Browsing Mode screen (B) appears. Tap **New Tab** (C, +). The Start Page for Private Browsing Mode (D) appears. You can then tap a thumbnail to open that site or tap in the address box and type a URL or a search term.

Private Browsing Mode uses a dark theme to distinguish it visually. Visual cues, such as the dark address box (E), make it easy to see when you are using Private Browsing Mode.

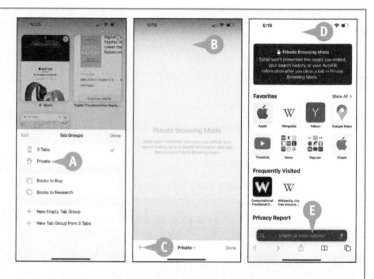

Switch Between Private Browsing Mode and Regular Browsing

After switching to Private Browsing Mode, you can open multiple tabs, as needed. You navigate in Private Browsing Mode by using the same techniques as for regular browsing.

To switch from Private Browsing Mode back to regular browsing, tap **Private Tabs** (F, ⊡) to display your currently open Private tabs. Tap **Tab Groups** (⌄) to display the Tab Groups screen, and then tap either your regular tabs (G) or a tab group (H). You can then tap the tab you want to view or tap **New Tab** (I, +) to open a new tab.

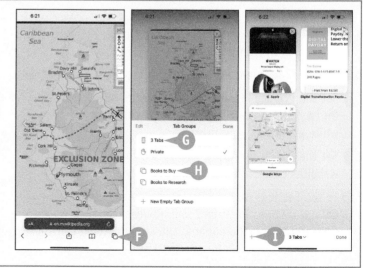

Tighten Up Safari's Security

To protect yourself against websites that infect computers with malware or try to gain your sensitive personal or financial information, turn on Safari's Fraudulent Website Warning feature. You can also turn off the JavaScript programming language, which can be used to attack your iPhone but which many websites require to function correctly. Additionally, you can block pop-up windows, which some websites use to display unwanted information; block new cookies and data; and set Safari to prevent cross-site tracking.

Tighten Up Safari's Security

1 On the Home screen, tap **Settings** (⚙).

The Settings screen appears.

2 Tap **Safari** (🧭).

The Safari screen appears.

A The AutoFill feature enables you to save information — such as your name, address, and credit card details — for filling out web forms quickly.

3 Set the **Block Pop-ups** switch to On (⬤) to block unwanted pop-up windows. Blocking pop-ups is usually helpful, but some websites require them to implement useful features.

4 Set the **Prevent Cross-Site Tracking** switch to On (⬤) or Off (◯), as needed. Setting this switch to On (⬤) is usually a good idea and is required for Privacy Report to block trackers.

5 Set the **Block All Cookies** switch to On (⬤) or Off (◯), as needed. See the tip for advice.

6 Set the **Fraudulent Website Warning** switch to On (⬤).

7 Set the **Privacy Preserving Ad Measurement** switch to On (⬤) if you want to allow measurement of ad efficacy while preserving your privacy.

8 Set the **Check for Apple Pay** switch to On (⬤) to let websites check whether Apple Pay is enabled.

B In the Settings for Websites area, you can change the default settings for Page Zoom, Request Desktop Website, Reader, Camera, Microphone, and Location. You can then override the defaults for specific sites.

9 Tap **Clear History and Website Data**.

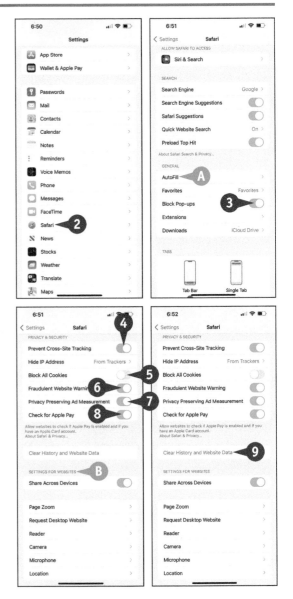

Note: If the Clear History and Website Data button is dimmed and unavailable, your iPhone has restrictions applied. If you manage the iPhone, you may be able to remove these restrictions through Screen Time.

A dialog opens.

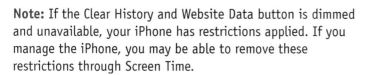

 Tap **Clear History and Data**.

The dialog closes.

Safari clears your browsing history and data.

Note: If iOS prompts you to close your open tabs outside your tab groups, tap **Close Tabs** or **Keep Tabs**, as appropriate.

⓫ Tap **Advanced**.

The Advanced screen appears.

⓬ Set the **JavaScript** switch to On (⬤) or Off ( ), as needed.

Note: Turning off JavaScript may remove some or most functionality of harmless sites.

⓭ Tap **Website Data**.

The Website Data screen appears.

Ⓒ You can tap **Remove All Website Data** to remove all website data.

⓮ Tap **Edit**.

A Delete icon (⊖) appears to the left of each website.

⓯ To delete a website's data, tap **Delete** (⊖), and then tap the textual **Delete** button that appears.

⓰ Tap **Done**.

What are cookies, and what threat do they pose?

A *cookie* is a small text file that a website places on a computer to identify that computer in the future. This is helpful for many sites, such as shopping sites in which you add items to a shopping cart, but when used by intrusive or malevolent sites, cookies can pose a threat to your privacy. You may want to set the **Block All Cookies** switch to On (⬤) to stop Safari from accepting cookies, but be warned that doing so will prevent some legitimate sites from working properly.

Manage Your App and Website Passwords

Your iPhone can store your app and website passwords so that Safari and other apps can enter them automatically when needed, reducing the need for you to type passwords manually.

The Passwords screen in the Settings app enables you to view the list of password entries your iPhone has stored. You can view and edit a password entry, which lets you copy the password, update it, or change the sites for which it is used; delete a password; or add a new password entry.

Manage Your App and Website Passwords

1 On the Home screen, tap **Settings** (⚙).

The Settings screen appears.

2 Tap **Passwords** (🔑).

Note: Before displaying the Passwords screen, the iPhone authenticates you. Normally, this happens via Face ID and takes only moments. If Face ID repeatedly fails, you will need to enter your passcode.

The Passwords screen appears.

Ⓐ You can tap **Search** (🔍) and type a search term to search for a particular password.

3 Tap the password entry you want to view.

The screen for the password entry appears.

Ⓑ You can view the password — for example, to refresh your memory.

Note: For security, iOS blocks the screenshot utility from capturing passwords, so the Password field in the example screen appears blank.

Ⓒ You can copy the username or password by tapping and holding it and then tapping **Copy Username** or **Copy Password** on the pop-up toolbar.

Ⓓ You can tap **Delete Password** to delete the password.

4 If you need to edit the username, password, or list of websites, tap **Edit**.

192

The fields open for editing.

5 Edit the username or password as needed.

6 Tap **Done**.

Editing Mode closes.

7 Tap **Passwords** (⟨).

The Passwords screen appears again.

Note: You can delete a password entry by swiping it left and then tapping **Delete**.

8 To add a new password, tap **Add Password** (+).

The Add Password screen appears.

9 Type or paste the website address.

10 Type or paste the username.

11 Type or paste the password.

12 Tap **Done**.

The Passwords screen appears again.

What does the Edit button on the Passwords screen enable me to do?

The Edit button on the Passwords screen enables you to delete multiple password entries at once instead of one at a time. Tap **Edit** to switch the Passwords screen to Editing Mode. You can then tap the selection circle (changes to ✓) for each password you want to delete and then tap **Delete** in the upper-left corner of the screen.

Using the Sign In with Apple Feature

Many apps and websites require you to create an account and sign in to it before you can use them. Each account typically requires a valid e-mail address and a password; ideally, each password should be unique, but the more passwords you have, the harder it is to remember them.

One solution to this problem is to use a password manager, but your iPhone offers a neater solution: the Sign In with Apple feature, which simplifies the process of signing into apps and websites — and even lets you hide your e-mail address from apps and websites.

Understanding the Requirements for Sign In with Apple

Sign In with Apple uses your existing Apple ID, the credentials you use to sign in to iCloud. Normally, you configure your iPhone to use your Apple ID when first setting up the iPhone. You can verify that your iPhone is using your Apple ID by tapping **Settings** (⚙) on the Home screen and making sure that "Apple ID" (A) appears on the Apple ID button, the one that bears your name and picture at the top of the Settings screen.

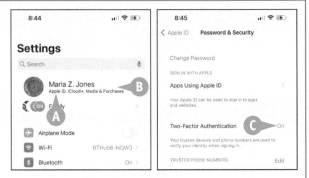

Sign In with Apple requires you to have enabled two-factor authentication on your iPhone. Two-factor authentication is a security feature that requires you to use a trusted device to receive a verification code when signing in to your account on a new device for the first time. Until you enable two-factor authentication, your iPhone prompts you relentlessly to do so; and once you have enabled two-factor authentication, you cannot disable it again. You can verify that your iPhone has two-factor authentication enabled by tapping **Settings** (⚙), tapping **Apple ID** (B), and then tapping **Password & Security**. On the Password & Security screen, check that the Two-Factor Authentication button shows On (C).

Sign In to an App or Website Using Sign In with Apple

When you go to sign in to an app or website that supports Sign In with Apple, a button such as Continue with Apple (D) or Sign In with Apple appears. Tap this button to start creating an account using your Apple ID. Enter your name (E) the way you want it to appear. Then tap **Share My Email** (F, changes to ✅) if you want to use your e-mail address, or tap **Hide My Email** (G, changes to ✅) if you want to have Apple create a unique address on its relay service and forward messages from the app or website to your e-mail address. Tap **Continue** (H) and follow any other prompts that appear.

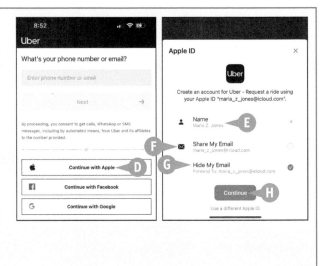

See Which Apps Are Using Your Apple ID

To see which apps are using your Apple ID, tap
Settings (⚙) on the Home screen. On the Settings
screen, tap **Apple ID**, the button at the top that contains
your name and picture. On the Apple ID screen, tap
Password & Security to display the Password & Security
screen. Here, tap **Apps Using Apple ID** (I) to display
the Apps Using Apple ID screen, which contains a list
of the apps.

Block Forwarded Messages or Stop Using Sign In with Apple for an App

To stop using Sign In with Apple for a particular app,
follow the instructions in the previous section to
display the Apps Using Apple ID screen.

Tap the app you want to stop using. A screen for that
app appears, such as the Bird screen shown here.

If you configured the Hide My Email feature for this
app, the Hide My Email section (J) appears. Here, the
This App Received button (K) shows the e-mail
address that Apple used for this app. You can tap
Manage Settings (L) to change the address used for
this app; you can create a new address or use one of
your existing ones.

To stop using Sign In with Apple for this app, tap
Stop Using Apple ID (M) and then tap **Stop Using**
(N) in the confirmation dialog that opens.

Read E-Mail

After you have set up Mail during the initial setup routine, as described in Chapter 1, or by adding other accounts, as explained in Chapter 4, you are ready to send and receive e-mail messages using your iPhone. This section shows you how to read your incoming e-mail messages. You learn to reply to messages and write messages from scratch later in this chapter.

The Mail app is effective and easy to use. However, you may want to try other e-mail apps that provide greater integration with particular e-mail services, such as Microsoft's Outlook app or Google's Gmail app.

Read E-Mail

Read a Message and View an Attached File

1 On the Home screen, tap **Mail** (✉).

Ⓐ The badge shows the number of unread messages.

The Mailboxes screen appears.

Note: If Mail does not show the Mailboxes screen, tap **Back** (‹) until the Mailboxes screen appears.

2 Tap the inbox you want to open.

Ⓑ To see all your incoming messages together, tap **All Inboxes**.

Ⓒ A blue dot indicates an unread message.

Ⓓ A paperclip icon (📎) indicates one or more attachments.

Ⓔ A gold star indicates the message's sender is one of your VIPs. See the second tip for information about VIPs.

Ⓕ You can tap **Filter** (☰) to filter the messages by Unread status, displaying only unread messages. You can then tap **Unread** to apply a different filter.

3 Tap a message.

The message opens.

Ⓖ You can tap **Previous** (⌃) or **Next** (⌄) to display another message.

4 If the message has an attachment, tap it.

196

The attachment opens in the viewer.

Note: Mail's viewer can display many types of attached files, but not all files.

Note: If Mail has hidden the controls at the top of the screen, tap the screen to display the controls.

5 If you want to send the file to an app or share it with others, tap **Share** (⬆️).

The Share sheet opens.

6 Tap the means of sharing, such as **Word** (📄) or **Pages** (📝) for a Word document.

7 Tap **Done**.

The message appears again.

Access New Messages Quickly from the Home Screen

1 On the Home screen, tap and hold **Mail** (✉️).

The pop-up panel opens.

H You can also tap another button, such as **VIP**.

2 Tap **All Inboxes**.

The All Inboxes screen appears.

Reply to or Forward an E-Mail Message

M ail makes it easy to reply to an e-mail message or forward it to others. If the message had
multiple recipients, you can choose between replying only to the sender of the message and
replying to the sender and all the other recipients in the To field and the Cc field, if there are any.
Recipients in the message's Bcc field, whose names you cannot see, do not receive your reply.

Reply to or Forward an E-Mail Message

Open the Message You Will Reply to or Forward

1 On the Home screen, tap **Mail** (📧).

The Mailboxes screen appears.

Note: When you launch Mail, the app checks for new
messages. This is why the number of new messages you
see on the Mailboxes screen sometimes differs from the
number on the Mail badge on the Home screen.

2 Tap the inbox you want to see.

The inbox opens.

Ⓐ The To icon (🔟) indicates that you are a To
recipient of the message.

Ⓑ The Cc icon (ⅽⅽ) indicates that you are a Cc
recipient of the message.

Ⓒ The absence of a label means you are a Bcc recipient
of the message.

3 Tap the message you want to open.

The message opens.

4 Tap **Action** (↩).

The Action dialog opens.

Note: You can also reply to or forward a message by
using Siri. For example, say "Reply to this message" or
"Forward this message to Alice Smith," and then tell Siri
what you want the message to say.

Reply to the Message

1 In the Action dialog, tap **Reply**.

 To reply to all recipients, tap **Reply All**. Reply to all recipients only when you are sure that they need to receive your reply. Often, it is better to reply only to the sender.

A screen containing the reply appears.

 Mail automatically adds your signature, if you have one.

2 Type your reply to the message.

3 Tap **Send** (⬆).

Mail sends the message.

Note: After you tap **Send** (⬆), the Undo Send button appears at the bottom of the Mail screen for 10 seconds. You can tap **Undo Send** to cancel sending the message. Mail opens the message for editing, so you can change it as needed.

Forward the Message

1 In the Action dialog, tap **Forward**.

A screen containing the forwarded message appears.

2 Type the recipient's address.

 Alternatively, you can tap **Add Contact** (⊕) and choose the recipient in your Contacts list.

3 Type a message if needed.

Usually, it is helpful to tell the recipient or recipients why you are forwarding the message to them, as the reason may not be obvious.

4 Tap **Send** (⬆).

Mail sends the message.

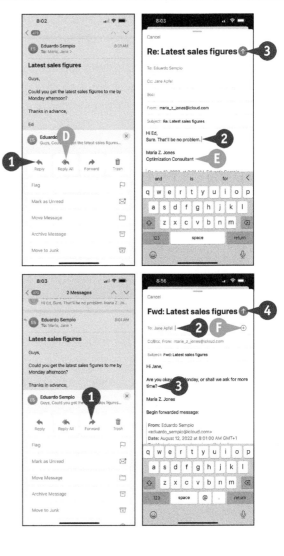

TIPS

Can I reply to or forward only part of a message?
Yes. The quick way to do this is to select the part of the message you want to include before tapping **Action** (↩). Mail then includes only your selection. Alternatively, you can start the reply or forwarded message and then delete the parts you do not want to include.

How do I check for new messages?
In a mailbox, tap and drag your finger down the screen, pulling down the messages. When a progress circle appears at the top, lift your finger. Mail checks for new messages.

Organize Your Messages in Mailbox Folders

To keep your inbox or inboxes under control, you should organize your messages into mailbox folders.

You can quickly move a single message to a folder after reading it or after previewing it in the message list. Alternatively, you can select multiple messages in your inbox and move them all to a folder in a single action. You can also delete any message you no longer need.

Organize Your Messages in Mailbox Folders

Open Mail and Move a Single Message to a Folder

1 On the Home screen, tap **Mail** (📩).

The Mailboxes screen appears.

2 Tap the mailbox you want to open.

The mailbox opens.

Ⓐ The Replied arrow (↩) indicates you have replied to the message.

Ⓑ The Forwarded arrow (↪) indicates you have forwarded the message.

3 Swipe left on the message you want to move.

The swipe controls appear.

Ⓒ You can delete the message by tapping **Trash** (🗑).

4 Tap **More** (⋯).

The Action dialog opens.

5 Tap **Move Message** (📁).

Note: If the message is from a VIP, the Move Message dialog opens. Tap **Move to "Starred"** to move the message to the Starred mailbox, or tap **Other Mailbox** to display the Move This Message to a New Mailbox screen.

The Move This Message to a New Mailbox screen appears.

6 Tap the mailbox to which you want to move the message.

Mail moves the message.

Move Multiple Messages to a Folder

 In the mailbox, tap **Edit**.

 Tap each message you want to move (changes to).

Note: You can tap either the selection button ( ) or the message preview.

3 Tap **Move**.

The Move These Messages to a New Mailbox screen appears.

4 Tap the destination mailbox.

D To move the messages to a mailbox in another account, tap **Back** (<). On the Accounts screen, tap the appropriate account to display the mailboxes in the account, and then tap the destination mailbox.

Note: Mail studies your history of moving messages so it can suggest the folder you may want for a particular message, saving you scrolling through all your folders.

The mailbox appears again, now without the messages you moved.

TIP

What does the Mark command in the Action dialog do?

Tap **Mark** to display the Mark dialog. You can then tap **Flag** to set a flag on the message — for example, to indicate that you need to pay extra attention to it. The flag ( ) then appears on the message. In the Mark dialog, you can also tap **Mark as Unread** to mark the message as not having been read, even though you have opened it; if the message is marked as unread, you can tap **Mark as Read** instead. You can also mark a message as unread or read by swiping right on it in the message list and then tapping **Unread** ( ) or **Read** ( ), as appropriate.

Write and Send E-Mail Messages

Your iPhone is great for reading and replying to e-mail messages you receive, but you can also write new messages. You can use the data in the Contacts app to address your outgoing messages quickly and accurately. If the recipient's address is not one of your contacts, you can type the address manually. You can attach files to an e-mail message to send them to the recipient.

Mail enables you to undo the sending of a message within ten seconds of you tapping **Send**. This feature, new in iOS 16, is great for fixing mistakes that you identify immediately.

Write and Send E-Mail Messages

① On the Home screen, tap and hold **Mail** (✉).

The pop-up panel appears.

② Tap **New Message** (✍).

Note: You can also tap **Mail** (✉) and then tap **New Message** (✍) to start a new message.

The New Message screen appears.

Ⓐ If you have created a signature, Mail inserts it automatically in the new message.

③ Tap **Add Contact** (⊕).

Ⓑ If the person you are e-mailing is not a contact, type the address in the To area. You can also start typing here and then select a matching contact from the list that the Mail app displays.

The Contacts list appears.

Note: If necessary, change the Contacts list displayed by tapping **Lists**, making your choice on the Lists screen, and then tapping **Done**.

Note: Contacts that appear in gray have no e-mail address.

④ Tap the contact you want to send the message to.

Note: If the contact has multiple e-mail addresses, the contact's info appears. Tap the address you want to use.

Ⓒ The contact's name appears in the To area.

Note: You can add other contacts to the To area by repeating steps **3** and **4**.

⑤ If you need to add a Cc or Bcc recipient, tap **Cc/Bcc, From**.

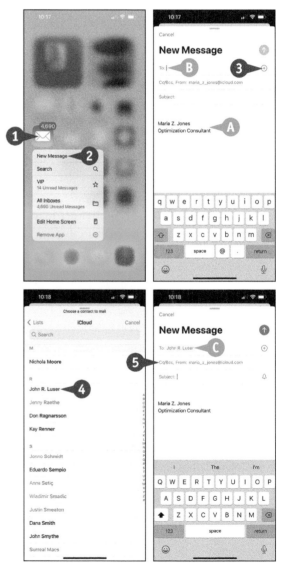

The Cc, Bcc, and From fields expand.

6 Tap the Cc area or Bcc area, and then follow steps **4** and **5** to add a recipient.

D To change the e-mail account you are sending the message from, tap **From**, and then tap the account to use.

E You can use the Hide My Email feature to create a random address that hides your real email address.

7 Tap **Subject**, and then type the message's subject.

F You can tap **Notifications** (🔔 changes to 🔔) to receive notifications when someone responds to the e-mail conversation.

8 Tap below the Subject line, and then type the body of the message.

Note: To stop working on a message temporarily, drag its title bar down to the bottom of the screen. You can then work with other messages. To resume work on the parked message, tap its title bar.

9 Tap **Send** (⬆).

Mail removes the message from the screen and plays the Swoosh sound but waits 10 seconds before actually sending the message.

G You can tap **Undo Send** within that 10-second period to stop Mail from sending the message. Mail opens the message for editing so that you can fix whatever is wrong.

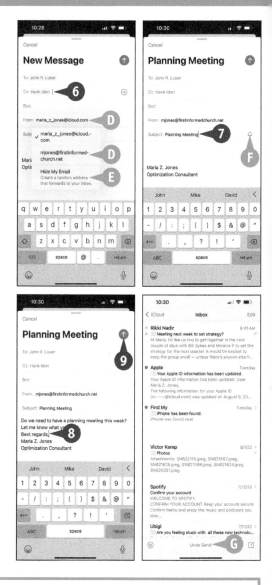

TIP

How do I attach a file to a message?

To attach a photo or video, tap and hold the message body area to display the contextual menu, and then tap **Insert Photo or Video**. On some iPhone models, you may need to tap **More** (**>**) before tapping **Insert Photo or Video**.

To attach a file from iCloud Drive, tap and hold the message body area to display the contextual menu, and then tap **Attach File**. On some iPhone models, you may need to tap **More** (**>**) before tapping **Attach File**.

To attach other types of files, start the message from the app that contains the file. Select the file, tap **Share** (⬆), and then tap **Mail** (✉). Mail starts a message with the file attached. You then address the message, add a subject and any text needed, and send the message.

CHAPTER 9

Keeping Your Life Organized

Your iPhone includes many apps for staying organized, such as the Calendars app, the Reminders app, and the Wallet app. Other apps help you find your way, stay on time, and track stock prices, weather forecasts, and your own health.

Browse Existing Events in Your Calendars

Your iPhone's Calendar app gives you a great way of managing your schedule and making sure you never miss an appointment.

After setting up your calendars to sync using iCloud or other calendar services, you can take your calendars with you everywhere and consult them whenever you need to. You can view either all your calendars or only those you choose.

Browse Existing Events in Your Calendars

Browse Existing Events in Your Calendars

1 On the Home screen, tap **Calendar** (🗓).

A In Light Mode, the black circle indicates the day shown; in Dark Mode, the circle is white. When the current date is selected, the circle is red.

B Your events appear on a scrollable timeline.

C An event's background color indicates the calendar it belongs to.

D You can tap **Today** to display the current day.

2 Tap the day you want to see.

The events for the day appear.

3 Tap the month.

The calendar for the month appears.

E You can tap the year to display the calendar for the full year, in which you can navigate quickly to other months.

4 Scroll up or down as needed, and then tap the date you want to display.

The date's appointments appear.

5 Tap **List** (:≡ changes to ▤).

The appointments appear as a list, enabling you to see more.

6 Tap an event to see its details.

The Event Details screen appears.

7 To edit the event, tap **Edit**.

The Edit screen appears, and you can make changes to the event. When you finish, tap **Done**.

Choose Which Calendars to Display

1 In the Calendars app, tap **Calendars** at the bottom of the screen.

2 Tap to place or remove a check mark next to a calendar you want to display or hide.

F Tap **Show All** to place a check mark next to each calendar for all accounts. Tap **Hide All** to remove all check marks.

G Similarly, tap **Show All** or **Hide All** for an account to display or hide the account's calendars.

H The Birthdays calendar automatically displays birthdays of contacts whose contact data includes the birthday.

I You can tap **Show Declined Events** (○ changes to ✓) to include invitations you have declined.

3 Tap **Done**.

The calendars you chose appear.

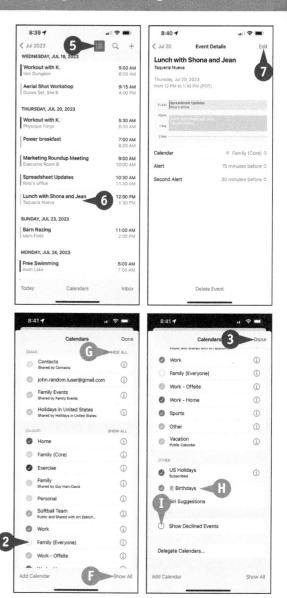

TIP

How can I quickly find an event?

In the Calendar app, tap **Search** (🔍). Calendar displays a list of your events. Type your search term. When Calendar displays a list of matches, tap the event you want to view.

Create New Events in Your Calendars

You can create calendar events on your computer, or online using a web interface such as that of iCloud, and then sync the events to your iPhone. But you can also create new events directly on your iPhone.

You can create either a straightforward, one-time event or an event that repeats on a schedule. You can also choose the calendar in which to store the event.

Create New Events in Your Calendars

1 On the Home screen, tap **Calendar** (🗓).

The Calendar screen appears.

2 Tap the day on which you want to create the new event.

Note: To start creating a new event straight from the Home screen, tap and hold **Calendar** (🗓) to display the pop-up panel, and then tap **Add Event**. You will need to select the date.

3 Tap **New** (+) to display the New Event screen.

Note: If New (+) is disabled, tap **Settings** (⚙) on the Home screen, tap **Mail** (✉), tap **Accounts**, tap the appropriate account, and set the **Calendars** switch to On (⬤).

4 Tap **Title** and type the title of the event.

5 Tap **Location or Video Call** to display the Location screen.

Note: If the Allow "Calendar" to Access Your Location? dialog opens when you tap **Location**, tap **Allow While Using App** to use locations.

A You can tap **Current Location** to use the current location.

6 Start typing the location.

7 Tap the appropriate match.

8 If the Starts date is incorrect, tap the date, and then tap the correct date.

B If this is an all-day appointment, set the **All-day** switch to On (⬤). Go to step **12**.

9 Tap the **Starts** time.

The time controls appear.

C If you need to change the time zone, tap **Time Zone**, type the city name, and then tap the time zone.

10 On the spin wheels, select the start time.

11 Tap **AM** or **PM**, as appropriate.

12 If you need to change the Ends date, tap the date, and then tap the end date.

13 Tap the **Ends** time, select the end time, and tap **AM** or **PM**, as appropriate.

14 If you want to allow travel time, tap **Travel Time**. On the Travel Time screen, set the **Travel Time** switch to On ( ); adjust the Starting Location setting, if needed; and then tap the time period, such as **30 minutes**. Tap **New Event** ( ) to return to the New Event screen.

15 Tap **Alert**.

The Alert pop-up menu opens.

16 Tap the appropriate item, such as **15 minutes before** or **At time of event**; these examples are with Travel Time turned off. If you turned on Travel Time, the choices are At Start of Travel Time, 5 Minutes Before Travel Time, and so on.

17 Tap **Calendar**.

The Calendar pop-up menu opens.

18 Tap the calendar to which you want to assign the event.

19 Tap **Add**.

The event appears on your calendar.

TIP

How do I set up an event that repeats every week?
On the New Event screen, tap **Repeat**. On the Repeat screen, tap **Every Week**, placing a check mark next to it, and then tap **Done**.

Work with Calendar Invitations

As well as events you create yourself, you may receive invitations to events that others create. When you receive an event invitation attached to an e-mail message, you can choose whether to accept the invitation or decline it. If you accept the invitation, you can add the event automatically to your calendar.

Work with Calendar Invitations

Respond to an Invitation from an Alert

1 When an invitation alert appears, tap and hold it.

Note: You can tap the invitation alert to open the invitation fully.

The pop-up panel displays the event's details, together with buttons for responding to the event.

2 Tap **Accept** (⊘), **Decline** (⊗), or **Maybe** (⊙), as needed.

A You can tap outside the pop-up panel to close it without tapping one of the response buttons.

Respond to an Invitation from the Inbox Screen

1 On the Home screen, tap **Calendar** (📅).

The Calendar screen appears.

2 Tap **Inbox**.

The Inbox screen appears.

B You can tap **Accept**, **Maybe**, or **Decline** to deal with the invitation without viewing the details.

C Calendar displays details of any conflict with an event.

3 Tap the invitation whose details you want to see.

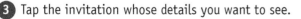

The Event Details screen appears.

4 If you decide to accept the invitation, tap **Calendar**.

The Calendar pop-up menu opens.

5 Tap the calendar to which you want to assign the event.

6 Tap **Alert**.

The Alert pop-up menu opens.

7 Tap the button for the alert interval. For example, tap **15 minutes before**.

D To control how the event's time appears in your calendar, tap **Show As**, and then tap **Busy** or **Free**, as appropriate, in the Show As pop-up menu.

8 Tap **Accept**.

Your calendar appears, showing the event you just accepted.

Track Your Commitments with Reminders

Your iPhone's Reminders app gives you an easy way to note your commitments and keep track of them. The Reminders app comes with a built-in list called Reminders, but you can create as many other lists as you need, giving each a distinctive color.

You can create a reminder with no due time or location or tie a reminder to a due time, arriving at or leaving a location, or both. Your iPhone can remind you of time- or location-based commitments at the appropriate time or place.

Track Your Commitments with Reminders

Open the Reminders App and Create Your Reminder Lists

 On the Home screen, tap **Reminders** (⋮).

The Reminders app opens, displaying the Lists screen.

Ⓐ If you have set up reminders or tasks on multiple accounts, such as iCloud and Exchange, a list appears for each account.

2 Tap **Add List**.

The Choose Account pop-up menu opens.

Note: If you have only one Reminders account, the Choose Account pop-up menu does not appear.

3 Tap the account in which you want to store the list.

The New List screen appears, with the placeholder name *New List* and the default icon, ⊜.

 Type the name for the list.

5 Tap the color to use for the list.

6 Optionally, tap an icon for the list instead of the default icon (⊜).

 Tap **Done**.

The list appears on the Lists screen.

8 Tap the list to open it.

Create a New Reminder

1 To create a new reminder in this list, tap **New Reminder** (⊕). This icon's color matches the color you assigned to the list.

Ⓑ You can tap **Lists** (〈) to return to the Lists screen so you can switch to another list.

The keyboard appears.

2 Type the text for the reminder.

Ⓒ You can tap **Add Note** and add a text note to the reminder.

3 Tap **Information** (ⓘ).

The Details screen appears.

4 Optionally, tap **Notes** and type any notes.

5 To create a date- or time-based reminder, set the **Date** switch to On (⬤○).

The calendar control appears.

6 Tap the date for the reminder.

7 To specify the time for the reminder, set the **Time** switch to On (⬤○).

8 Set the time.

9 Tap **AM** or **PM**, as appropriate.

10 If you need to repeat the reminder, tap **Repeat**, choose the repeat interval on the Repeat screen, and then tap **Details** to return to the Details screen.

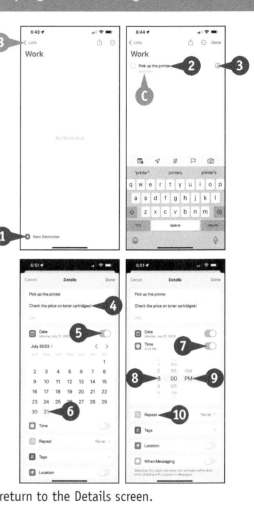

TIP

How do I sync my iPhone's reminders with my Mac's reminders?

You can sync your iPhone's reminders with your Mac's reminders — or your iPad's reminders — via your iCloud account, via one or more Exchange accounts, or via both types of accounts.

Swipe up from the bottom of the screen to display the Home screen, and then tap **Settings** (⚙) to display the Settings screen. Tap **Apple ID** (the button that bears your Apple ID name) to display the Apple ID screen. Tap **iCloud** (☁) to display the iCloud screen, and then set the **Reminders** switch to On (⬤○). On your Mac, click **Apple** (), and then click **System Settings** on macOS Ventura or **System Preferences** on earlier macOS versions. Click **Apple ID** and then **iCloud** (☁) to display the iCloud pane. On Ventura, set the **Reminders** switch to On (⬤○). On earlier macOS versions, select the **Reminders** check box (☑).

continued ▶

You can assign different priorities to your reminders to give yourself a quick visual reference of their urgency. You can also add notes to a reminder to keep relevant information at hand. When you have completed a reminder, you can mark it as completed. You can view your list of scheduled reminders for quick reference, and you can choose whether to include your completed reminders in the list. If you no longer need a reminder, you can delete it from the list.

Track Your Commitments with Reminders (continued)

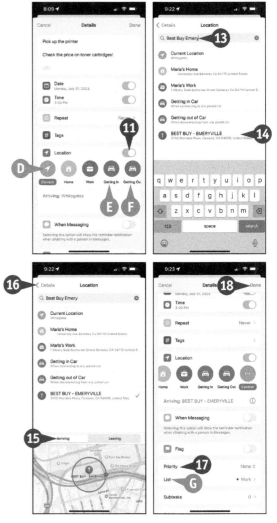

11 To create a location-based reminder, set the **Location** switch to On (●).

Note: If Reminders prompts you to allow it to use your current location, tap **Allow While Using App**.

D You can tap **Current** (◉) to use your current location.

E You can tap **Getting In** (◉) to specify getting in your vehicle at your current location.

Note: The Getting In location and Getting Out location require your vehicle to have Bluetooth with which your iPhone is paired.

F You can tap **Getting Out** (◉) to specify getting out of your vehicle at your current location.

12 For any other location option, tap **Custom** (●), which appears to the right of Getting Out (◉).

The Location screen appears.

13 Start typing the location in the search box.

14 Tap the appropriate location in the list of results.

The Location screen displays a map of the location.

15 Tap **Arriving** or **Leaving**, as needed.

16 Tap **Details** (<).

The Details screen appears again.

17 To assign a priority to the reminder, tap **Priority**; tap Low, Medium, High, or None; and then tap **Details** (<).

G To assign the reminder to a different list than the current list, tap **List**. On the List screen, tap the list you want to use.

18 Tap **Done**.

The new reminder appears on your list of reminders.

 Tap **New Reminder** (➕) to start creating a new reminder.

 When you finish a task, tap its button (◯ changes to ◉) to mark the reminder as complete.

Note: To delete a reminder, tap **Edit** on the screen that contains it. Tap **Delete** (➖) to the left of the reminder, and then tap **Delete**.

20 Tap **Lists** (‹) to switch to another reminder list.

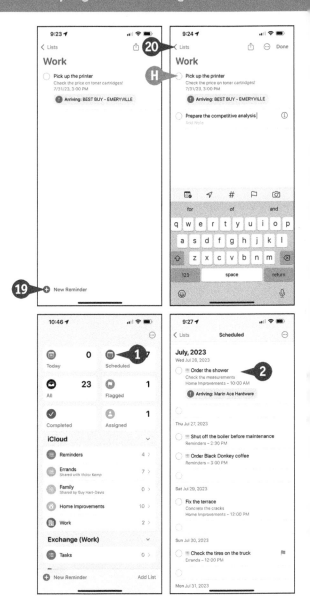

View a List of Your Scheduled Reminders

1 Tap **Scheduled** (▦).

The Scheduled list appears.

2 Tap the reminder you want to see.

Note: If you have many lists of reminders, you can arrange the lists in groups. To create a group, tap **Edit** on the Reminders screen, and then tap **Add Group** in the lower-left corner. On the New Group screen, type the name for the group, and then tap **Include**. On the Include screen, tap **Add** (➕) for each list you want to add to the new group.

TIP

How do I change the default list that Reminders puts my reminders in?
On the Home screen, tap **Settings** (⚙) to display the Settings screen. Tap **Reminders** (⁝) to display the Reminders screen, tap **Default List** to display the Default List screen, and then tap the list you want to make the default.

Keep Essential Documents at Hand with Wallet

allet is an app for storing payment cards and electronic versions of essential documents, such as insurance cards, airline boarding passes, movie tickets, and hotel reservations — even the keys for some cars. As explained in the section "Set Up and Activate Your iPhone" in Chapter 1, the iPhone's setup routine walks you through adding a payment card for Apple Pay to Wallet; you can add other cards later, as needed.

You can add documents to Wallet from built-in apps such as Mail and Safari, as shown in this section, or by using custom apps for shopping, booking hotels, and booking flights.

Keep Essential Documents at Hand with Wallet

Add a Document to Wallet

 In Mail, tap the message with the document attached.

The message opens.

 Tap the document's button.

The document appears.

 Tap **Add**.

Mail adds the document to Wallet.

The message appears again.

Note: In Safari, open the web page containing the document, and then tap **Add** to add the document to Wallet.

Open Wallet and Find the Documents You Need

 On the Home screen, tap **Wallet** (🔲).

The Wallet app opens.

The documents you have added appear.

 Tap the document you want to view.

Note: If a document has a specific expiration date, Wallet marks the document as expired once that date has passed. Scan your Wallet periodically for expired documents and remove any you find.

The document appears above the other documents. You can then hold its barcode in front of a scanner to use the document.

3 To see another document, tap the current top document and swipe down.

Wallet reshuffles the documents so you can see them all.

B You can also tap **Done** to return to the first Wallet screen and then tap the document you want to view.

Choose Settings for a Document or Delete It

1 Tap **More** (☉).

The More menu opens.

2 Tap **Pass Details** (ⓘ).

The Details screen appears.

3 Set the **Automatic Updates** switch to On (◯) if you want to receive updates to this document.

4 Set the **Allow Notifications** switch to On (◯) if you want to allow the document to raise notifications.

5 Set the **Suggest on Lock Screen** switch to On (◯) if you want notifications about the document to appear on the lock screen.

C If you have no further need for the document, tap **Remove Pass** to remove it.

6 Tap **Back** (ᐸ).

7 Tap **Done**.

TIP

What other actions can I take with documents in Wallet?
You can share a document with other people via e-mail, instant messaging, or AirDrop. To access these features, tap **Share** (⬆), and then tap **AirDrop**, **Mail**, or **Message** on the Share sheet that appears.

Find Your Location with Maps

Your iPhone's Maps app can pinpoint your location by using the Global Positioning System, known as GPS, or via triangulation using wireless networks. You can view your location on a road map, display a satellite picture with or without place labels, or view transit information. You can easily switch among map types to find the most useful one. To help you get your bearings, the Tracking feature in the Maps app can show you which direction you are facing.

Find Your Location with Maps

1 On the Home screen, tap **Maps** (⬤).

The Maps screen appears.

Ⓐ A blue dot shows your current location. The expanding circle around the blue dot shows that Maps is determining your location.

Note: It may take a minute for Maps to work out your location accurately. While Maps determines the location, the blue dot moves, even though the iPhone remains stationary.

2 Drag the gray handle down to collapse the Search pane.

3 Place your thumb and finger apart on the screen and pinch inward.

Note: To zoom in, place your thumb and finger on the screen and pinch apart.

The map zooms out, showing a larger area.

4 Tap **Location** (⬀ changes to ⬆), turning on the Location service.

5 Tap **Location** (⬆ changes to ⬥).

218

The Compass icon appears ( ). The red arrow indicates north.

 The map turns to show the direction the iPhone is facing so that you can orient yourself.

6 When you need to restore the map orientation, tap **Compass** ( ).

The map turns so that north is upward.

The Compass icon disappears.

7 Tap **Choose Map** ( ).

The Choose Map dialog opens.

 Explore is the view shown so far in this section.

 You can tap **Driving** to display a street map overlaid with driving information.

 You can tap **Transit** to a street map overlaid with transit information.

8 Tap **Satellite**.

The satellite map appears, showing photos with street and place names overlaid on them.

9 Tap **Close** ( ).

The Choose Map dialog closes.

 You can tap **3D** to switch to a three-dimensional view that enables you to tilt the map by sliding two fingers up and down.

Note: The satellite photos may be several years old and no longer accurate.

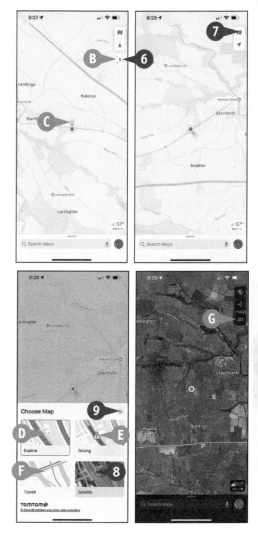

TIPS

How can I tell the scale of the map?

Place two fingers on the screen as if about to pinch outward or inward. Maps displays a scale in the upper-left corner of the screen.

How can I share my location?

Tap and hold the location you want to share. A dropped pin appears on the map as a red circle, and the Dropped Pin panel opens. Tap **Share** ( ) in the upper-right corner of the panel to display the Share sheet. You can then tap the means of sharing — such as AirDrop, Message, Mail, or Twitter — and follow the prompts to send or post your location.

Find Directions with Maps

Your iPhone's Maps app can give you directions to where you want to go. Maps can also show you current traffic congestion in some locales to help you identify the most viable route for a journey.

Maps displays driving directions by default, but you can make it display public transit directions and walking directions.

Find Directions with Maps

1 On the Home screen, tap **Maps** ( ).

The Maps screen appears.

2 Tap **Search Maps**.

The Directions screen appears.

3 Start typing your destination.

A list of suggested matches appears.

4 Tap the correct match.

A map of the destination appears.

5 Tap **Directions**.

The Directions screen appears.

By default, My Location appears as the starting point for the directions.

Note: If you want the directions to start from your current location, leave My Location as the starting point. Go to step **7**.

6 Tap **My Location** to display the Change Stop screen, start typing the new location, and then tap the correct match.

The Directions screen shows the new starting location, together with possible routes.

Ⓐ The active route and its time button appear in darker blue.

Ⓑ If multiple routes are available, you can tap a time button to view a different route. The time button changes to darker blue to indicate it is active.

7 To add a stop, tap **Add Stop**. Otherwise, go to step **9**.

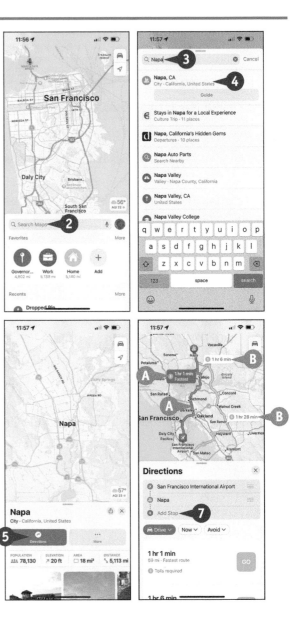

On the Add Stop screen that appears, start typing the location, and then tap the correct match.

Maps displays a map of the location.

 Tap **Add Stop** (⊕).

Maps displays the Directions screen, including the new stop.

 Maps updates the routes.

 If necessary, drag a stop up or down the Directions list to change the order.

Note: To reverse the direction of the journey, drag the start point to the end and the end point to the start.

D Maps updates the routes for the new stop order.

E You can tap the pop-up menu, and then tap **Drive** (🚗), **Walk** (🚶), Transit (🚆), **Cycle** (🚲), or **Ride Share** (🧍).

⑩ Tap **Go**.

The first screen of directions appears.

⑪ Swipe left to display the next direction.

Note: When you start navigating the route, the directions change automatically to reflect your progress.

⑫ To finish using the directions, swipe up from the bottom of the screen, and tap **End Route**.

The map appears again.

TIP

What else should I know about the directions for walking, cycling, or public transit?

You should be aware that walking directions may be incomplete or inaccurate. Before walking the route, check that it does not send you across pedestrian-free bridges or through rail tunnels. Similarly, try to check that cycling directions are complete before you attempt to follow them.

The Maps app provides transit information for only some routes. Even for these, it is advisable to double-check the information via online schedules, such as on the website or app of the transit company involved.

Using Maps' Favorites and Contacts

When you want to return to a location easily in the Maps app, you can create a favorite for the location.

Similarly, you can add a location to your contacts so that you can access the location either from the Contacts app or from the Maps app. You can either create a new contact or add the location to an existing contact. You can also return quickly to locations you have visited recently but for which you have not created a favorite or contact.

Using Maps' Favorites and Contacts

Create a Favorite in Maps

1 On the Home screen, tap **Maps** (⊿).

The Maps screen appears.

2 Find the place for which you want to create a favorite. For example, tap and drag the map, or search for the location you want.

3 Tap and hold the place for which you want to create a favorite.

A The Maps app drops a pin on the place.

The Dropped Pin panel opens.

4 Swipe up.

The Dropped Pin panel opens further.

5 Tap **Add to Favorites** (⋆).

6 Tap **Close** (×).

The panel closes.

Create a Contact in Maps

1 Find the place for which you want to create a contact. For example, tap and drag the map, or search for the location you want.

2 Tap and hold the appropriate place.

The Maps app drops a pin on the place.

The Dropped Pin panel opens.

3 Tap **Share** (⬆).

The Share sheet opens.

4 Swipe up.

5 Tap **Create New Contact** (⊕).

B You can tap **Add to Existing Contact** (⊕) and then tap the contact to which you want to add the location instead.

The New Contact screen appears.

6 Type the first name for the contact record, as needed.

7 Type the last name or description for the contact record, as needed.

8 Add any other information the contact record requires.

9 Tap **Done**.

The Maps app creates the contact record for the location.

The Dropped Pin panel appears again.

10 Tap **Close** (×).

The Dropped Pin panel closes.

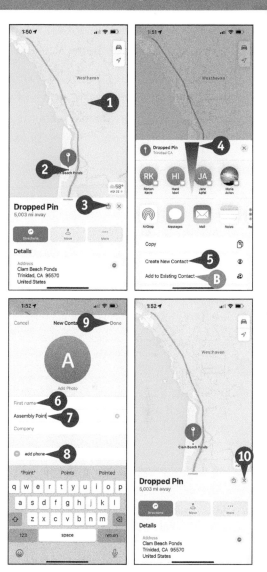

TIP

How do I go to a location for which I have created a favorite or a contact?

In the Maps app, tap **Search Maps** to display the Search screen. Start typing the name of the favorite or contact, and then tap the appropriate search result.

Take Notes

Your iPhone is a great device for taking notes no matter where you happen to be. The Notes app enables you to create notes stored in an e-mail account — such as your iCloud account — or on your iPhone.

You can create straightforward notes in plain text for any account you add to Notes. For notes stored on Exchange, IMAP, or Google accounts, you can also add formatting. For notes stored in iCloud, you can add check circles, photos, web links, and sketches.

Take Notes

1 On the Home screen, tap **Notes** (⬜).

The Notes app opens.

Note: To change the account or folder in which you are working, tap **Back** (<), and then tap the account or folder you want to use.

2 Tap **New** (✑).

A new note opens.

3 Type the title and the first few paragraphs of the note.

A By default, Notes applies to the first paragraph the Title style, which uses larger text and boldface. See the second tip if you want to change the style for the first paragraph.

B The second paragraph receives the Body style.

4 When you want to change styles or insert a nontext item, tap **More** (⊕).

The More bar appears.

5 Tap **Formatting** (Aα).

C You can tap **Table** (⊞) to add a table.

D You can tap **Add Photo** (⊙) to add a new photo, an existing photo, or a scanned document to the note. This adds the photo or document as a separate item attached to the note.

E You can tap **Sketch** (Ⓐ) to draw a sketch in the note.

F You can tap **Close** (✕) when you no longer need the More bar displayed.

224

The Format pane appears.

6 Tap the style you want to apply to the paragraph.

G The paragraph takes on the style.

7 Tap **Close** (✕).

The Format pane closes.

8 Tap **return**.

The insertion point moves to a new paragraph.

9 Tap **Check circle** (⊘).

H The Notes app inserts a check circle on the current line.

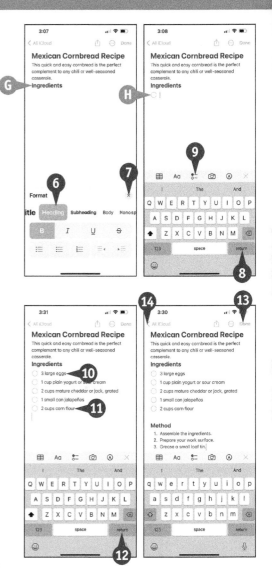

10 Type the text to accompany the check circle.

11 Tap **return** to create a new line, and then type further check-circle paragraphs, as needed.

12 When you finish using check circles, tap **return** twice.

The Notes app creates a new paragraph and discontinues the check circles.

13 When you finish working on the note, tap **Done**.

The Notes app hides the keyboard.

14 Tap **Back** (‹) one or more times. The name varies depending on the folder you are using.

The Notes screen appears again, and you can work with other notes.

TIPS

How do I tell Siri the account for new notes?
On the Home screen, tap **Settings** (⚙), and then tap **Notes** (▭). To store notes on your iPhone rather than online, set the **"On My iPhone" Account** switch to On (⬤). Tap **Default Account**, and then tap the appropriate account or tap **On My iPhone**. The Notes widget in Today View also uses this default account.

What other settings can I configure for Notes?
You can choose the default style for the first line in each new note. Open the Notes screen in the Settings app as explained in the previous tip, tap **New Notes Start With**, and then tap the appropriate style — **Title**, **Heading**, **Subheading**, or **Body** — on the New Notes Start With screen.

Using Stocks, Weather, Clock, and Compass

The iPhone includes several built-in apps that enable you to keep track of important information throughout the day. You can use the Stocks app to track stock prices in almost real time. You can use the Weather app to learn the current weather conditions and forecast for your current location and other locations. You can use the Clock app's World Clock, Alarm, Bedtime, Stopwatch, and Timer features to track and measure time. You can use the Compass app to get your bearings, measure angles, and learn your approximate elevation.

Using the Stocks App

The Stocks app enables you to track a customized selection of stock prices.

Tap **Stocks** (🎵) on the Home screen to launch the Stocks app. The Stocks screen appears, showing the default selection of stocks. At the bottom is a news section that you can expand by swiping up. To view more information on a stock, tap it.

To change the stocks displayed, tap **More** (A, ⋯), and then tap **Edit Watchlist**. On the Stocks configuration screen that appears, tap **Search** (B, 🔍). Type the name or stock symbol of the stock you want to add, tap the matching entry in the list to display the information panel, tap **More** (⋯), and then tap **Add to Watchlist**. You can tap a stock's handle (C, ≡) and drag it up or down to change the order. Tap **Remove** (D, ➖) and then **Remove** (E, 🗑) to remove a stock from the watchlist. Tap **Done** (F) to return to the Stocks screen.

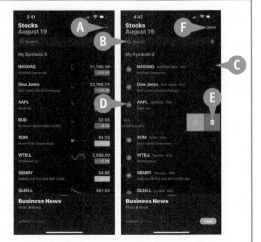

Using the Weather App

The Weather app lets you stay in touch with current weather conditions and forecasts for multiple locations.

Tap **Weather** (⬤) or the Weather widget on the Home screen to launch the Weather app. You can then swipe left or right at the top of the screen, or tap the dots (G) at the bottom of the screen, to display the city you want to see. Swipe the timeline (H) left to see later hours. Swipe up to display further details, such as sunrise and sunset times, humidity, and wind.

To customize the locations, tap **Cities** (I, ≡). You can then tap **Search** (J, 🔍) to start adding a location, swipe a location left and tap **Remove** (K, 🗑) to remove it, or tap and hold and then drag to move a city up or down the list. Tap **More** (L, ⬤) and then **Celsius °C** or **Fahrenheit °F** to toggle between Celsius and Fahrenheit. When you finish customizing the list, tap the city (M) whose weather you want to display.

Using the Clock App

The Clock app, which you can launch by tapping **Clock** (🕐) on the Home screen, has four main features: World Clock (N), Alarm (O), Stopwatch (P), and Timer (Q).

Use World Clock to track the time in different cities. To remove a city, swipe its button left and then tap **Delete** (R). To add a city, tap **Add** (S, ⊞) and select the city on the Choose a City screen. To change the order of the list, tap **Edit** and drag cities up or down by their handles (≡); tap **Done** when you finish.

Use Alarm to set as many alarms as you need, each with a different schedule and your choice of sound. Tap **Add** (T, ⊞) to display the Add Alarm screen, set the details for a new alarm, and then tap **Save**. On the Alarm screen, you can set each alarm's switch (U) to On (▣) or Off (▢), as needed.

Use Stopwatch to time events to the hundredth of a second. Swipe left or right to switch between the analog-look stopwatch and the digital-look stopwatch.

Use Timer to count down a set amount of time and play a sound when the timer ends. To play music or other media for a set amount of time, tap **When Timer Ends**, tap **Stop Playing** on the When Timer Ends screen, and then tap **Set**.

Using the Compass App

The Compass app, which you can launch by tapping **Utilities** (⁑) on the Home screen and then tapping **Compass** (🧭) in the Utilities folder, makes it easy to get your bearings, your GPS location, and your elevation. You can measure an angle by tapping to fix the bearing and then turning your iPhone toward the target point; the red arc (V) shows the angle. You can tap the GPS location (W) to switch to the Maps app and display the map for that location. You can learn your approximate elevation by looking at the Elevation readout (X).

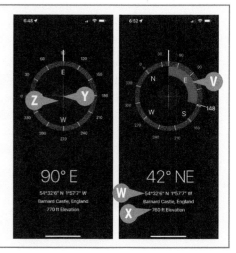

To get as accurate a bearing as possible, hold your iPhone flat, so that the small white crosshair (Y) appears centered in the gray bubble (Z) in the middle of the compass circle.

Using the Health App

The Health app integrates with third-party hardware and apps to enable you to keep tabs on many different aspects of your health, ranging from your weight and blood pressure to your nutrition, activity levels, and body mass index. Tap **Health** (♥) on the Home screen to launch the Health app.

Navigate the Health App's Screens

The Health app contains three main screens, the Summary screen, the Sharing screen, and the Browse screen.

The Summary screen appears at first, showing the Favorites list (A), the Highlights list (B), the Get More from Health list, and the Apps list.

The Sharing screen, which you can display by tapping **Sharing** (C, 👥 changes to 👥), provides tools for sharing your health data with your doctor (D) or with other people (E) as well as for requesting others to share their health data with you (F).

The Browse screen, which you can display by tapping **Browse** (G, ▦ changes to ▦) at the bottom of the screen, contains the Health Categories list (H) and the Health Records list.

Set Up Your Health Profile and Medical ID

Tap **Account** (⊙, your initials, or your chosen photo) to display the Account screen. Here you can enter your medical details; connect to a provider to see your health records; specify privacy settings for apps, research studies, and devices; and export all your health data to share with medical professionals.

Start by tapping **Health Details** (I) and entering basic details, such as your date of birth and blood type, on the Health Details screen. Then tap **Medical ID** (J) to display the Medical ID screen. Tap **Edit** in the upper-right corner to open the screen for editing. You can then enter your medical conditions, medical notes, allergies and reactions, medications, and emergency contact information. In the Emergency Access section at the bottom of the screen, set the **Show When Locked** switch to On (⬤) if you want to allow your medical ID to be viewed from the iPhone's Power Off screen. Tap **Done** (K) when you finish editing your medical ID information.

Set Up Your Favorites List

To give yourself quick access to the Health items you find most useful, add those items to your Favorites list on the Summary screen. If the Summary screen is not already displayed, tap **Summary** (♥ changes to ♥) to display it. Then tap **Edit** to the right of the Favorites heading to display the Edit Favorites screen.

Tap **Existing Data** (L) to view the items that have data, or tap **All** (M) to view all items. Tap **Favorite** (N, ☆ changes to ★) to add an item to the Favorites list. Tap **Done** (O) when you finish.

From the Favorites screen, you can tap an item to view its current data. For example, tap **Activity** to display the Activity screen (P), where you can examine your data for the Move, Exercise, and Stand targets.

Add Data Points

The Health app can automatically accept data points from sources you approve, but you can also add data points manually. For example, if you weigh yourself on a manual scale or have your blood pressure taken, you can add your latest readings to the Health app so that you can track your weight and blood pressure over time.

Tap the appropriate button — for example, tap **Blood Pressure** — on the Favorites screen to display the Blood Pressure screen. Tap **Add Data** (Q) to display the data-entry screen, such as the Blood Pressure screen shown here, input the data (R), and then tap **Add** (S). If the values are abnormal, the Confirm Data dialog opens to prompt you to confirm the values; tap **Confirm** (T) if they are correct.

Manage Files with the Files App

The Files app enables you to work with files stored on your iPhone; files stored on network servers, such as macOS Server; and files stored on online storage services, such as iCloud Drive, OneDrive, and Dropbox. You can quickly locate files by using the Recents screen, by using the Browse screen, or by searching by keyword. You can also recover recently deleted files by using the Recently Deleted Location. You navigate the Files app using similar techniques to those for navigating file-opening and file-saving features within apps.

Manage Files with the Files App

Open the Files App

1 On the Home screen, tap **Files** (▦).

The Files app opens.

2 Tap **Browse** (▤ changes to ▤).

The Browse screen appears.

Ⓐ The Recently Deleted (🗑) location contains files that you have deleted recently, somewhat like the Trash on macOS or the Recycle Bin on Windows. To retrieve a deleted file, tap **Recently Deleted** (🗑), tap and hold the file, and then tap **Recover** on the command bar that appears.

Ⓑ The Shared screen (▣) contains files that others have shared with you.

Browse Files and Open Files

1 Tap **Recents** (🕐 changes to 🕐).

The Recents screen appears.

Ⓒ You can search your recent files by tapping **Search** (🔍) and then typing a search term.

Ⓓ Your most recent files appear at the top.

2 Tap **Browse** (▤ changes to ▤).

The Browse screen appears.

Ⓔ You can search all your files by tapping **Search** (🔍) and then typing a search term.

3 Tap the location you want to browse. This example uses iCloud Drive.

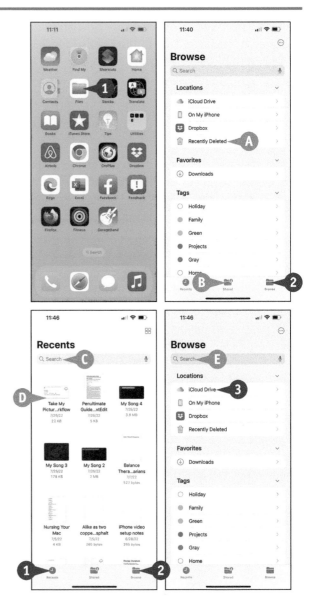

The screen for the location appears.

④ Tap **More** (⋯).

The More menu opens.

Ⓕ You can change the sort order by tapping **Name**, **Date**, **Size**, **Kind**, or **Tags**.

Ⓖ You can reverse the current sort order by tapping the sort type that shows the check mark (✓).

Ⓗ You can tap **List** (☰) to display the files and folders as a list or tap **Icons** (⊞) to display them as icons.

⑤ Tap the folder you want to open.

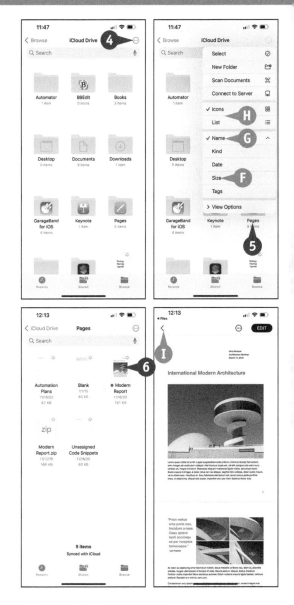

The folder opens.

⑥ Tap the file you want to open.

The file opens in the default app for the file type, assuming your iPhone has such an app.

The app appears, and you can work on the file.

Note: You can open only files for which your iPhone contains a suitable app. If there is no suitable app, Files displays the file for viewing if it has a suitable viewer, but you cannot change the file.

Ⓘ You can tap **Back** (《 or 〈) to return to the Files app.

TIP

Can I move or delete multiple files at once?
Yes, you can take several actions with multiple files in the same folder. First, navigate to that folder. Tap **More** (⋯), and then tap **Select** (⊘) to switch to Selection Mode. Tap each item to select it (changes to ✓). After selecting the items, tap the appropriate button at the bottom of the screen — **Duplicate** (⊞), **Move** (📁), **Share** (⬆), or **Delete** (🗑); or tap **More** (⋯), and then tap **Compress** (🗜), **New Folder with Item** (📁), or **Copy** (📋) — and then follow the prompts to complete the action.

continued ▶

A s well as opening a file, the Files app enables you to take other actions with a file, such as renaming it, copying it and pasting a copy, duplicating it in the same location, or moving it to another location. Files also enables you to use tags to group and sort your files. Files comes with default tags with color names, such as Red and Orange, but you can customize the names and create new tags as needed.

Manage Files with the Files App (continued)

Take Other Actions with a File

1 Tap and hold the file you want to affect.

The pop-up menu opens.

J Tap **Copy** (🖺) to copy the file. After copying the file, navigate to the location in which you want to paste the copy, tap and hold open space, and then tap **Paste** on the control bar.

K Tap **Duplicate** (🗐) to create a duplicate file in the same folder.

L Tap **Move** (🗁) to display a screen for moving the file. Tap the location, and then tap **Move**.

M Tap **Delete** (🗑) to delete the file.

N Tap **Get Info** (ⓘ) to display information about the file.

O Tap **Quick Look** (👁) to display a preview of the file.

P Tap **Rename** (✏) to display the Rename Document screen. Type the new name, and then tap **Done**.

Q Tap **Share** (⬆) to open the Share sheet for sharing the file.

R Tap **Compress** (🗇) to create a zip file containing the file.

2 Tap **Tags** (◇).

The Tags screen appears.

3 Tap each tag you want to apply to the file. Also tap any applied tag that you want to remove.

4 Tap **Done**.

The Files app displays the folder from which you started.

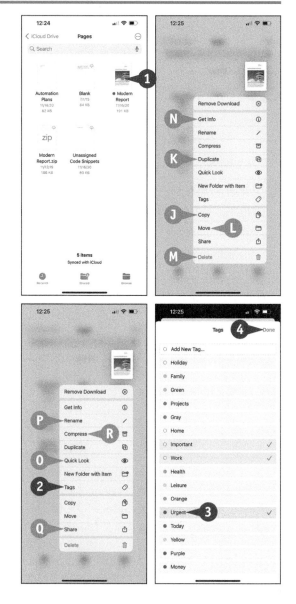

Organize Your Locations and Tags

1 Tap **Browse** (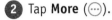 changes to ▮).

The Browse screen appears.

2 Tap **More** (⋯).

The menu opens.

3 Tap **Edit**.

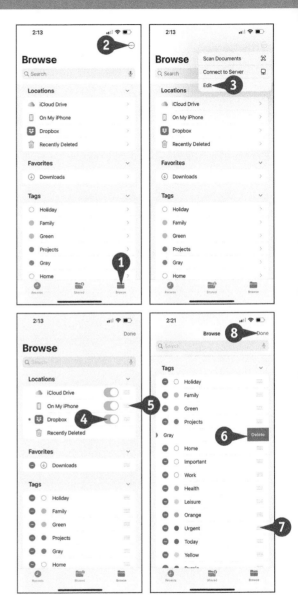

The Browse screen switches to Edit Mode.

4 In the Locations list, set a switch to Off (◯) changes to ⬤) if you want to hide the location.

Note: If you have configured a compatible app but it has not appeared in the Locations list, set its switch here to On (⬤) to enable it.

5 Tap a handle (≡) and drag a location up or down, as needed.

6 In the Tags list, tap **Delete** (⊖) and then tap **Delete** to delete a tag.

7 To change the tag order, tap the handle (≡) and drag the tag up or down the list.

8 When you finish editing the Browse screen, tap **Done**.

The Browse screen switches off Edit Mode.

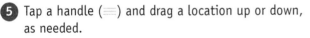

TIP

Can I create my own tags?

Yes, you can create your own tags when saving new files in the apps. For example, when you save a new document in Pages, you can create custom tags for it.

You cannot create new tags directly in the Files app, but you can rename the built-in tags. Tap **Browse** (▮ changes to ▮) to display the Browse screen, tap **More** (⋯), and then tap **Edit** to switch to Edit Mode. You can then tap a tag, type a new name for it, and tap **Done** on the keyboard.

Understanding Shortcuts and Automation

Your iPhone includes the Shortcuts app, which gives you two ways of executing tasks quickly and effortlessly. The first way of executing tasks is using shortcuts, sequences of actions that run at the tap of a button or a widget. iOS comes with many prebuilt shortcuts, but you can also build your own custom shortcuts to take exactly the actions you want.

The second way of executing tasks is by using automations. Like a shortcut, an automation is a sequence of actions; the difference is that an automation runs automatically when an event occurs rather than when you tap a button.

Open the Shortcuts App and Navigate the Interface

To get started with shortcuts, tap **Shortcuts** (🔵) on the Home screen. The Shortcuts app opens, usually displaying the My Shortcuts screen. At first, this screen may contain only the Starter Shortcuts list (A), which provides quick examples. You can add other shortcuts to this screen as needed. When you want to run a shortcut, you tap its button on the My Shortcuts screen. To see more shortcuts, tap **Shortcuts** (B, ‹), and then tap **All Shortcuts** (🗂).

On the Automation screen, the Create Personal Automation feature (C) lets you configure the Shortcuts app to automatically trigger sequences of software tasks when certain conditions are met. You can also create automated tasks to be performed with HomeKit-compatible devices using the Home app's interface, again when certain conditions are met. To get started, tap **Set Up Home Hub** (D).

Explore Built-In Shortcuts in the Gallery

Before creating any shortcuts of your own, spend a few minutes exploring the prebuilt shortcuts. Tap **Gallery** (E, 🔖 changes to 🔖) to display the Gallery screen.

At the top of this screen, you can search (F) using keywords. Searching can be a great way to find out which shortcuts are available for a particular app or task you have in mind.

If you simply want to see the types of shortcuts on offer, browse through the sections on the Gallery screen. Scroll down to find a category of interest, and then scroll left to explore the shortcuts it contains; tap **See All** (G) to display a screen showing the entire category.

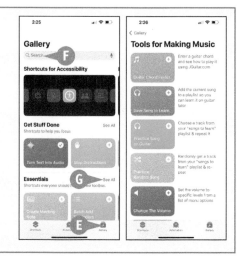

Add Shortcuts to the My Shortcuts Screen

When you find a shortcut you want to use on the Gallery screen, add it to the My Shortcuts screen. Tap the shortcut in the Gallery to display the information screen for the shortcut. Here, you can read the information about the shortcut (H); tap **More** (I, such as ... — the color varies) to display information about the actions the shortcut takes (J), and then tap **Done** (K); and tap **Add Shortcut** (L, ⊕) to add the shortcut to the My Shortcuts screen.

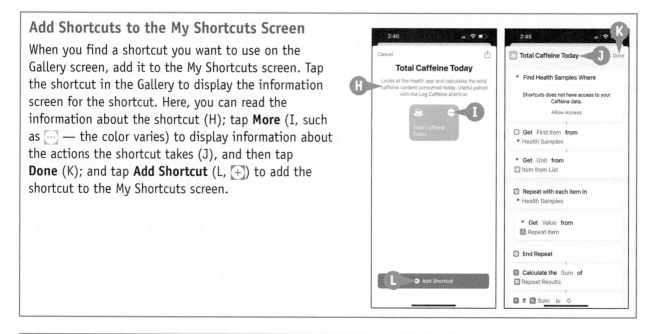

Configure or Modify a Shortcut

The Shortcuts app enables you to configure an existing shortcut or modify what it does. To start configuring or modifying a shortcut, tap **Shortcuts** (⬛ changes to ⬛) to display the Shortcuts screen, and then tap **My Shortcuts** (⬛) to display the My Shortcuts screen. Then tap **Details** (...) on the shortcut to open the shortcut in the shortcut editor.

You can then tap an item in an action (M) to configure that item, or tap **Remove** (N, ×) to remove an action.

To rename the shortcut or change its icon, tap **Menu** (O, ⌄), and then tap **Rename** (P, ✏️) or **Choose Icon** (Q, 🖼️), respectively. From the menu, you can also tap **Add to Home Screen** (R, ⊕) to add the shortcut to the Home screen so that you can run it quickly.

When you finish configuring the shortcut, tap **Done** (S) to close the shortcut editor.

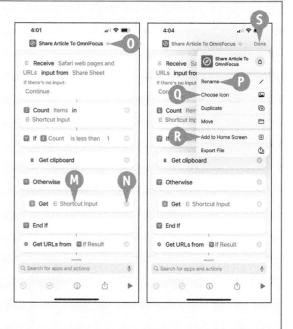

Create a Custom Shortcut

The Shortcuts app enables you to create custom shortcuts that perform exactly the actions you want. You can browse an extensive selection of actions, arrange the actions you need into the right order, and customize what the actions do. You can then assign your new shortcut a name and a *glyph* — an icon — with a colored background.

As with prebuilt shortcuts, you can run your custom shortcuts either from the My Shortcuts screen in the Shortcuts app or directly from the iPhone's Home screen.

Create a Custom Shortcut

1 On the Home screen, tap **Shortcuts** (⬛).

The Shortcuts app opens.

2 Tap **Shortcuts** (▦ changes to ▦).

The My Shortcuts screen appears.

Note: If the Shortcuts screen appears, tap **My Shortcuts** (⬔) to display the My Shortcuts screen.

3 Tap **Create Shortcut** (+).

The shortcut editor screen appears, showing a new shortcut with the default name New Shortcut.

4 Tap **Menu** (⌄) to open the menu.

5 Tap **Rename** (✎), type the new name, and then tap **done** on the on-screen keyboard.

6 Tap **Menu** (⌄) to open the menu.

7 Tap **Choose Icon** (🖼) to display the Icon screen, select an icon, and then tap **Done**.

8 Tap **Add Action** (⊕).

The Action screen appears.

9 Locate the action you want to add to the shortcut.

A You can tap **Search for apps and actions** and type a keyword to search for.

B You can tap **Categories** to view categories of shortcuts.

C You can tap **Apps** to display a list of apps, and then tap the app you want.

D You can browse the **Suggestions From Your Apps** list to see suggested actions based on your iPhone usage.

10 To follow this example, tap **Scripting** (⟡) in the Categories list.

The contents of the Scripting category appear.

11 Tap the action you want to add. For the example, scroll down to the Device section and tap **Get Battery Level** (🔲).

The shortcut editor screen appears, with the action added to the shortcut.

12 Add further actions, as needed. For the example, swipe the handle up to display the Scripting screen, scroll down to the Notification section, and then tap **Show Alert** (⚙️).

13 For the example, for the Show Alert action, tap the default alert of "Do you want to continue?" and type in its place **The battery level is now**.

14 Continuing the example, go to the Variables list and tap **Battery Level**, adding the variable after "is now."

15 Finally, type **%.** to complete the information for the alert.

16 Tap **Done**.

The shortcut appears on the My Shortcuts screen.

17 Tap the new shortcut.

E The shortcut performs its actions — in this example, displaying a dialog that shows the battery level percentage.

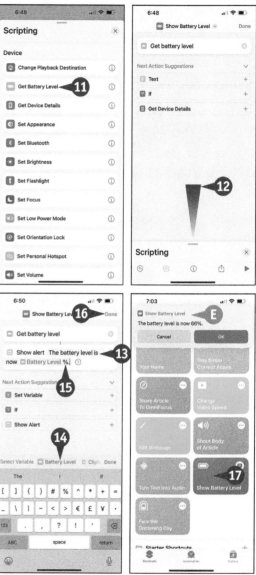

TIP

How do I run a custom shortcut from the Home screen?
On the My Shortcuts screen, tap **Details** (⋯) on the shortcut to display the screen for the shortcut. Tap **Menu** (⌄) to open the menu, and then tap **Add to Home Screen** to display the preview panel. Here, the Home Screen Name and Icon box shows the default icon and name for the shortcut. To change the icon, tap it; tap **Take Photo**, **Choose Photo**, or **Choose File**, as appropriate; and follow the prompts. To change the text, tap it, and then edit it as needed. When icon and text are satisfactory, tap **Add**.

CHAPTER 10

Enjoying Music, Videos, and Books

As well as being a phone and a powerful handheld computer, your iPhone is also a full-scale music and video player. To play music and listen to radio, you use the Music app; to play videos, you use the TV app. You can read digital books and PDF files using the Books app.

Navigate the Music App and Set Preferences

The Music app enables you to enjoy music you have loaded on your iPhone, music you have stored on Apple's iTunes Match service, and music on the Apple Music Radio service.

The Music app packs a wide range of functionality into its interface. The For You feature presents a selection of music customized to your tastes. The Browse feature gives you easy access to a wide variety of music online. The Radio feature allows you to listen to Apple Music Radio.

Navigate the Music App and Set Preferences

1 On the Home screen, tap **Music** (🎵).

The Music app opens.

Note: The Music app's screens vary depending on whether you subscribe to the Apple Music service.

2 If Library is not selected, tap **Library** (🎵 changes to 🎵).

The Library screen appears, showing your music library.

Ⓐ You can tap an item, such as Playlists or Artists, to browse the library.

Ⓑ The Recently Added section shows items added recently.

3 Tap **Edit**.

The Library screen opens for editing.

4 Tap an empty selection circle to select it (changes to ✅), adding that item to the Library list.

5 Tap a selected selection circle to deselect it (✅ changes to), removing that item from the Library list.

6 Drag a selection handle (☰) up or down to move an item in the list.

7 Tap **Done**.

The Library screen displays the customized list.

8 Tap **Listen Now** (▶ changes to ▶).

The Listen Now screen appears, showing music suggestions for you.

C You can tap **Account** (icon or your chosen picture) to display the Account screen, on which you can edit your nickname for the account and set a photo to use.

9 Swipe up to scroll down to see other categories, such as Made for You and New Releases.

10 Swipe left to scroll a category to see more of its contents.

11 Tap **Radio** ((•)) changes to ((•))).

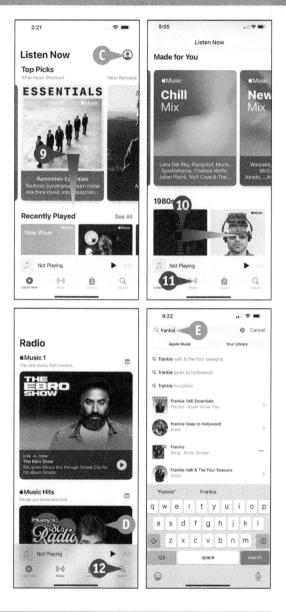

The Radio screen appears.

D You can tap a station to start it playing.

Note: See the section "Listen to Apple Music Radio," later in this chapter, for more information on the Radio feature.

12 Tap **Search** (Q changes to Q).

The Search screen appears.

E You can tap the Search box and type or dictate a search term.

TIP

How does the Search function work?

The Search function enables you to search both your own music and the Apple Music service. Tap **Search** (Q changes to Q) to display the Search screen, and then type your search terms in the box at the top of the screen. Tap the **Apple Music** tab button to see matching searches you can perform on Apple Music; you can then tap a search to perform it. Tap the **Your Library** tab button to see matching items in your music, broken down into categories such as Artists, Albums, or Songs. When you locate the item you want, tap the item to go to it.

Play Music Using the Music App

Y ou use the Music app to play back music from your iCloud Library or music you have loaded on your iPhone using iTunes. You can play music by song or by album, as described in this section. You can play songs in exactly the order you want by creating a custom playlist, as described in the later section, "Create a Music Playlist and Add Songs." You can also play by artist, genre, or composer.

Play Music Using the Music App

1 On the Home screen, tap **Music** (♫).

The Music app opens.

2 Tap **Library** (📚 changes to 📖).

The Library screen appears.

3 Tap the button for the means by which you want to browse your library. This example uses **Songs** (♫), so the Songs screen appears.

A If the songs are sorted by artist or recent addition, tap **Sort** and then tap **Title** in the dialog that opens.

4 Tap the letter that starts the name of the item you want to play.

That section of the list appears.

Note: You can also swipe or drag your finger up the screen to scroll down.

Note: Tap above the letter A in the navigation letters to go back to the top of the screen.

5 Tap the song you want to play.

The song starts playing.

B The song appears on the Now Playing button.

C You can tap **Pause** (❚❚) to pause the song.

D You can tap **Next** (▶▶) to skip to the next song.

6 Tap **Now Playing**. You can tap either the song name or the album image.

The Now Playing panel opens.

7 Tap and drag the progress bar to move through the song.

8 Tap and drag the volume control to change the volume. You can also press **Volume Up** or **Volume Down**, the iPhone's physical buttons.

9 Tap **Lyrics** (🗨 changes to 💬) to display the lyrics, if the song file contains them.

E The lyrics appear.

10 Tap **Lyrics** (🗨 changes to 💬).

Music hides the lyrics again.

11 Tap **More** (⋯) to open the More panel.

Note: The More panel's contents vary depending on how your library is configured and where the current song is stored.

F You can tap **Delete from Library** (🗑) to delete the song from your iPhone's library.

G You can tap **Add to a Playlist** (➕☰) to add the song to a new or existing playlist.

H You can tap **SharePlay** to share the song — for example, to listen to the song with your friends on a FaceTime call.

I You can tap **Love** (♡) or **Suggest Less Like This** (🖤).

12 Tap **List** (☰ changes to ≔) to open the List panel.

J You can tap **Shuffle** (⤬) to play songs in random order.

K You can tap **Repeat** (⟳) to repeat the current song or current list.

L The Playing Next section shows upcoming songs. You can tap a song to play it or drag a handle (═) to rearrange the list.

How else can I control playback?
Swipe down from the upper-right corner of the screen to display Control Center. You can control playback using the playback buttons. To access further controls, including the progress bar and the volume control, tap the song title or band name. If you have Apple Watch, you can use the Now Playing app to control the iPhone's playback.

Why does Music show "Not Playing" when audio is playing?
This happens when another app is playing audio. The *Now Playing/Not Playing* readout indicates only the Music app's own playing status.

Play Videos Using the TV App

To play videos — such as movies, TV shows, or music videos — you use the iPhone's TV app, which you can set up to use your existing TV provider. You can play a video on the iPhone's screen, which is handy when you are traveling; on a TV to which you connect the iPhone; or on a TV connected to an Apple TV box.

iOS's Picture-in-Picture Mode enables you to shrink the playing video down to a thumbnail so that you can continue to use other apps on your iPhone while watching the video.

Play Videos Using the TV App

Set Up the TV App

 On the Home screen, tap **TV** (📺).

The TV app opens.

Note: You can also play videos included on web pages. To do so, swipe up to display the Home screen, tap **Safari**, navigate to the page, and then tap the video.

Ⓐ You can tap **Account** (ⓐ) to display the Account screen, from which you can manage your subscriptions.

② Tap the video source. For this example, you would tap **Library** (🗄 changes to 🗄).

The Library screen appears.

③ Tap the video category, such as **Home Videos** (🎥).

The category screen appears.

④ Tap the video you want to view.

The details screen for the video appears.

Ⓑ You can tap **Remove Download** (⬇) to remove a downloaded video from your iPhone.

⑤ Tap **Play** (▶).

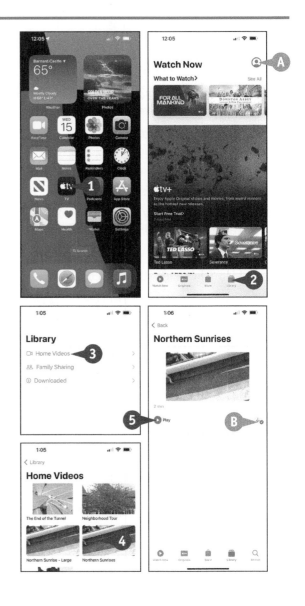

The video starts playing.

Note: The playback controls appear for a few seconds and then disappear automatically.

Note: If the video is in landscape format, turn your iPhone sideways to switch to landscape orientation.

6 When you need to control playback, tap the screen.

The playback controls appear.

C You can drag the progress bar to move through the video.

D You can drag the volume control to change the volume.

E You can tap **Pause** (❙❙) to pause playback. Tap **Play** (▶) to resume playback.

F You can tap **Rewind** (⏪) to rewind the video.

G You can tap **Fast-Forward** (⏩) to fast-forward the video.

7 To switch to Picture-in-Picture view, tap **Picture-in-Picture** (▣).

The video appears in a small window.

H You can work in your apps or on the Home screen.

I You can drag the picture-in-picture window to a different position.

J You can tap **Restore** (▣) to restore the Video app to full screen.

8 Tap **Close** (✖) when you want to close the video.

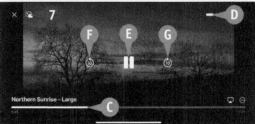

TIPS

How do I play videos on my television from my iPhone?

If you have an Apple TV or AirPlay-compatible device, use AirPlay, as explained in the next section, "Play Music and Videos Using AirPlay." Otherwise, use the Apple Lightning Digital AV Adapter and an HDMI cable to connect your iPhone to a TV.

What other video content can I watch on my iPhone?

You can also use your iPhone to watch or listen to *podcasts*, which are video or audio programs released via the Internet. The Podcasts app enables you to access podcasts covering many different topics.

Play Music and Videos Using AirPlay

Using the AirPlay feature, you can play music from your iPhone on remote speakers connected to an AirPlay-compatible device such as an AirPort Express or Apple TV. Similarly, you can play video from your iPhone on a TV or monitor connected to an Apple TV. Even better, you can use the iOS feature called *Screen Mirroring* to display an iPhone app on a TV or monitor. For example, you can display a web page in Safari on your TV screen.

Play Music and Videos Using AirPlay

Play Music on External Speakers or an Apple TV

1 On the Home screen, tap **Music** (🎵).

The Music app opens.

2 Navigate to the song you want to play. For example, tap **Library** (🎵 changes to 🎵), and then tap **Songs** (♪).

3 Tap the song.

The song starts playing.

The song's details appear on the Now Playing button.

4 Tap **Now Playing**.

The Now Playing screen appears.

5 Tap **AirPlay** (◉).

The AirPlay dialog opens.

6 Tap the AirPlay device on which you want the music to play.

Your iPhone starts playing music on the device via AirPlay.

Note: When you want to stop using AirPlay, tap **AirPlay** (◉), and then tap **iPhone** (▯).

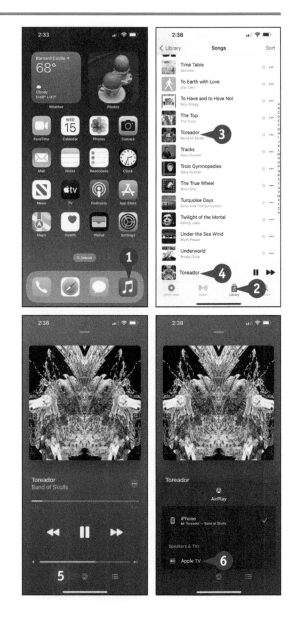

Play Video or an App on an Apple TV

1 Open the app you want to use. This example uses **Notes** ().

2 Swipe down from the upper-right corner of the screen.

Control Center opens.

3 Tap **Screen Mirroring** ().

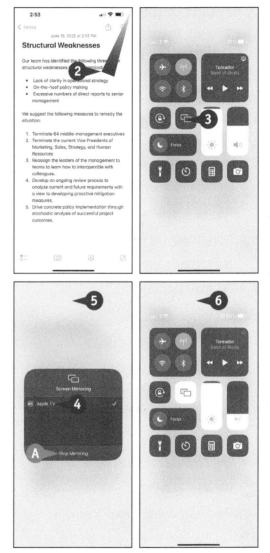

The Screen Mirroring panel opens.

4 Tap the Apple TV you want to use.

The iPhone's screen appears on the screen connected to the Apple TV.

A The Stop Mirroring button appears.

5 Tap outside the Screen Mirroring panel.

The Screen Mirroring panel closes.

6 Tap in the app above Control Center.

Control Center closes, and the app appears full screen.

Note: When you are ready to stop screen mirroring, open Control Center, tap **Screen Mirroring** (), and then tap **Stop Mirroring**.

TIPS

Can AirPlay play music through multiple sets of speakers at the same time?
Yes. In the AirPlay dialog, select the first set of speakers, and then select each other set. After establishing the connections, AirPlay displays a single entry with the names of both devices, such as Mac mini + AirPort Express. Tap this entry when you want to display the full list.

How else can I play audio through speakers without a cable?
You can play audio through Bluetooth speakers. Pair and then connect the speakers, as explained in the section "Using Bluetooth Devices with Your iPhone" in Chapter 6. Tap AirPlay (⊚) in Music or another app, and then tap the speakers in the Speakers & TVs section of the AirPlay dialog.

Create a Music Playlist and Add Songs

Instead of playing individual songs or playing an album's songs from start to finish, you can create a playlist that contains only the songs you want in your preferred order. Playlists are a great way to enjoy music on your iPhone. Playlists you create on your iPhone appear on your other devices that share your iCloud account, and vice versa.

To help identify a playlist, you can add a new photo or an existing photo. Alternatively, you can let the Music app create a thumbnail from the covers of the songs you add to the playlist.

Create a Music Playlist and Add Songs

1 On the Home screen, tap **Music** (🎵).

The Music screen appears.

2 Tap **Library** (🎵 changes to 🎵).

The Library screen appears.

3 Tap **Playlists** (≡♪).

The Playlists screen appears.

4 Tap **New Playlist**.

The New Playlist screen opens.

5 Tap **Playlist Name** and type the name for the playlist.

6 Optionally, tap **Description** and type a description for the playlist.

7 Optionally, tap **Photo** (📷), tap **Take Photo** (📷) or **Choose Photo** (🖼️), and follow the prompts to add a photo.

8 Tap **Add Music** (➕).

The first Add Songs screen appears.

A You can search for music by tapping **Search** ($\mathbb{Q}$) and typing your search term.

9 Tap the button for the means by which you want to browse your library. This example uses **Songs**.

The appropriate screen appears, such as the Songs screen.

10 Tap each song you want to add ($\oplus$ changes to $\checkmark$).

11 Tap **Done**.

The New Playlist screen appears.

12 Rearrange the songs as needed by dragging each song up or down by its handle ($\equiv$).

B You can remove a song by tapping **Remove** ($\ominus$) and then tapping the textual Remove button that appears.

13 Tap **Done**.

The Playlists screen appears.

C You can tap the playlist to open it so that you can play it.

TIP

How can I add songs to an existing playlist?

Navigate to the song you want to add, and then tap and hold it. In the panel that opens, tap **Add to a Playlist** ($\boxdot$). The Add to a Playlist screen appears, showing your playlists. Tap the playlist to which you want to add the song. You can use the same technique to add a whole album to a playlist. Alternatively, you can tap **New Playlist** to start creating a new playlist.

Listen to Apple Music Radio

The Radio feature in the Music app enables you to listen to the Apple Music Radio service. Apple Music Radio has two main parts, one free and one paid. The free part comprises the Beats 1 global radio station and other live radio stations. The paid part is curated, on-demand radio stations and custom radio stations, which require a subscription to the Apple Music service. At the time of this writing, an individual subscription costs $9.99 per month; a family subscription, which covers up to six people, costs $14.99 per month.

Listen to Apple Music Radio

1 On the Home screen, tap **Music** (♫).

The Music app opens.

2 Tap **Radio** ((•)) changes to ((•))).

The Radio screen appears.

3 Swipe up to scroll down.

Other sections appear, including the More to Explore section.

4 Tap the genre you want to browse.

The list of stations in that genre appears.

Note: To share a station, tap and hold the station and then tap **Share Station** (⬆) on the panel that appears.

5 Tap the station you want to play.

A The current song on that station starts playing.

6 Tap **Now Playing**, the button that shows the current song's name.

The Now Playing screen appears.

 You can navigate by using the playback controls. For example, tap **Pause** (❚❚) to pause playback, or drag the playhead to move through the song.

 Tap **Lyrics** (💬 changes to 💬).

The Lyrics pane appears.

 The current line appears in white font.

8 Tap **Lyrics** (💬 changes to 💬).

Note: You may need to tap the screen to display the Lyrics button and the other playback controls.

The Lyrics panel closes.

9 Tap **List** (☰ changes to 目).

The List panel appears.

 The Playing Next list shows the upcoming track or tracks.

10 Tap **More** (⋯).

Note: You can also tap **More** (⋯) on the Now Playing panel.

The More panel opens.

 You can take various actions, such as tapping **Copy** (🗐) to copy the song details, tapping **SharePlay** (📺) to share playback, tapping **Share Song** (🖄) to share the song information, or tapping **Create Station** (•))) to create a station based on the song.

11 Tap outside the More panel.

The More panel closes.

TIP

What do the Share Station and Share Song commands do?

The Share Station command enables you to share a link to a station on Apple Music Radio. Similarly, the Share Song command lets you share a link to a song on the iTunes Store. You can use various means of sharing, such as sending the link via Mail or Messages, posting it to Facebook or Twitter, or simply setting yourself a reminder to listen to — or avoid — the music.

Read Digital Books with the Books App

The Books app enables you to read e-books or PDF files that you load on the iPhone from your computer or sync via iCloud by enabling Books on your Mac and your iPhone to use iCloud. You can also read e-books and PDFs you download from online stores, download from web pages, or save from e-mail messages.

If you have already loaded some e-books, you can read them as described in this section. If Books contains no books, tap **Store** and browse the Book Store or sync books from your computer using iTunes.

Read Digital Books with the Books App

1 On the Home screen, tap **Books** (📖).

Books opens, and the Reading Now screen appears.

Note: If the book you want to read appears on the Reading Now screen, tap the book to open it. Go to step **6**.

2 Tap **Library** (📚 changes to 📚).

The Library screen appears.

Ⓐ To change the collection of books displayed, you can tap **Collections** (≡) and then tap the appropriate collection, such as **Books** (📖) or **PDFs** (📄).

3 To view the books as a list, tap **List** (☰ changes to ☰) at the top of the screen.

Ⓑ You can tap **Search** (🔍) to locate the book you want.

The list of books appears.

Ⓒ You can tap **Sort** and then tap **Recent**, **Title**, **Author**, or **Manually** to sort the books differently.

4 Tap the book you want to open.

The book opens.

Note: When you open a book, Books displays your current page. When you open a book for the first time, Books displays the book's cover, first page, or default page.

5 To display the next page, tap the right side of the page.

Note: To display the previous page, tap the left side of the page.

The next page appears.

6 Tap **Controls** (≡).

The control panel appears.

D To change the font, tap **Themes & Settings** (ᴀA) and use the controls in the Themes & Settings dialog.

E To search in the book, tap **Search Book** (Q), and then type your search term.

F To set a bookmark on the current page, tap **Bookmark** (◻ changes to ◼). The bookmark icon appears on the Controls icon (≡°).

7 To jump to another part of the book, tap **Contents** (:≡).

The table of contents appears.

8 Tap the part of the book you want to display.

That part of the book appears.

G You can tap **Back** (◉) to return to the page you were reading previously. Similarly, you can tap **Go Forward** (◉) to go forward to the page from which you have gone back.

Note: To find free books on the Book Store, tap **Browse Sections** (≡), and then tap **Special Offers & Free** in the Book Store Sections list. Other sources of free e-books include ManyBooks.net (www.manybooks. net), Project Gutenberg (www.gutenberg.org), and the Baen Free Library (www.baen.com/library).

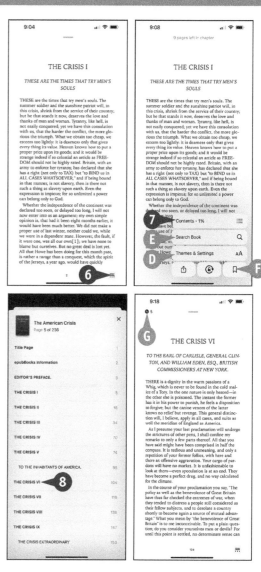

TIPS

How do I put my Mac's Books library on my iPhone manually?

Sync your books using Finder on macOS. After connecting your iPhone to your Mac and displaying the iPhone control screens, click **Books** and then work with the controls on that screen.

Can I use the Books app to read Kindle books?

No, the Books app cannot display Kindle books. To read Kindle books or listen to Audible audiobooks, install Amazon's free Kindle app from the App Store. Beware online converters that promise to convert Kindle files to EPUB files usable in Books or other e-book reader apps; these converters are unlikely to work and may attempt to install malware.

CHAPTER 11

Working with Photos and Video

Your iPhone's Camera app enables you to take high-quality still photos and videos. You can edit photos or apply filters to them, trim video clips down to length, and easily share both photos and videos.

Take Photos with the Camera App

Your iPhone includes one or more rear cameras and a front, or screen-side, camera. The rear cameras have more features than the front camera and on some iPhone models have higher resolution. Both cameras can take photos and videos; the front camera works for video calls, too.

To take photos using the camera, you use the Camera app. This app includes a digital zoom feature for zooming in and out; a flash that you can set to On, Off, or Auto; and a High Dynamic Range (HDR) feature that combines several photos into a single photo with adjusted color balance and intensity.

Take Photos with the Camera App

1 On the Home screen, tap **Camera** ().

Note: From the lock screen, you can open the Camera app by swiping left.

    The Camera app opens and displays whatever is in front of the lens.

2 Aim the iPhone so that your subject appears in the middle of the photo area. To focus on an item not in the center of the frame, tap that item to move the focus rectangle to it.

Note: If you need to take tightly composed photos, get a tripod mount for the iPhone. You can find various models on Amazon, eBay, and photography sites.

Ⓐ You can tap the zoom buttons to zoom to .5X, 1X, 2X, 2.5X, or 3X using different lenses, depending on the iPhone model.

Note: The iPhone SE third generation's rear camera has only a single lens.

3 If you need to zoom in, tap and hold any of the zoom buttons.

Ⓑ The zoom track appears.

4 Drag along the zoom track to zoom.

Note: You can also zoom in by placing two fingers together on the screen and pinching outward. To zoom out, pinch inward.

The Camera app displays the result of adjusting the zoom.

5 Tap **Take Photo** (○).

Note: You can drag **Take Photo** (○) left to take a burst of photos.

C The Camera app takes the photo and displays a thumbnail.

6 Tap the thumbnail.

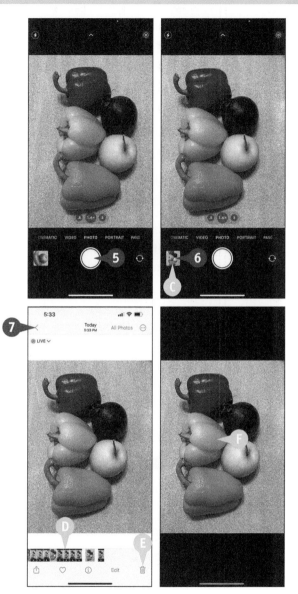

The photo appears.

Note: You can swipe left on the photo to display earlier photos and then swipe right to go forward again.

D You can tap a thumbnail to display another photo.

E You can tap **Delete** (🗑) to delete the current photo.

F After a few seconds, the controls disappear. Tap the screen to display them again.

7 Tap **Back** (‹) when you want to go back to the Camera app.

How do I switch to the front-facing camera?
Tap **Switch Cameras** (⟳) to switch from the rear-facing camera to the front-facing camera. The image that the front-facing camera is seeing appears on-screen, and you can take pictures as described in this section. HDR is available for the front-facing camera; flash is available only on some iPhone models. Tap **Switch Cameras** (⟳) again when you want to switch back to the rear-facing camera.

Using Night Mode and the Flash

To enable you to take high-quality photos in low-light conditions, all iPhone models includes flash modules that you can either control manually or let the Camera control automatically. The iPhone 14, iPhone 13, and iPhone 12 models also include a feature called Night Mode that activates automatically in low light. To gather enough light, Night Mode uses long exposure times — up to several seconds — so using a tripod or other support is advisable.

Night Mode is not available on the iPhone SE third generation. Some Night Mode features are available only on particular iPhone models.

Using Night Mode and the Flash

Using Night Mode

Note: To get good results, mount the iPhone on a tripod or other support when using Night Mode.

1 In the Camera app, aim the lens and compose the photograph, zooming if necessary. See the previous section, "Take Photos with the Camera App," for details.

Ⓐ If the light level is low, the Night Mode indicator illuminates, showing the exposure time in seconds (such as ● 3s).

2 Tap **Show Controls** (●).

The Controls bar appears above the Take Photo button.

3 Tap **Night Mode** (●).

Ⓑ The Night Mode controls appear above the Take Photo button.

Ⓒ The Night Mode label appears.

4 If you want to change the exposure, drag the **Exposure** slider left or right.

Note: You normally would change the exposure only after taking a photo using automatic exposure and finding it overexposed or underexposed.

Ⓓ The adjusted exposure time appears.

5 Tap **Take Photo** (○).

The Camera app takes the photo.

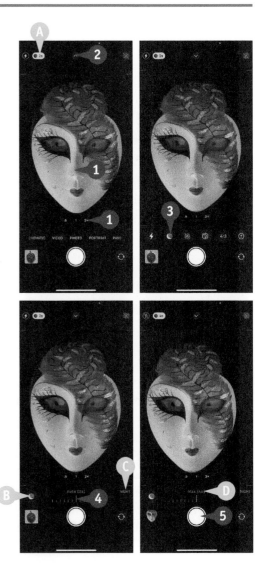

Using the Flash

1 In the Camera app, tap **Show Controls** (⬆).

The Controls bar appears above the Take Photo button.

2 Tap **Flash** (⚡, ⚡, or ⚡).

Note: The Flash icon in the upper-left corner of the screen shows the flash status: Flash Off (⚡), Flash On (⚡), or Flash Auto (⚡). Tap the current icon to change the setting. You may need to use the Controls bar to access all three settings.

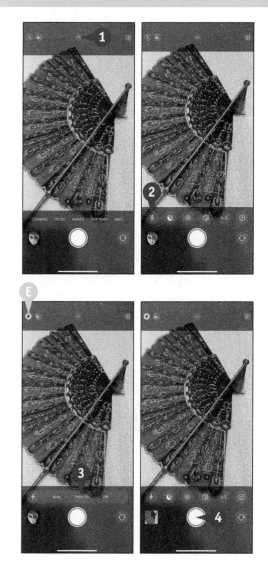

The Flash controls appear.

3 Tap the flash setting you want. In this example, you would tap **On**.

E The flash is now set to On.

4 Tap **Take Photo** (⬜).

The Camera app takes the photo.

Note: Depending on the lighting conditions and what the camera sensors are seeing, the Camera app may activate the flash if you have not set it to Off. If you want to use Night Mode instead of flash, turn the flash off.

TIPS

How should I choose between Night Mode and flash?
Use Night Mode when your subject is distant or static and you can set up your iPhone on a tripod or other support that will keep it still through a multisecond exposure. Use flash for all other low-light conditions or for fill-in lighting — for example, to illuminate the face of a backlit subject.

What other types of photos can I take using Night Mode?
On the iPhone 12, iPhone 13, and iPhone 14, you can use the front camera to take Night Mode selfies. With the rear cameras, you can capture time-lapse videos in Night Mode. On the iPhone 12, iPhone 13, and iPhone 14 Pro models, you can also use Portrait Mode in Night Mode.

Configure Camera Settings to Suit You

I f you will take many photos and videos, spend a few minutes optimizing the Camera app's settings for your specific needs. Your choices include capturing using the high-efficiency HEIF/HEVC format, setting the resolution and frame rates for video and slow-motion video, displaying the on-screen grid, and using the Smart HDR feature to improve exposure and color balance in your photos.

Configure Camera Settings to Suit You

1 On the Home screen, tap **Settings** (⚙).

The Settings screen appears.

2 Tap **Camera** (📷).

The Camera screen appears.

3 Tap **Formats**.

The Formats screen appears.

4 In the Camera Capture section, tap **High Efficiency** if you want to use the HEIF format for photos and the HEVC format for video. Otherwise, tap **Most Compatible**.

5 If the Photo Capture section appears, set the **Apple ProRAW** switch to On (⬤) to capture full-resolution photos in Apple's ProRAW format.

6 If the Video Capture section appears, set the **Apple ProRes** switch to On (⬤) to capture video in Apple's professional HDR ProRes format.

7 Tap **Camera** (‹).

The Camera screen appears again.

8 Set the **Record Stereo Sound** switch to On (⬤) if you want to record sound in stereo. This is usually helpful.

9 Set the **Use Volume Up for Burst** switch to On (⬤) if you want to be able to press **Volume Up** to take a burst of photos.

Note: The regular action for taking a burst of photos is to slide **Take Photo** (⭕) to the left.

10 Set the **Scan QR Codes** switch to On (⬤) if you will use the Camera app to scan QR codes.

11 Tap **Record Video**.

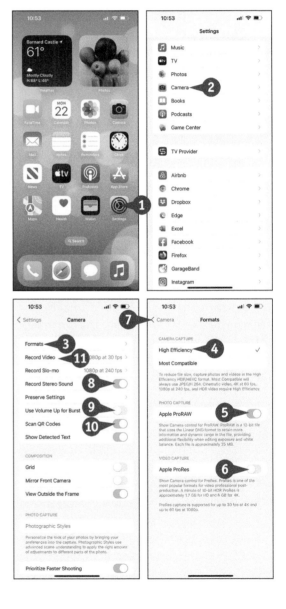

The Record Video screen appears.

12 Tap the video resolution and frame rate you want to use as the default.

A Look at the list to see approximately how much space the different resolutions and frame rates take up per minute of video. Fps stands for *frames per second*.

13 Set the **HDR Video** switch to On (⬤) if you want to enable HDR video.

B You can set the **Show PAL Formats** switch to On (⬤) to make the formats list show formats that use the Phase Alternating Line, PAL, standard widely used in Europe, Africa, Asia, and South America.

14 Tap **Auto FPS**.

The Auto FPS screen appears.

15 Tap **Off**, **Auto 30 fps**, or **Auto 30 & 60 fps** to specify the shooting speed in low light.

16 Tap **Record Video** (⟨).

The Record Video screen appears again.

17 Set the **Lock Camera** switch to On (⬤) if you want to prevent the iPhone from switching camera modules as you zoom while recording.

Note: If your iPhone has only one rear camera module, the Lock Camera switch does not appear.

18 Tap **Camera** (⟨).

The Camera screen appears again.

19 Tap **Record Slo-mo**.

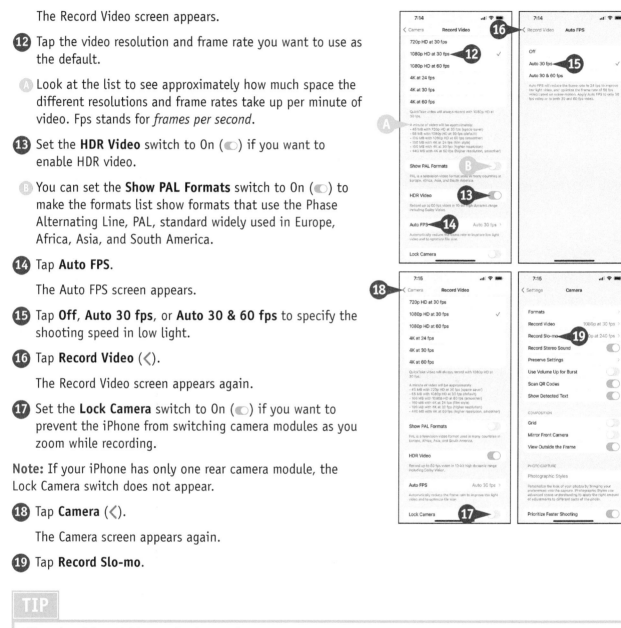

TIP

What do 720p, 1080p, and 4K mean?

720p, 1080p, and 4K are the resolutions. 720p resolution uses 1280×720-pixel resolution. 1080p resolution uses 1920×1080-pixel resolution. 4K uses 3840×2160-pixel resolution. The resolutions and frame rates available on the Record Video screen vary by iPhone model.

continued ▶

S et the switches on the Preserve Settings screen to control which settings persist from one Camera session to the next instead of reverting to the defaults at the start of each Camera session. Which switches are available here depends on your iPhone model. The Camera Mode switch enables you to keep the Camera app in the last mode you used, which may help you shoot photos more quickly. Similarly, the Creative Controls switch lets you preserve settings such as filters, aspect ratios, light settings, and depth settings, while the Exposure Adjustment switch lets you keep your exposure adjustments across sessions.

Configure Camera Settings to Suit You (continued)

The Record Slo-Mo screen appears.

20 Tap the resolution and frame rate at which you want to record slow-motion video.

21 Tap **Camera** (<).

The Camera screen appears again.

22 Tap **Preserve Settings**.

The Preserve Settings screen appears.

23 Set the **Camera Mode** switch to On (⬤) to preserve the camera mode setting instead of reverting to Photo Mode.

24 Set the **Creative Controls** switch to On (⬤) to preserve settings such as filters, aspect ratio, and light.

25 Set the **Exposure Adjustment** switch to On (⬤) to preserve the exposure adjustment and display the exposure adjustment indicator.

26 Set the **Night Mode** switch to On (⬤) to preserve exposure settings in Night Mode.

27 Set the **Portrait Zoom** switch to On (⬤) to preserve zoom settings in Portrait Mode.

28 Set the **Apple ProRAW** switch to On (⬤) to keep using the Apple ProRAW format rather than resetting to the default formats with each new Camera session.

29 Set the **Live Photo** switch to On (⬤) to preserve the Live Photo setting.

30 Tap **Camera** (<).

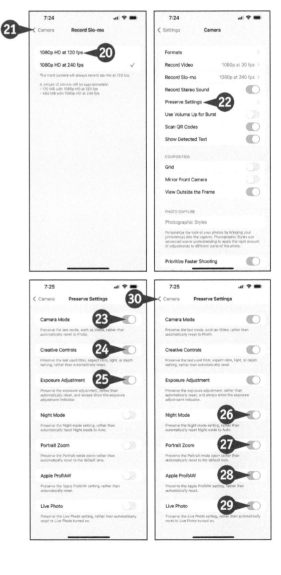

The Camera screen appears again.

31 In the Composition section, set the **Grid** switch to On (⬤) if you want to display the grid.

32 Set the **Mirror Front Camera** switch to On (⬤) if you want the front camera to display a mirror image instead of an image with left and right switched.

33 Set the **View Outside the Frame** switch to On (⬤) if you want the Camera app to capture any extra data available on its sensor but outside the frame as it is currently cropped.

34 Tap **Photographic Styles**.

The Photographic Styles screen appears.

35 Swipe left.

The next style appears.

You can swipe left again to display other styles.

36 When you find the style you want, tap the **Use** button, such as **Use "Rich Contrast"**.

The Camera screen appears again.

37 Set the **Prioritize Faster Shooting** switch to On (⬤) to allow the Camera app to reduce image quality to facilitate faster shooting.

38 Set the **Lens Correction** switch to On (⬤) to correct lens distortion on the front and ultrawide cameras.

39 Set the **Macro Control** switch to On (⬤) to display a control for switching to the ultra-wide lens to capture macro shots and clips.

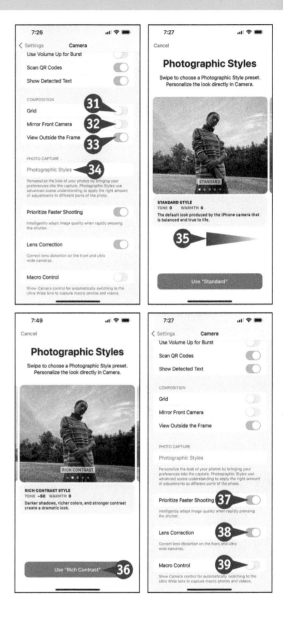

TIP

How is the View Outside the Frame feature helpful?
Capturing all the data available to the camera's sensor, including any data outside the frame as it is currently cropped, gives you more flexibility in editing the photo later. For example, you may be able to straighten the photo without losing any of your carefully composed frame. The downside is that the photo contains more data and so occupies more of your iPhone's storage.

The Camera app includes an on-screen grid to help you compose your photos. The grid has nine squares, which can assist you in composing your photos according to the Rule of Thirds or other compositional guidelines. You can also use the grid lines simply to help orient your iPhone accurately with horizontal and vertical lines on objects.

The Camera app also enables you to take photos in different aspect ratios, such as square photos, and capture panoramas. Panoramas can be especially effective for capturing landscapes.

Shoot with the Grid and Different Aspect Ratios

Note: If you have not already displayed the grid, tap **Settings** (⚙) to display the Settings screen, tap **Camera** (📷) to display the Camera screen, and then set the **Grid** switch to On (⬤) in the Composition section.

　On the Home screen, tap **Camera** (📷).

The Camera app opens and displays what the lens is currently viewing.

Ⓐ The grid lines appear.

② Use the grid lines to align the lens with horizontal or vertical lines on your subject or to position key features or objects at the intersections of gridlines.

③ Tap **Take Photo** (◯).

The Camera app takes the photo.

Ⓑ You can tap the thumbnail to open the photo.

Shoot with Different Aspect Ratios

1 In the Camera app, tap **Show Controls** (⊙).

The Controls bar appears above the Take Photo button.

2 Tap **Aspect Ratio** (⊙).

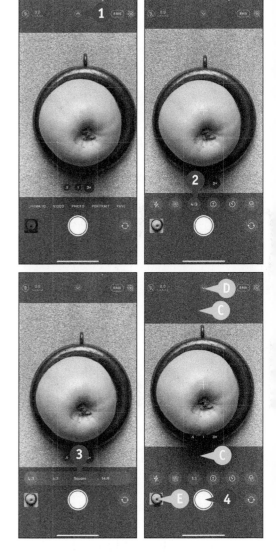

The Aspect Ratio controls appear.

3 Tap the aspect ratio you want, such as **Square** or **16:9**. This example uses **Square**.

Ⓒ The Camera app crops the preview to the aspect ratio you chose.

Ⓓ You can tap **Hide Controls** (⊙) if you want to hide the Controls bar.

4 Tap **Take Photo** (◯).

The Camera app takes the photo.

Ⓔ You can tap the thumbnail to open the photo.

TIP

How do I take panorama photos?

Tap **Pano** on the Modes bar. Holding the iPhone in portrait orientation, aim at the left end of the panorama. Tap **Take Photo** (◯); gradually move the iPhone to the right, keeping the white arrow on the horizontal line; and then tap **Stop** (◼).

The Camera app often does a great job of capturing panoramas, but sometimes the results are disappointing. If you take a poor panorama photo, try again, keeping the iPhone as steady as possible. A monopod can be helpful for panoramas, as you can plant its foot and gradually rotate it and the iPhone — and yourself, unless you want the panorama to include a selfie.

Take Live Photos and Timed Photos

The Camera app's Live Photo feature enables you to capture several seconds of video around a still photo. Live Photo is great for photographing moving subjects or setting the scene.

The self-timer feature lets you set the app to take a photo after a delay of three seconds or ten seconds, which is good for group shots and for avoiding camera shake.

Take Live Photos and Timed Photos

Open the Camera App, Take a Live Photo, and View It

1 On the Home screen, tap **Camera** (📷).

The Camera app opens.

2 Tap **Live** (◉ changes to ◉).

Note: Live Photo starts recording video as soon as you enable the feature. Live Photo discards the video except for the segments before and after photos you shoot.

Ⓐ The Live badge appears briefly.

3 Tap **Take Photo** (◯).

The Camera app captures the Live Photo.

4 Tap the photo's thumbnail.

The photo opens.

The Live Photo segment plays.

5 Tap and hold the photo to play the Live Photo segment again.

6 Tap **Back** (‹).

The Camera app appears again.

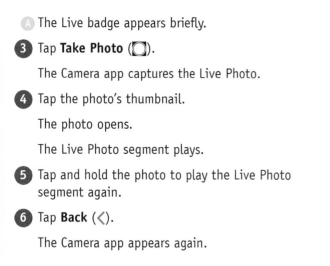

Take a Timed Photo

 Tap **Show Controls** (⌃).

The control bar appears.

2 Tap **Timer** (⏲).

The Timer settings appear.

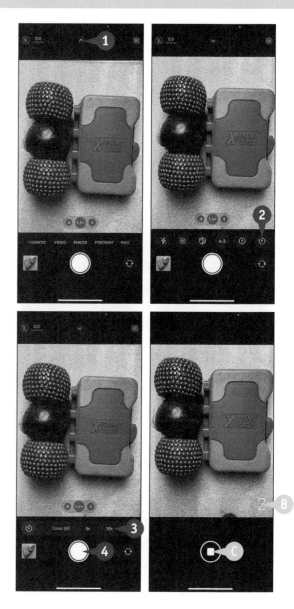

3 Tap **3s** or **10s** to set the delay.

The delay appears at the top of the screen.

4 Tap **Take Photo** (◯).

Ⓑ The Camera app displays an on-screen countdown of seconds.

Ⓒ You can tap **Stop** (◯) to stop the countdown.

Note: The rear flash flashes to indicate the countdown to the subject.

When the countdown ends, the Camera app takes a photo.

Note: The timer remains set until you change it.

TIP

How do I take time-lapse movies?

Tap **Time-Lapse** on the Modes bar; if you cannot see Time-Lapse, drag the current setting to the right first. Set the iPhone up on a tripod or other steady holder, aim it at the subject, and then tap **Start** (■). When you have captured enough, tap **Stop** (■) to stop shooting.

Using Portrait Mode

The Camera app includes Portrait Mode, a mode optimized for taking portraits. After switching to Portrait Mode, you can apply special lighting presets to make the subject look the way you want. You can also edit or remove the Portrait Mode effect after taking a photo.

You can use Portrait Mode either with the main camera on the back of the iPhone or with the front-facing "selfie" camera.

Using Portrait Mode

1 On the Home screen, tap **Camera** (📷).

The Camera app opens.

2 Tap **Portrait**.

The Camera app switches to Portrait Mode.

A On some iPhone models, the Camera app switches to its 2X, 2.5X, or 3X lens, making the subject appear larger. The telephoto lens also gives better focus separation.

B The readout shows the current lighting effect.

3 Tap and hold **Lighting Effect**. The icon displayed varies depending on which effect is currently selected.

The Lighting Effect wheel appears.

4 Rotate the Lighting Effect wheel clockwise or counterclockwise.

Note: You can also tap **Lighting Effect** to display the wheel and then tap an icon on it.

C The next lighting effect appears.

D The preview shows the lighting effect applied.

5 Release the Lighting Effect wheel when you find the effect you want.

6 Tap **Take Photo** (⚪).

7 Tap the photo thumbnail.

268

The photo opens.

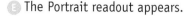 The Portrait readout appears.

8 Tap **Edit**.

The photo opens for editing.

9 Tap **Lighting Effect**. As before, the icon varies, depicting the selected lighting effect.

The Lighting Effect Wheel appears.

10 Rotate the Lighting Effect wheel to change the effect.

11 To adjust the intensity of the effect, scroll the bar left or right.

12 Tap **Done**.

The photo closes.

How do I blur the background in a photo?

Tap **Portrait** to switch the Camera app to Portrait Mode. Tap **Aperture** (f changes to f) in the upper-right corner of the screen to display the Aperture controls, and then drag the slider left or right to adjust the effective aperture to control the amount of background separation from the subject. This simulates a "bokeh" effect, blurring the background to make the subject stand out from it.

Apply Filters to Your Photos

You can use the Filter feature in the Camera app to change the look of a photo by applying a filter such as Vivid, Dramatic Warm, Mono, Silvertone, or Noir.

You can apply a filter either before taking the photo or after taking it. If you apply the filter before taking the photo, you can remove the filter afterward; the filter is an effect applied to the photo, not an integral part of the photo.

Apply Filters to Your Photos

1 On the Home screen, tap **Camera** (📷).

The Camera app opens.

2 Compose your shot, and then tap **Show Controls** (⌃).

The Controls bar appears.

3 Tap **Filters** (◗).

Note: You may need to scroll the Controls bar left to display the Filters icon.

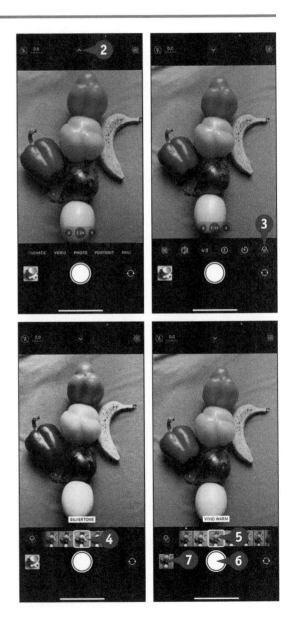

The Filters bar appears.

4 Tap the filter you want to preview.

The Camera app applies the filter to the display.

5 Tap the filter you want to apply.

The Camera app applies the filter.

6 Tap **Take Photo** (◯).

The Camera app takes the photo.

7 Tap the photo's thumbnail.

The photo appears.

8 Tap **Edit**.

The Adjust screen appears, showing the editing tools.

9 Tap **Filters** (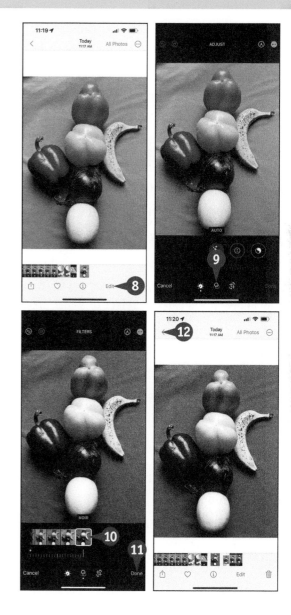).

The Filters screen appears.

10 Tap the filter you want to apply.

Note: Tap **Original** if you want to remove filtering.

The Camera app applies the filter to the photo.

11 Tap **Done**.

iOS saves the change to the photo.

12 Tap **Back** (<) to return to the Camera app.

Is it better to apply a filter before taking a photo or after taking it?
This is up to you. Sometimes it is helpful to have the filter effect in place when composing a photo so that you can arrange the composition and lighting to complement the filtering. Other times, especially when you do not have time to experiment with filters, it is more practical to take the photos and then try applying filters afterward.

To improve your photos, you can use the powerful but easy-to-use editing tools your iPhone includes. These tools include rotating a photo to a different orientation, straightening it by rotating it a little, and cropping off the parts you do not need.

You can access the editing tools either through the Recently Added album in the Photos app or through the Photos app. To start editing a photo, you open the photo by tapping it and then tapping **Edit**.

Edit Your Photos

Open a Photo for Editing

1 On the Home screen, tap **Photos** (✳).

The Photos app opens.

2 Navigate to the photo you want to edit.

Ⓐ If the photo is part of a burst, the Burst readout appears. You can tap **Select** to select another photo from the burst instead of the default photo.

3 Tap **Edit**.

The Adjust screen appears.

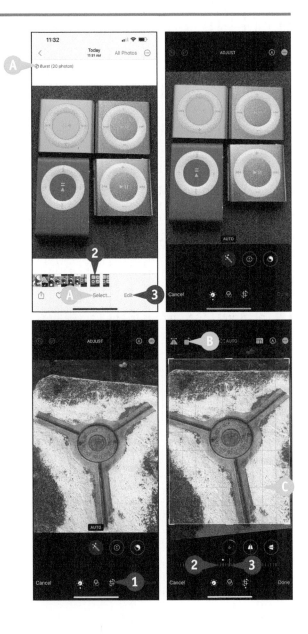

Crop, Rotate, and Straighten a Photo

1 Tap **Crop** (🗗).

The tools for cropping, straightening, and rotating appear.

Ⓑ You can tap **Rotate** (◻) to rotate the photo 90 degrees clockwise.

2 Tap and hold the degree bar.

Ⓒ The fine grid appears, providing horizontal and vertical lines for reference as you straighten the photo.

3 Drag the degree bar left or right to straighten the photo.

④ Tap and hold an edge or corner of the crop box.

Ⓓ The nine-square grid appears. This is to help you compose the cropped photo.

⑤ Drag the edge or corner of the crop box to select only the area you want to keep.

Note: After adjusting the crop box to the size needed, you can drag the photo to change the part that will be cropped.

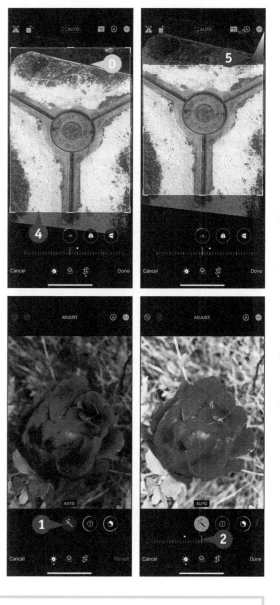

Enhance the Colors in a Photo

① Tap **Auto-Enhance** (changes to 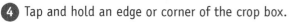).

iOS calculates a suitable enhancement and applies it.

Note: Tap **Auto-Enhance** again (changes to) if you want to remove the enhancement.

② Optionally, drag the slider left or right to adjust the degree of enhancement.

TIP

What does the three-rectangles button on the cropping screen do?
The button with three rectangles (▥) is the Aspect button. Tap **Aspect** (▥) when you need to crop to a specific aspect ratio, such as a square or the 16:9 widescreen aspect ratio. On the Aspect bar that appears, tap the constraint you want to use. iOS adjusts the current cropping to match the aspect ratio. You may then need to move the portion of the photo shown to get the composition you want. If you adjust the cropping, tap **Aspect** (▥) again and reapply the aspect ratio.

continued ▶

The Red-Eye Reduction feature enables you to restore unwanted red eyes to normality. The Enhance feature enables you to adjust a photo's color balance and lighting quickly using default algorithms that analyze the photo and try to improve it. The Enhance feature often works well, but for greater control, you can use the Light settings and the Color settings to tweak the exposure, highlights, shadows, brightness, black point, contrast, vibrancy, and other settings manually.

Edit Your Photos (continued)

Remove Red Eye from a Photo

Note: You may need to zoom in on the photo to touch the red-eye patches accurately.

1 Tap **Red-Eye Reduction** (◌ changes to ◌).

   iOS prompts you to tap each eye.

2 Tap each red eye.

   iOS removes the red eye.

3 Tap **Red-Eye Reduction** (◌ changes to ◌).

   iOS turns off the Red-Eye Reduction tool.

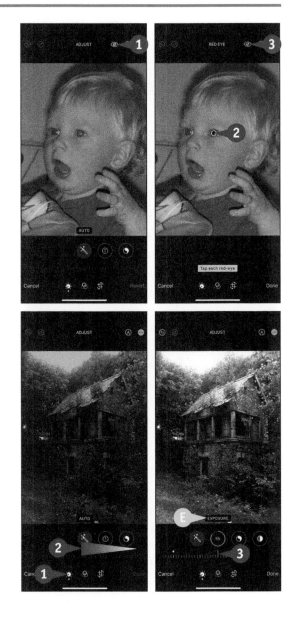

Fine-Tune a Photo

1 Tap **Adjust** (▣).

   The Adjust controls appear.

Note: You may want to try tapping **Auto-Enhance** and then adjusting the automatic enhancements manually. This section demonstrates making the changes from scratch.

2 Swipe left on the Adjust controls to bring the control you want to adjust to the middle of the screen, at which point it becomes active.

Ⓔ The name of the active control appears, such as **Exposure**.

3 Drag the slider left or right to adjust the intensity of the active effect. For example, if the photo is too dark, you might increase the exposure to lighten it, as in this example.

4 Scroll the Adjust controls farther left to display more controls.

5 Tap the active control to enable or disable its effect.

Note: Photos remembers the setting for a disabled effect, so when you reenable an effect, it has the same value as before you disabled it.

ⓕ The white dot indicates the zero point, at which the effect is disabled.

Note: A partial white ring () indicates a negative value for the setting; a partial yellow ring (🔅) indicates a positive value; a gray ring indicates the effect has a zero value or is disabled.

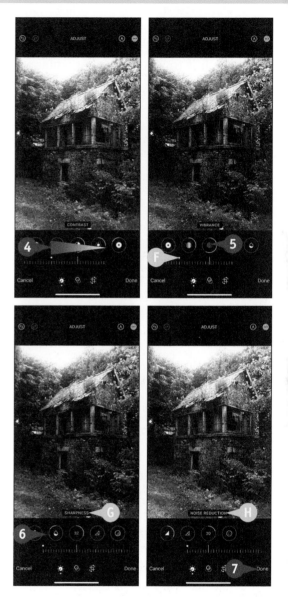

6 Adjust other settings as needed to make the photo look the way you want.

ⓖ You can tap **Sharpness** (◨) to adjust the level of manufactured additional detail in the photo. This will not fix a blurry image but will accentuate existing detail.

ⓗ You can tap **Noise Reduction** (◉) to reduce "noise," artifacts caused by taking photos in inadequate lighting. Reducing noise may also remove detail you want to keep.

7 Tap **Done**.

Photos displays the photo with the edits you have applied.

Photos preserves the original photo, and you can revert to it if you want.

How do I get rid of changes I have made to a photo?
Tap **Cancel** in the lower-left corner of the Adjust screen, and then tap **Discard Changes** in the confirmation dialog that opens.

Capture a Video Clip and Trim It

As well as capturing still photos, the Camera app can capture high-quality, full-motion video in either portrait orientation or landscape orientation. You launch the Camera app as usual and then switch it to Video Mode for regular-speed shooting or to Slo-Mo Mode to shoot slow-motion footage. You can use flash, but it is effective only at close range for video. After taking the video, you can edit the clip by trimming off any unwanted frames at the beginning and end.

Capture a Video Clip and Trim It

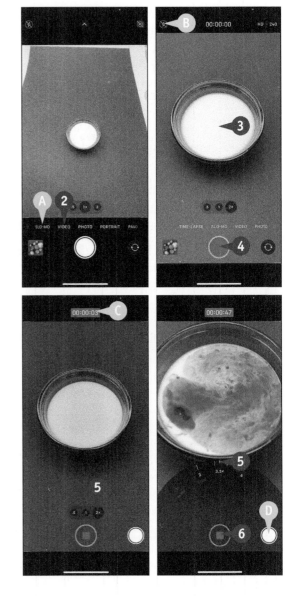

① On the Home screen, tap **Camera** (📷).

The Camera screen appears, showing the image the lens is seeing.

Note: You can start shooting video quickly by tapping and holding **Take Photo** (◯). When you have time, it is better to tap **Video** to switch to the video view first, because the video camera has a different field of view than the still camera, and you may need to recompose the shot.

② Tap **Video**.

Ⓐ Tap **Slo-Mo** if you want to shoot slow-motion footage. This example uses **Slo-Mo**.

The video image and video controls appear.

③ Aim the camera at your subject.

Ⓑ If you need to use the flash for the video, tap **Flash** (⚡, ⚡, or 🚫), and then tap **Auto** or **On**.

Note: To focus on a particular area of the screen, tap that area.

④ Tap **Record** (◉).

Ⓒ The camera starts recording, and the time readout shows the time that has elapsed.

⑤ To zoom in, tap and hold the Zoom readout and then drag along the zoom track.

Note: You can also zoom by placing your thumb and forefinger on the screen and pinching apart or pinching together.

Ⓓ To take a still photo while shooting video, tap **Take Photo** (◯).

⑥ To finish recording, tap **Stop** (◉).

The Camera app stops recording and displays a thumbnail of the video's first frame.

 7 Tap the thumbnail.

The video appears and starts playing automatically.

Note: Tap anywhere on the screen to display the video controls. These disappear automatically after a few seconds of not being used.

 8 To trim the video clip, tap **Edit**.

The controls for editing the video appear.

 9 Tap the left trim handle and drag it to the right until the frame appears where you want the trimmed clip to start.

10 Tap the right handle and drag it to the left until the frame appears where you want the trimmed clip to end.

11 Tap **Done**.

The Trim panel appears.

12 Tap **Save Video as New Clip** (📹).

Ⓔ You can tap **Save Video** (📹) if you prefer to overwrite the existing video.

Note: Tap **Play** (▶) if you want to play back the trimmed video.

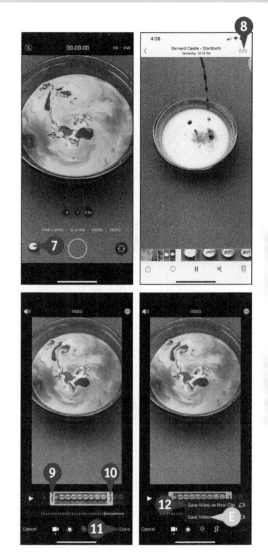

TIPS

How can I pause shooting a video?
As of this writing, you cannot pause while shooting in the Camera app. Either shoot separate video clips or trim out unwanted footage afterward.
Alternatively, you can use a third-party camera app that offers this capability.

What does the bar of miniature pictures at the bottom of the video playback screen do?
The navigation bar gives you a quick way of moving forward and backward through the video. Tap the thumbnails and drag them left or right until the part of the video you want to view is at the vertical blue playhead bar. You can use the navigation bar either when the video is playing or when it is paused.

Browse Photos Using Years, Months, and Days

You can use the Photos app to browse the photos you have taken with your iPhone's camera, photos you have synced using iTunes or via iCloud's Shared Albums feature, and images you save from e-mail messages, instant messages, or web pages.

You can browse your photos by dates and locations using the smart groupings that Photos creates. Each Year grouping contains Months, which contain Days, which contain your photos. Alternatively, you can browse by albums, as explained in the section "Browse Photos Using Albums," later in this chapter.

Browse Photos Using Years, Months, and Days

1 On the Home screen, tap **Photos** (✳).

The Photos app opens.

2 Tap **Library** (▣ changes to ▣).

The Photos screen appears, showing the Years list.

A photo represents each year.

3 Tap the year you want to open.

The Months screen for the year appears.

A photo represents each month.

4 Tap the month you want to open.

Note: Scroll up or down as needed to see other months.

The Days screen for the month appears.

5 Tap the photo you want to view.

The photo opens.

 You can tap **Edit** to edit the photo, as explained earlier in this chapter.

Ⓑ You can tap **Share** (⬆) to share the photo, as explained later in this chapter.

Ⓒ You can tap **Favorite** (♡ changes to ❤ or ❤ changes to ♡) to make the photo a favorite or demote it from being a favorite.

Ⓓ You can tap **Trash** (🗑) to delete the photo.

Note: The Trash icon does not appear for photos you cannot delete, such as photos in a shared photo stream.

❻ In the thumbnail bar, tap the photo you want to view.

Note: You can also swipe left or right to display other photos.

The photo appears.

❼ Tap **Back** (<).

The Days screen appears.

Note: You can scroll up or down to display other days.

❽ Tap **Months**.

The Months screen appears.

Note: You can scroll up or down to display other months.

❾ Tap **Years**.

The Years screen appears, and you can navigate to another year.

TIP

How can I move a photo to a different year?
To move a photo to a different year, you need to change the date set in the photo's metadata. You cannot do this with the Photos app, but you can change the date with a third-party app such as Pixelgarde, which is free from the App Store as of this writing. Alternatively, if you sync the photos from your computer, you can change the date in the photo on your computer. For example, in Photos on the Mac, select the photo, click **Image** on the menu bar, and then click **Adjust Date and Time**.

Browse Photos Using Memories

The Memories feature in the Photos app presents a movie of photos from a particular period of time, such as a given year or a trip to a certain geographical location.

You can customize the settings for a memory. You can either customize them quickly by choosing roughly how long a memory should be and what atmosphere it should have or take complete control and specify exactly which items to include and which music to play.

Browse Photos Using Memories

1 On the Home screen, tap **Photos** (✳).

The Photos app opens.

2 Tap **For You** (📇 changes to 📇).

The For You screen appears.

A You can tap **See All** to display the Memories screen, which contains the full list of memories.

3 Swipe left to display other memories.

4 Tap the memory you want to view.

The memory starts playing.

B You can tap **Pause** (⏸) to pause playback.

C You can tap **Choose Music** (🎵) to change the default music for the memory.

D You can tap **Choose Photos** (🎞) to display a screen for choosing which photos to include in the memory.

E You can tap **More** (⊙) to open the menu, from which you can take other actions, such as editing the title of the memory and making the current photo the key photo, the photo that Photos displays as the cover of the memory.

Browse Photos Using the Map

The Camera app automatically stores location information — the longitude, the latitude, and the direction the camera was facing — in each photo and video you take, enabling the Photos app to sort your photos and videos by their locations. Starting from any photo, you can display other nearby photos, identifying them by their locations on the map. You can then browse the photos taken in a particular location.

Browse Photos Using the Map

 1 In the Photos app, navigate to the photo from which you want to start browsing.

2 Swipe up.

The Places section for the photo appears.

A The map in the Places section shows the area in which the photo was taken.

3 Tap the location.

The Map screen appears, showing the location.

4 Tap **Show Nearby Photos**.

Note: Zoom in or out on the map as needed by placing your thumb and finger on the screen and moving them apart or pinching them together.

B You can tap **Grid** to display the places as a list.

5 Tap the place you want to view.

The photos in the place appear, and you can tap a photo to display it full screen.

Your iPhone's Photos app includes a feature called Shared Albums that enables you to share photos easily with others via iCloud and enjoy the photos they are sharing. You can add other people's shared albums to the Photos app on your iPhone by accepting invitations. You can then browse the photos those people are sharing.

The section "Share Your Shared Albums," later in this chapter, shows you how to share your own photos via Shared Albums.

Browse Photos Using Shared Albums

Accept an Invitation to a Shared Album

1 When you receive an invitation to subscribe to shared photos, open the e-mail message in Mail.

2 Tap **Subscribe**.

The Photos app becomes active.

Note: If the Turn On Shared Albums dialog opens after you tap **Subscribe**, tap **Settings**. The Photos screen in the Settings app then appears. In the Albums section, set the **Shared Albums** switch to On (⬤).

The For YOu screen appears.

3 Tap the notice that announces you joined the shared album.

The album opens.

Ⓐ You can tap **People** (👥) to view the list of people with whom the album is shared.

4 Tap the thumbnail for the photo you want to view.

The photo opens.

Ⓑ You can tap **Share** (🖳) to share the photo with others.

Ⓒ You can tap **Add a comment** if you want to add a comment on the photo.

Ⓓ You can tap **Like** (👍) to like the photo.

Note: Swipe left or right to display other photos.

5 Tap **Back** (‹).

The album's screen appears again.

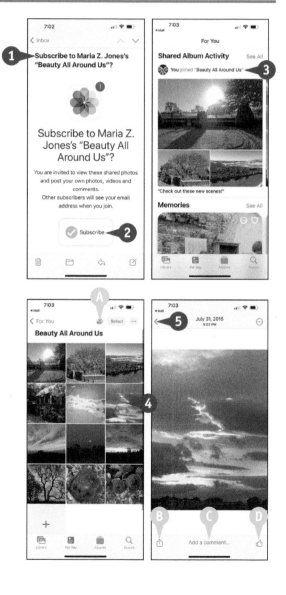

Browse the Latest Activity on Shared Albums

1 In the Photos app, tap **For You** (📇 changes to 📇).

The For You screen appears.

2 In the Shared Album Activity section, tap **See All**.

Note: The Activity item shows new activity on your shared albums. When you add a shared album, the Activity thumbnail shows the new album's thumbnail.

The Activity screen appears.

3 Swipe up to scroll down.

Other items appear.

4 Tap a photo.

The photo opens.

5 Tap **Activity** (<).

The Activity screen appears.

6 When you finish browsing the latest activity, tap **For You** (<).

The For You screen appears.

Note: To remove a shared album, first open the Photos app. Tap **Albums** (📷 changes to 📷) to display the Albums screen, and then navigate to the shared album. Tap **People** to display the People screen, and then tap **Unsubscribe**. In the confirmation dialog that opens, tap **Unsubscribe** again.

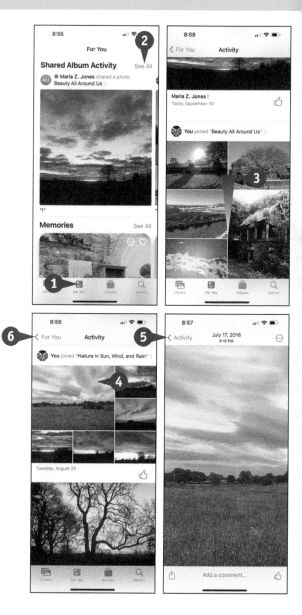

How else can I share my photos?

You can create an iCloud Shared Photo Library. This is a feature Apple has announced but not delivered as of this writing. To set up an iCloud Shared Photo Library, either follow the prompts when you first launch Photos after upgrading to a version that contains the new feature; or tap **Settings** (⚙️) on the Home screen, tap **Photos** (❀), go to the Library section, and tap the button for starting to create an iCloud Shared Photo Library.

Browse Photos Using Albums

A long with browsing by collections and browsing shared albums, you can browse your photos by albums. The Camera app automatically stores each conventional photo you take in the All Photos album, each burst photo in an album called Bursts, and each video in an album called Videos. You can also create other albums manually from your photos or sync existing albums from your computer.

Browse Photos Using Albums

Open the Photos App and Browse an Album

1 On the Home screen, tap **Photos** (✻).

The Photos app opens.

2 Tap **Albums** (▤ changes to ▤).

The Albums screen appears.

3 Tap the album you want to browse. This example uses The Fall of Summer album.

Note: The All Photos album contains all the photos you take; photos you save from web pages, e-mail messages, instant messages, and social media apps; and photos you edit from other people's streams.

The album opens.

Note: The People album contains faces identified in photos. You can browse the photos in which a particular person appears.

4 Tap the photo you want to view.

The photo opens.

Note: Swipe left to display the next photo or right to display the previous photo.

5 Tap **Back** (‹).

The album appears.

6 Tap **Albums** (‹).

The Albums screen appears.

Create an Album

1 In the Photos app, tap **Albums** (changes to).

The Albums screen appears.

2 Tap **New** (+).

A pop-up panel opens, giving you the choice between creating a regular album and a shared album. You can also create a folder.

3 Tap **New Album** (📷) or **New Shared Album** (📷), as appropriate. This example uses New Album (📷).

The New Album dialog opens.

4 Type the name to give the album.

5 Tap **Save**.

The screen for adding photos appears.

6 Tap the source of the photos. For example, tap **Albums**, and then tap the album.

7 Tap each photo to add to the collection, placing ✓ on each.

8 Tap **Add**.

A The album appears on the Albums screen.

TIPS

How can I move through a long list of photos more quickly?
You can move through the photos more quickly by using momentum scrolling. Tap and flick up with your finger to set the photos scrolling. As the momentum drops, you can tap and flick up again to scroll further. Tap and drag your finger in the opposite direction to stop the scrolling.

How can I recover photos I deleted by mistake?
Tap **Albums**, scroll down to the Utilities area, and then tap **Recently Deleted**. In the Recently Deleted album, tap **Select**, tap the photos, and then tap **Recover**.

Share Your Shared Albums

Photos enables you to create shared photo albums, invite people to subscribe to them, and add photos.

You can also control whether subscribers can post photos and videos to your shared photo album, decide whether to make the album publicly available, and choose whether to receive notifications when subscribers comment on your photos or post their own.

Share Your Shared Albums

1 On the Home screen, tap **Photos** (🌸).

The Photos app opens.

2 Tap **Albums** (▦ changes to ▦).

The Shared screen appears.

3 Tap **New** (+).

A pop-up panel appears.

4 Tap **New Shared Album** (🗂).

The iCloud dialog opens.

5 Type the name for the album.

6 Tap **Next**.

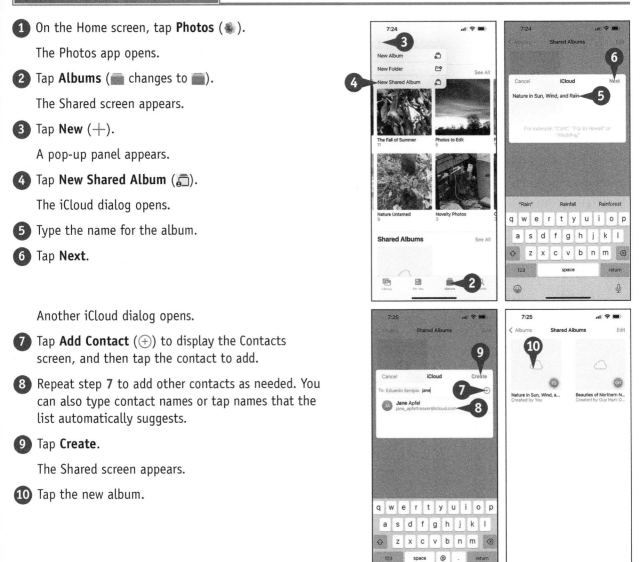

Another iCloud dialog opens.

7 Tap **Add Contact** (⊕) to display the Contacts screen, and then tap the contact to add.

8 Repeat step **7** to add other contacts as needed. You can also type contact names or tap names that the list automatically suggests.

9 Tap **Create**.

The Shared screen appears.

10 Tap the new album.

The album's screen appears.

11 Tap **Add** (+).

The Photos screen appears, with the selection controls displayed.

12 Navigate to another album if necessary. For example, tap **Albums**, and then tap the album.

13 Tap each photo you want to add.

14 Tap **Add**.

Another iCloud dialog opens.

15 Type the text you want to post with the photos.

16 Tap **Post**.

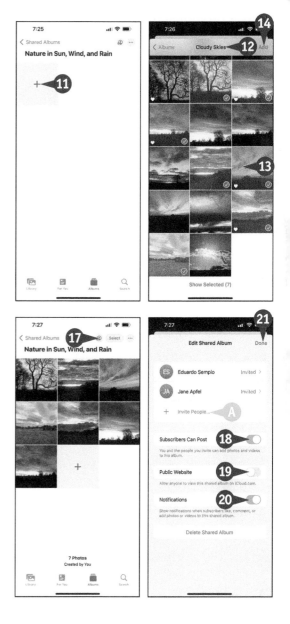

The album's screen appears.

17 Tap **People** (👥).

The Edit Shared Album screen appears.

Ⓐ To invite others to the album, tap **Invite People** (+).

18 Set the **Subscribers Can Post** switch to On (⚪) or Off (⚪), as needed.

19 Set the **Public Website** switch to On (⚪) or Off (⚪) to control whether to make the album publicly accessible on the iCloud.com website.

20 Set the **Notifications** switch to On (⚪) or Off (⚪), as needed.

21 Tap **Done**.

If I make a photo album public, how do people find the website?
When you set the **Public Website** switch on the People screen for a photo album to On (⚪), a Share Link button appears. Tap **Share Link** to display the Share sheet, and then tap the means of sharing you want to use — for example, Messages, Mail, Twitter, or Facebook.

After taking photos and videos with your iPhone's camera or after loading photos and videos on the iPhone using iTunes, you can share them with other people.

This section explains how to tweet photos to your Twitter account, assign photos to contacts, use photos as wallpaper, and print photos. Chapter 6 explains how to share items via the AirDrop feature.

Share and Use Your Photos and Videos

Select the Photo or Video to Share

1. On the Home screen, tap **Photos** ( ).

2. On the Photos screen, tap the item that contains the photo or video you want to share. For example, tap **Albums** (changes to), and then tap **Favorites**.

3. Tap the photo or video you want to share.

4. Tap **Share** ( ) to display the Share sheet.

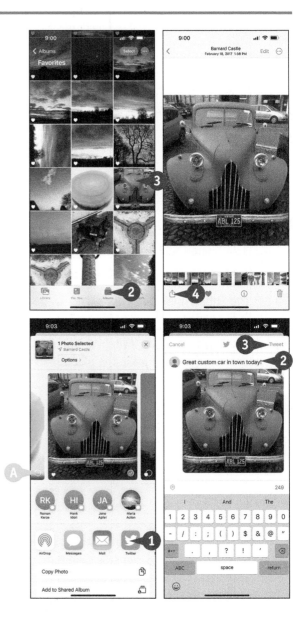

Share a Photo on Twitter

A. You can tap the selection button (changes to) to include another item in the sharing.

1. On the Share sheet, tap **Twitter** ( ).

   The Twitter dialog opens.

2. Type the text of the tweet.

3. Tap **Tweet**.

   Your iPhone posts the tweet to Twitter.

Assign a Photo to a Contact

1 On the Share sheet, scroll down and tap **Assign to Contact** (👤).

The list of contacts appears.

2 Tap the contact to which you want to assign the photo.

The screen for moving and scaling the photo appears.

3 If necessary, move the photo so that the relevant part appears centrally.

4 If necessary, pinch in to shrink the photo or pinch out to enlarge it.

5 Tap **Choose**.

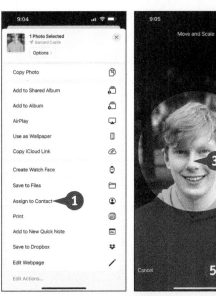

Set a Photo as Wallpaper

1 On the Share sheet, tap **Use as Wallpaper** (📱).

The screen for moving and scaling the photo appears.

2 Move the photo to display the part you want.

3 If necessary, pinch in to shrink the photo or pinch out to enlarge it.

Ⓑ You can swipe left to change the filter applied to the photo.

4 Tap **Done**.

The Set Wallpaper dialog appears.

5 Tap **Set as Wallpaper Pair**.

How do I print a photo?

Display the photo you want to print, and then tap **Share** (⬆️) to display the Share sheet. Tap **Print** (🖨️) to display the Printer Options screen. If the Printer readout does not show the correct printer, tap **Select Printer**, and then tap the printer. Back on the Printer Options screen, tap **Print** to print the photo.

CHAPTER 12

Advanced Features and Troubleshooting

This chapter shows you how to keep your iPhone's software up to date, how to back up and restore your iPhone, how to reset its settings, and how to use Lockdown Mode. You also learn to troubleshoot Wi-Fi connections, locate your iPhone when it goes missing, manage your Apple ID, and take screenshots or screen recordings.

Capture Screenshots or Screen Recordings

iOS enables you to capture screenshots and screen recordings. A screenshot is a still image that shows whatever appears on the screen and is great for capturing and sharing information easily. A screen recording is a video of what happens on-screen and is useful for demonstrating how to take particular actions.

The screenshot functionality uses a keypress and is enabled by default. The screen recording functionality uses a button that does not appear in Control Center by default but that you can quickly add.

Take a Screenshot

To take a screenshot of what is currently displayed on the screen, press **Side** and **Volume Up** at the same time. A thumbnail of the screen capture (A) appears in the lower-left corner of the screen for a few seconds and then disappears.

If you want to mark up the screenshot immediately or share it, tap this thumbnail to open the screenshot for editing. To mark up the screenshot, use the icons (B) at the bottom of the screen. At the top of the screen, tap **Undo** (C, 🔄) to undo your last action, tap **Redo** (D, 🔄) to redo the last action you undid, tap **Delete** (E, 🗑️) to delete the screenshot, or tap **Share** (F, ⬆️) to share it.

Add the Screen Recording Control to Control Center

First, add the Screen Recording control to Control Center so that you can access it. This control is not in Control Center by default, but you may have added it already.

On the Home screen, tap **Settings** (⚙️) to display the Settings screen. Tap **Control Center** (G, 🎛️) to display the Control Center screen, and then look to see if Screen Recording (◉) appears in the Included Controls section at the top of the screen.

If it does not, go to the More Controls section, and then tap **Add** (H, ➕) to the left of Screen Recording (I, ◉) to move it to the Included Controls list.

Start a Screen Recording

Swipe down from the upper-right corner of the screen to display Control Center. Tap **Screen Recording** (J, ⊙). A three-second countdown timer starts. Swipe up from the bottom of the screen to close Control Center unless you want to record it. A red Stop button (⬤) appears briefly in the upper-left corner of the screen in place of the clock readout. The red button then displays the clock readout.

Perform the actions you want to record. When you finish, tap the clock readout (K, `11:56`) to open the Screen Recording dialog, and then tap **Stop** (L).

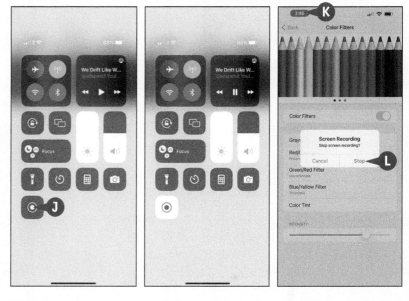

Watch a Screen Recording

After you end a screen recording, a banner appears telling you that iOS has saved the screen recording. You can tap this banner to go straight to the screen recording in the Photos app.

To open the screen recording later, tap **Photos** (✿) on the Home screen. In the Photos app, tap **Albums** (M, 💼 changes to 💼), and then tap **Screen Recordings** (N, ⊙) to display the screen recordings.

Tap the screen recording (O) you want to play back.

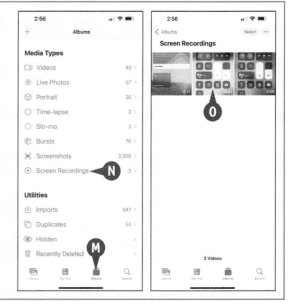

Update Your iPhone's Software

Apple frequently releases new versions of the iPhone's software to fix problems, improve performance, and add new features. To keep your iPhone running well and to add any new features, you should normally update its software when a new version becomes available. However, if you run a mission-critical app on your iPhone, you may prefer to wait until the app's developer confirms the update is fully compatible with the app.

The easiest way to update is directly on the iPhone. If you use your computer to manage your iPhone, you can also perform the update using your computer.

Update Your iPhone's Software

Ⓐ The badge on the Settings icon indicates that a Settings notification is waiting for you. Often, this means an update is available.

① On the Home screen, tap **Settings** (⚙️).

The Settings screen appears.

② If Software Update Available appears, tap **Software Update Available** and go to step 4. If not, tap **General** (⚙️).

The General screen appears.

③ Tap **Software Update**.

The Software Update screen appears.

④ To configure Automatic Updates settings, tap **Automatic Updates**.

The Automatic Updates screen appears.

5 Set the **Download iOS Updates** switch to On (🔵) to make iOS automatically download updates when it has a Wi-Fi connection.

6 Set the **Install iOS Updates** switch to On (🔵) if you want your iPhone to install updates automatically overnight when your iPhone is charging and connected to Wi-Fi.

7 Set the **Install Security Responses & System Files** switch to On (🔵) to have your iPhone automatically install Apple's Rapid Security Response fixes and updates to essential iOS system files.

8 Tap **Back** (〈).

The Software Update screen appears again.

9 Tap **Install Now**.

The installation of the update begins.

After iOS verifies the update and installs the files, your iPhone restarts.

Ⓑ The Software Update Complete screen confirms that your iPhone has been updated.

10 Tap **Continue**.

You will need to enter your passcode to sign in following the restart.

Note: After updating iOS, update your iPhone's apps as well, because there may be new versions that require the iOS update. See the section "Update and Remove Apps" in Chapter 7 for instructions.

TIP

How do I update my iPhone's software using my computer?

Connect your iPhone to your computer via the USB cable. On macOS Catalina or later versions, click **iPhone** (▯) under Locations in the Sidebar in a Finder window; the General screen appears. On earlier macOS versions or Windows, click **iPhone** (▯) on the navigation bar in iTunes; the Summary screen appears. Click **Check for Update** in the upper area. If the dialog that opens tells you that a new software version is available for the iPhone, click **Update** to download and install the update; verify that the update has completed before you disconnect the iPhone from the computer. If the dialog says your iPhone is up to date, click **OK**, and then disconnect the iPhone.

Extend Your iPhone's Runtime on the Battery

To extend your iPhone's runtime on the battery, you can reduce the power usage by dimming the screen; turning off Wi-Fi, Bluetooth, and cellular data when you do not need them; and setting your iPhone to go to sleep quickly. When the battery reaches 20 percent power, your iPhone prompts you to turn on Low Power Mode, which disables background app refreshing, slows down the processor, and turns off some demanding graphical features. You can also enable Low Power Mode manually anytime you want.

Extend Your iPhone's Runtime on the Battery

Dim the Screen

1 Swipe down from the upper-right corner of the screen.

Control Center opens.

2 Swipe down the **Brightness** control.

The screen brightness decreases.

3 Tap the bar at the bottom of the screen.

Control Center closes.

Note: You can also save power by avoiding — or reducing your usage of — resource-intensive apps such as games and video conferencing.

Turn Off Wi-Fi, Bluetooth, and Cellular Data

1 Swipe down from the upper-right corner of the screen.

Control Center opens.

Ⓐ You can turn off all communications by tapping **Airplane Mode** (changes to).

2 To turn off Wi-Fi, tap **Wi-Fi** (changes to).

3 To turn off Bluetooth, tap **Bluetooth** (changes to).

4 To turn off cellular data, tap **Cellular Data** (changes to).

5 Tap the bar at the bottom of the screen.

Control Center closes.

Turn On Low Power Mode Manually

1 On the Home screen, tap **Settings** (⚙️).

The Settings screen appears.

2 Tap **Battery** (🔋).

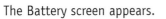

The Battery screen appears.

3 Set the **Low Power Mode** switch to On (changes to ⚪).

Your iPhone enables Low Power Mode.

B The battery icon appears yellow (such as 🔋) to indicate that the iPhone is using Low Power Mode.

Note: For quick access to Low Power Mode, add its icon to Control Center. From the Home screen, tap **Settings** (⚙️), tap **Control Center** (🎛️), and then tap **Customize Controls**. On the Customize screen, tap **Add** (➕) to the left of Low Power Mode.

TIP

What else can I do to save power?

If you do not need your iPhone to track your location, you can turn off the GPS feature. On the Home screen, tap **Settings** (⚙️), and then tap **Privacy & Security** (✋) to display the Privacy & Security screen. Tap **Location Services** (📍) to display the Location Services screen, and then set the **Location Services** switch to Off ( ).

You can also set a short time for Auto-Lock. On the Home screen, tap **Settings** (⚙️), tap **Display & Brightness** (🔡), and then tap **Auto-Lock**. Tap a short interval — for example, **1 Minute**.

Back Up and Restore Using Your Computer

When you sync your iPhone with your computer, Finder or iTunes automatically backs up the iPhone's data and settings, unless you have chosen to back up your iPhone to iCloud instead. You can also run a backup manually as explained here. If your iPhone suffers a software or hardware failure, you can use Finder or iTunes to restore the data and settings to your iPhone or to a new iPhone or an iPad. You must turn off the Find My iPhone feature before restoring your iPhone.

Back Up and Restore Using Your Computer

Back Up Your iPhone

1 Connect your iPhone to your computer via the USB cable or via Wi-Fi.

The iPhone appears in the Sidebar in Finder on macOS Catalina or later versions, or on the navigation bar in iTunes on earlier macOS versions or on Windows.

2 Click **iPhone** () in the Sidebar or on the navigation bar.

The iPhone's management screens appear.

3 On macOS Catalina or later versions, click **General** to display the General screen. On earlier macOS versions or on Windows, click **Summary** to display the Summary screen.

4 Click **Back Up Now**.

iTunes backs up your iPhone.

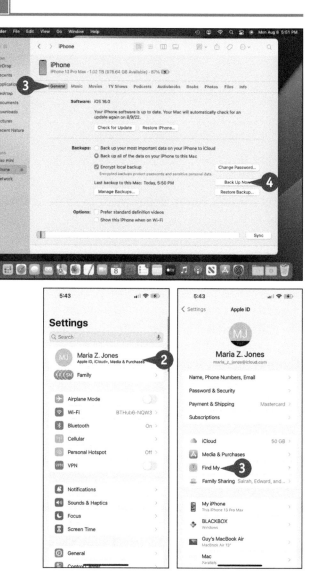

Turn Off the Find My iPhone Feature on Your iPhone

1 On the Home screen, tap **Settings** ().

The Settings screen appears.

2 Tap **Apple ID**, the button bearing your Apple ID name.

The Apple ID screen appears.

3 Tap **Find My** () to display the Find My screen.

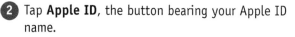

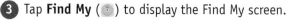

4 Tap **Find My iPhone**.

5 Set the **Find My iPhone** switch to Off (⊙ changes to ⊙).

The Apple ID Password dialog opens.

6 Type the password for your Apple ID.

7 Tap **Turn Off**.

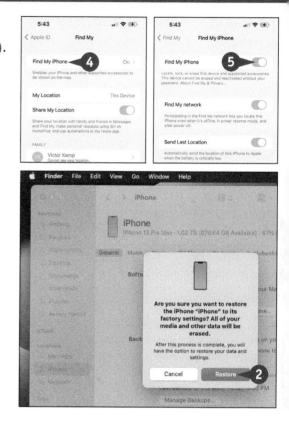

Restore Your iPhone

1 On the General screen in Finder or the Summary screen in iTunes, click **Restore iPhone**.

A dialog asks you to confirm that you want to restore the iPhone to its factory settings.

2 Click **Restore** or **Restore and Update**, depending on which button appears.

Finder or iTunes backs up the iPhone's data, restores the software on the iPhone, and returns the iPhone to its factory settings.

Note: Do not disconnect the iPhone during the restore process. Doing so can leave the iPhone in an unusable state.

3 On the Welcome to Your New Phone screen, click **Restore from this backup** (⊙ changes to ⊙).

4 Click ⊕ and choose your iPhone by name.

5 Click **Continue**.

Finder or iTunes restores the data and settings to your iPhone.

Your iPhone restarts, appears in Finder or iTunes, and then syncs.

6 Disconnect the iPhone.

TIP

How can I protect confidential information in my iPhone's backups?

On the General screen in Finder or the Summary screen in iTunes, click **Encrypt local backup** (☐ changes to ☑). In the dialog that opens, type the password, and then click **Set Password**. iTunes then encrypts your backups using strong encryption.

Apart from protecting your confidential information, encrypting your iPhone also saves your passwords during backup and restores them to the iPhone when you restore the device.

Back Up and Restore Using iCloud

Instead of, or as well as, backing up your iPhone to your computer, you can back it up to iCloud, preferably via Wi-Fi, but optionally — if you have a generous data plan — via the cellular network. If your iPhone suffers a software or hardware failure, you can restore its data and settings from backup.

You can choose which items to back up to iCloud. You do not need to back up apps, media files, or games you have bought from the iTunes Store, because you can download them again.

Back Up and Restore Using iCloud

1 On the Home screen, tap **Settings** (⚙️).

The Settings screen appears.

2 Tap **Apple ID**, the button bearing your Apple ID name.

The Apple ID screen appears.

3 Tap **iCloud** (☁️).

Note: The 5GB of storage in a standard free iCloud account is enough space to store your iPhone's settings and your most important data and files.

The iCloud screen appears.

A If you need more storage space, tap **Manage Account Storage** to display the iCloud Storage screen, and then tap **Change Storage Plan**.

4 Tap **Photos**.

The Photos screen appears.

5 Set the **Sync this Phone** switch to On (⬤) if you want to store your photos in iCloud.

6 If you enable iCloud Photos, tap **Optimize iPhone Storage** or **Download and Keep Originals**, as needed.

7 Set the **Shared Albums** switch to On (⬤) if you want to share albums with others via iCloud.

8 Tap **iCloud** (<).

The iCloud screen appears again.

9 Tap **Show All**.

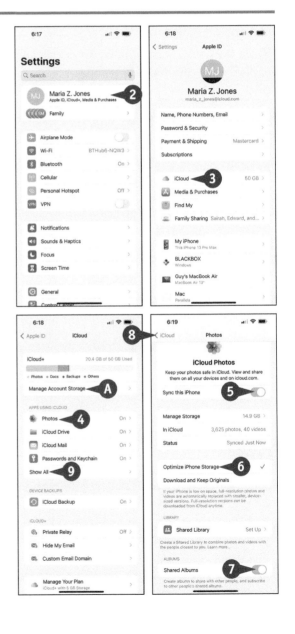

The Apps Using iCloud screen appears.

B To configure an app that has more than an On/Off switch, tap the app's button, and then work on the screen that appears.

10 Set each app's switch to On (⬤) or Off ( ), as needed.

11 In the nameless lower sections, set each app's switch to On (⬤) or Off ( ), as needed.

12 Tap **iCloud** (‹).

The iCloud screen appears again.

13 Tap **iCloud Backup** (⟳).

The iCloud Backup screen appears.

14 Set the **Back Up This iPhone** switch to On (⬤).

15 Set the **Back Up Over Cellular** switch to On (⬤) only if you have an unlimited or very generous data plan.

16 If you want to back up your iPhone now, tap **Back Up Now**.

Your iPhone begins backing up its contents to iCloud.

TIP

How do I restore my iPhone from its iCloud backup?

First, reset the iPhone to factory settings. On the Home screen, tap **Settings** (⚙), tap **General** (⚙), tap **Transfer or Reset iPhone**, and then tap **Erase All Content and Settings**. On the Erase This iPhone screen, tap **Continue**. When the iPhone restarts and displays its setup screens, choose your language and country. On the Set Up iPhone screen, tap **Restore from iCloud Backup**, and then tap **Next**. On the Apple ID screen, enter your Apple ID, and then tap **Next**. On the Choose Backup screen, tap the backup you want to use — normally, the most recent backup — and then tap **Restore**.

Reset Your iPhone's Settings

If your iPhone malfunctions, you can reset its network settings, reset the Home screen's icons, reset your keyboard dictionary, reset your location and privacy settings, or reset all settings to eliminate tricky configuration issues. If your iPhone has intractable problems, you can back it up, erase all content and settings, and then set it up from scratch. You can also erase your iPhone before selling or giving it to someone else; you must turn off Find My iPhone first.

Reset Your iPhone's Settings

Display the Reset Screen

1 On the Home screen, tap **Settings** (⚙).

The Settings screen appears.

Note: If your iPhone is not responding to the screen, press **Volume Up** once, press **Volume Down** once, and then press and hold **Side** until the iPhone restarts.

2 Tap **General** (⚙).

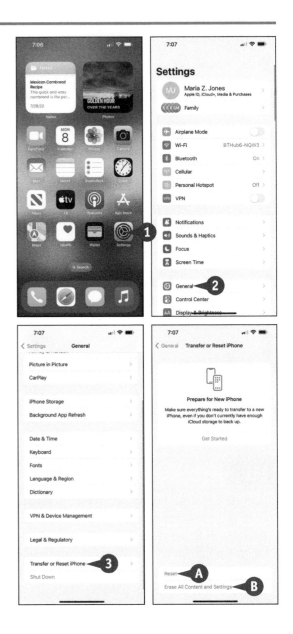

The General screen appears.

3 Tap **Transfer or Reset iPhone**.

The Transfer or Reset iPhone screen appears.

A You can tap **Reset** to display the Reset dialog, which enables you to reset all settings, the network settings, the keyboard dictionary, the Home screen layout, or Location & Privacy settings.

B You can tap **Erase All Content and Settings** to start the process of wiping your iPhone clean.

Reset Your iPhone's Network Settings

1 On the Transfer or Reset iPhone screen, tap **Reset**.

The Reset dialog opens.

2 Tap **Reset Network Settings**.

Note: If your iPhone prompts you to enter your passcode at this point, do so.

A dialog opens, warning you that this action will delete all network settings and return them to their factory defaults.

3 Tap **Reset Network Settings**.

iOS resets your iPhone's network settings.

Restore Your iPhone to Factory Settings

Note: If you intend to sell or give away your iPhone, turn off Find My iPhone before restoring your iPhone to factory settings. See the second tip.

1 On the Transfer or Reset iPhone screen, tap **Erase All Content and Settings**.

The Erase This iPhone screen appears.

Note: Enter your passcode if prompted to do so.

2 Tap **Continue**, and then follow the prompts to complete the erasure.

iOS wipes your media and data and restores your iPhone to factory settings.

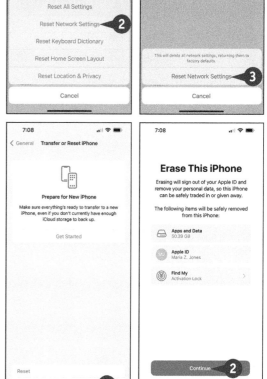

TIPS

Does the Reset All Settings command delete my data and my music files?

No. When you reset all the iPhone's settings, the settings go back to their defaults, but your data remains in place. But you need to set the iPhone's settings again, either by restoring them using Finder or iTunes or by setting them manually, to get your iPhone working the way you prefer.

How do I turn off the Find My iPhone feature?

Tap **Settings** (⚙️), tap **Apple ID** — the button bearing your Apple ID name — and then tap **Find My** (🔵). On the Find My screen, tap **Find My iPhone** to display the Find My iPhone screen, and then set the **Find My iPhone** switch to Off (🔵 changes to ⚪).

Troubleshoot Wi-Fi Connections

To avoid exceeding your data plan, use Wi-Fi networks whenever they are available instead of using your cellular connection.

Normally, your iPhone automatically reconnects to Wi-Fi networks to which you have previously connected it and maintains those connections without problems. If Wi-Fi does not seem to be working properly on your iPhone, your first recourse should be to turn Wi-Fi off and then turn it back on. You may also need to tell your iPhone to forget a network and then rejoin the network manually, providing the password again.

Troubleshoot Wi-Fi Connections

Turn Wi-Fi Off and Back On

1 On the Home screen, tap and hold **Settings** (⚙️).

The contextual menu opens.

2 Tap **Wi-Fi** (🛜).

The Wi-Fi screen appears.

3 Set the **Wi-Fi** switch to Off ( ).

Note: Alternatively, use Control Center to toggle Wi-Fi off and back on. Swipe diagonally down from the upper-right corner of the screen to open Control Center, tap **Wi-Fi** (🛜 changes to 🛜), and then tap **Wi-Fi** again (🛜 changes to 🛜).

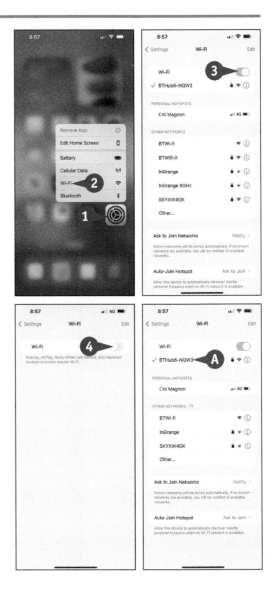

Your iPhone turns off Wi-Fi.

4 Set the **Wi-Fi** switch to On (⚪).

Your iPhone turns Wi-Fi back on.

A Your iPhone connects automatically to the network it was previously using.

You can now check whether the network connection is working satisfactorily.

For example, open Safari and access a website.

If the network connection is not working satisfactorily, continue troubleshooting with the following subsection.

Forget a Network and Then Rejoin It

1 On the Wi-Fi screen, tap **Information** (ⓘ) to the right of the network.

The network's screen appears.

2 Tap **Forget This Network**.

Note: If turning Wi-Fi off and then back on does not resolve a Wi-Fi problem, try turning Airplane Mode on briefly and then turning it off again. Swipe down from the upper-right corner of the screen to open Control Center, tap **Airplane Mode** (✈ changes to ✈), and then tap **Airplane Mode** again (✈ changes to ✈).

The Forget Wi-Fi Network dialog opens.

3 Tap **Forget**.

The iPhone removes the network's details.

The Wi-Fi screen appears.

4 Tap the network's name.

The Enter Password screen appears.

5 Type the password for the network.

6 Tap **Join**.

The iPhone joins the network.

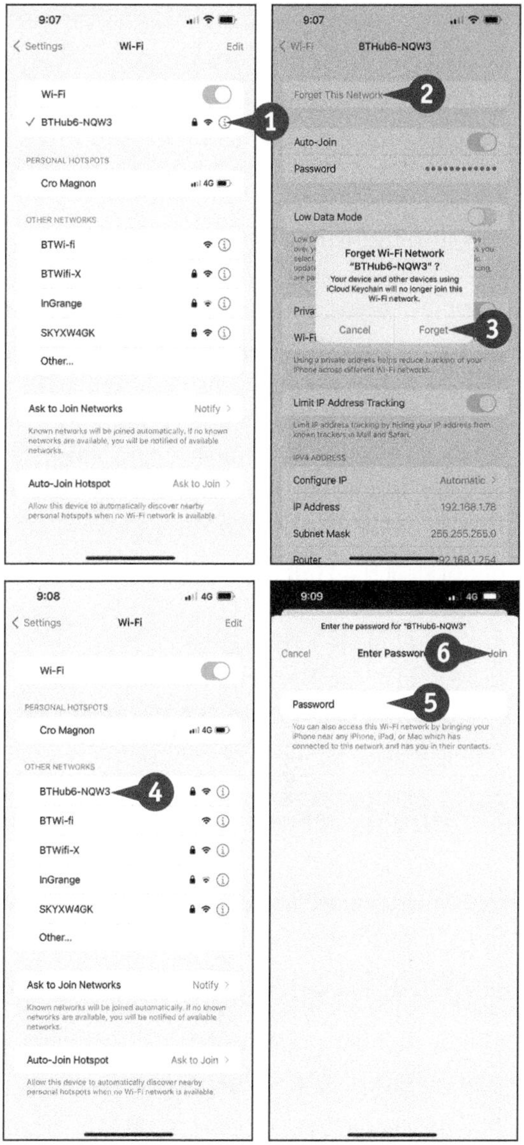

TIP

What else can I do to reestablish my Wi-Fi network connections?
If you are unable to fix your Wi-Fi network connections by turning Wi-Fi off and back on or by forgetting and rejoining the network, as described in this section, try restarting your iPhone. If that does not work, reset your network settings, as described earlier in this chapter, and then set up each connection again manually.

Locate Your iPhone with Find My iPhone

Through your iCloud account, you can use Apple's Find My iPhone feature to locate your iPhone if it has been lost or stolen. You can play a sound to help locate the iPhone. You can display a message on the iPhone — for example, to tell the finder how to contact you. And if you determine someone has taken your iPhone, you can remotely wipe its contents to prevent anyone from hacking into your data.

To use Find My iPhone, you must verify that the Find My iPhone feature is enabled and suitably configured on your iPhone.

Configure the Find My iPhone Feature

On the Home screen, tap **Settings** (⚙) to display the Settings screen, and then tap **Apple ID**, the button that bears your Apple ID name. On the Apple ID screen, tap **Find My** (◉) to display the Find My screen, and then tap **Find My iPhone** (A) to display the Find My iPhone screen.

Verify that the **Find My iPhone** switch (B) is set to On (⬤), enabling the Find My iPhone feature. Set the **Find My network** switch (C) to On (⬤) to use Apple's Find My network, which lets you find the iPhone even when it is offline, it has been powered off, or it has been erased. Set the **Send Last Location** switch (D) to On (⬤) to have the iPhone automatically send its location to Apple when the battery runs critically low.

Locate Your iPhone Using Find My iPhone

You can use the Find My Phone service using most any web browser, such as Safari, Microsoft Edge, Firefox, or Chrome. On a Mac, on an iPad, or on an iPhone other than the missing one, you can also use the Find My app, which is installed by default. This section illustrates using Find My iPhone in a web browser.

Open a web browser window to the iCloud website, www.icloud.com. On the Sign In to iCloud web page, type your Apple ID and password, and then click **Sign In** (➔). On the main iCloud screen, which shows available apps and services, click **Find iPhone** (◉) to display the Find My iPhone screen. If prompted to sign in here, do so, using two-step verification if necessary.

Click the pop-up menu (E) at the top — normally, it shows All Devices at first — and then click the iPhone (F) you want to track.

Locate Your iPhone Using Find My iPhone (continued)

The Find My iPhone locates your iPhone — if possible — and displays its location (G) and the Info dialog (H).

From the Info dialog, you can take three actions:

- **Play a sound on the iPhone.** Click **Play Sound** (◀›). This feature is primarily helpful for locating your iPhone if you have mislaid it somewhere nearby, but it may also cause someone else to pick up your iPhone if you have lost it elsewhere.

- **Lock your iPhone with a passcode.** Click **Lost Mode** (🔒) in the Info dialog to display the Lost Mode dialog (I), and then enter a passcode (J) to lock the iPhone. Follow the prompts to re-enter the passcode, provide a contact phone number for reaching you on another phone, customize the default message (K), and click **Done** (L). Via iCloud, iOS locks the iPhone using the passcode for security.

- **Remotely erase your iPhone.** Click **Erase iPhone** (🗑) in the Info dialog, and then click **Erase** (M) in the Erase This iPhone? dialog that opens. If this iPhone is the last trusted device for your Apple ID, the Erase Last Trusted Device? dialog opens instead of the Erase This iPhone? dialog. Read the warning about having to use your Recovery Key to access your Apple ID. If you are sure you want to erase the iPhone, click **Erase**.

Manage Your Apple ID

Your iPhone uses your Apple ID for authentication and authorization. Using the Apple ID screen in the Settings app, you can review your Apple ID information and change it if necessary. For example, you may need to change your display name, add a payment method or shipping address, or verify that two-factor authentication is enabled for security. You can also edit the phone numbers and e-mail addresses at which you are reachable via iMessage and FaceTime.

Manage Your Apple ID

1 On the Home screen, tap **Settings** (⚙) to display the Settings screen.

2 Tap **Apple ID**, the button that shows your Apple ID name, to display the Apple ID screen.

A To add a photo or update an existing photo, tap the account icon. In the Photo dialog that opens, tap **Take Photo** or **Choose Photo**, as appropriate, and then follow the prompts.

Note: At the bottom of the Apple ID screen is a Sign Out button that you can tap to sign out of your account.

3 Tap **Name, Phone Numbers, Email**.

Note: If the Sign In to iCloud dialog opens, type your password, and then tap **OK**.

The Name, Phone Numbers, Email screen appears.

B You can tap **Name** and edit your name.

C You can add phone numbers and e-mail addresses to the Reachable At list by tapping **Edit** and then tapping **Add Email or Phone Number**.

4 In the Subscriptions section, set the switches to On (🔘) or Off ( ) to control which messages you receive.

5 Tap **Back** (〈).

The Apple ID screen appears again.

6 Tap **Password & Security** to display the Password & Security screen.

D You can tap **Change Password** and follow the prompts to change your Apple ID password.

7 Verify that the Two-Factor Authentication button shows On. If not, follow the prompts to enable two-factor authentication.

E You can tap **Edit** and then change your trusted phone numbers.

F You can tap **Get Verification Code** to get a code for signing in on another device or at iCloud.com.

8 Tap **Apple ID** (〈) to display the Apple ID screen.

9 Tap **Payment & Shipping**.

The Manage Payments screen appears.

G You can tap **Add Payment Method** to add a payment method.

H You can tap **Add Shipping Address** to add a shipping address.

10 Tap **Apple ID** (〈) to display the Apple ID screen.

11 Tap the button for your iPhone.

The Device Info screen appears.

12 Verify that the Find My iPhone button shows On. If not, tap **Find My iPhone** and set the **Find My iPhone** switch to On (⬤).

I You can view your phone's details.

13 Tap **Apple ID** (〈) to display the Apple ID screen.

J You can tap **Media & Purchases** (🅐) to configure account settings, such as payment methods and personalized recommendations.

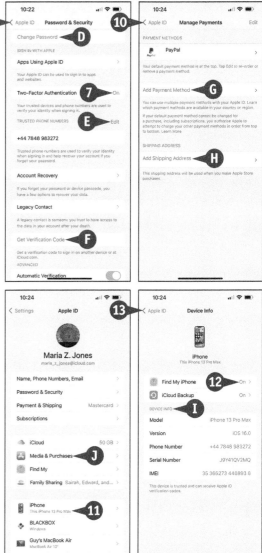

TIP

Where is the setting for getting rid of unused apps?
On the Home screen, tap **Settings** (⚙) to display the Settings screen, and then tap **App Store** (🅐) to display the App Store screen. Then set the **Offload Unused Apps** switch to On (⬤) if you want iOS to delete apps you have not used for a while. iOS keeps any documents you created in the app.

Lock Down Your iPhone Against Serious Hackers

iOS 16 includes a feature called Lockdown Mode that you can turn on to protect your iPhone against heavy-duty hackers, such as those from security services or from hostile nation-states. Lockdown Mode disables some elements of the iPhone's functionality that may offer security holes to skilled and determined attackers.

Apple intends Lockdown Mode for people who face an extreme level of cyberattack, such as human-rights activists, crusading journalists, public figures, and — who knows? — secret agents. If you do not fall into one of these groups, you likely do not need Lockdown Mode, but there is nothing to stop you from trying it.

Lock Down Your iPhone Against Serious Hackers

① On the Home screen, tap **Settings** (⚙).

The Settings screen appears.

② Tap **Privacy & Security** (✋).

The Privacy & Security screen appears.

③ Tap **Lockdown Mode**.

The Lockdown Mode screen appears.

④ Read the information about when Apple intends Lockdown Mode to be used.

Ⓐ You can tap **Learn more** to display details of the restrictions that Lockdown Mode imposes on your iPhone.

⑤ Tap **Turn On Lockdown Mode**.

A screen with specific information about Lockdown Mode appears.

6 At the bottom of the screen, tap **Turn On Lockdown Mode**.

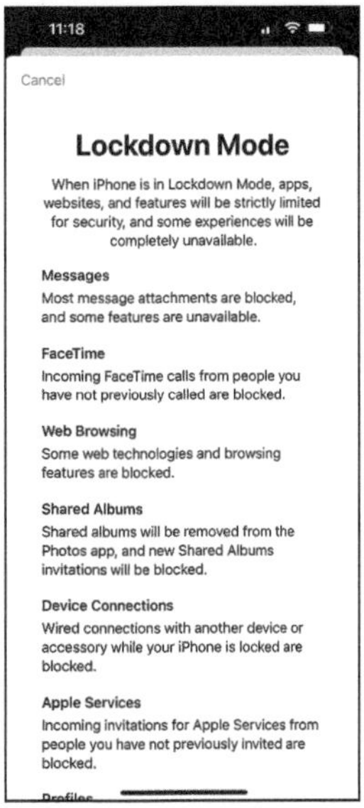

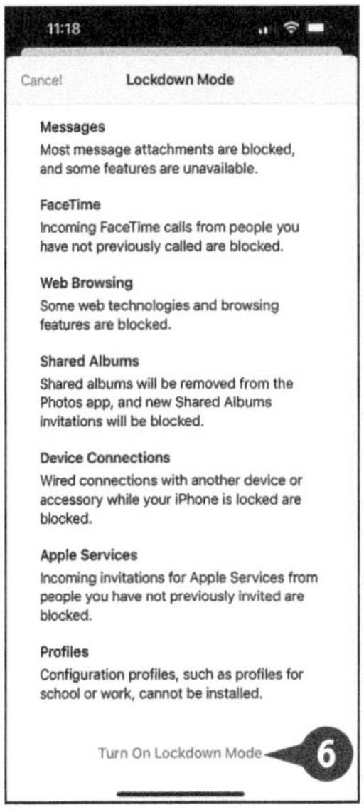

The Turn On Lockdown Mode? dialog opens.

7 Tap **Turn On & Restart**.

A screen appears prompting you for your passcode.

Note: For security, iOS prevents the keypad from being included in the screen capture shown here.

8 Type your passcode.

Your iPhone restarts in Lockdown Mode.

You can unlock your iPhone with your passcode as usual, and you can use most of your iPhone's functions. However, iOS disables potentially insecure features.

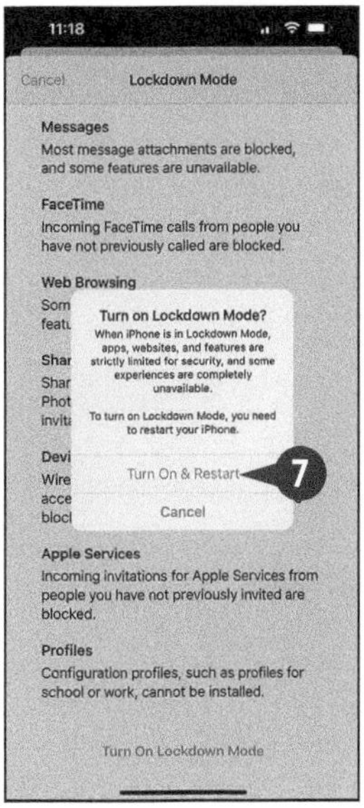

TIP

How do I turn off Lockdown Mode?

You turn off Lockdown Mode much the same way you turn it on: Tap **Settings** (⚙) to display the Settings screen, tap **Privacy & Security** (✋) to display the Privacy & Security screen, and then tap **Lockdown Mode** to display the Lockdown Mode screen. Tap **Turn Off Lockdown Mode** on the Lockdown Mode screen, tap **Turn Off & Restart** in the Turn Off Lockdown Mode? dialog, and then type your passcode to authenticate yourself. Your iPhone restarts with Lockdown Mode off. Once you unlock your iPhone with your passcode, all the hardware and software features should be fully functional once more.

Index